Leif Svalesen

# The Slave Ship
# *Fredensborg*

Translated by Pat Shaw
and Selena Winsnes

Indiana University Press
Bloomington and Indianapolis

Copyright © 2000 by H. Aschehoug & Co. (W. Nygaard), Oslo
English-language translation first published in North America
and the United Kingdom in 2000 by Indiana University Press,
601 North Morton Street, Bloomington, IN 47404

Editorial Direction: Tove Storsveen
Graphic Design: Ane Valderhaug/ Nini Anker
Jacket illustration: Map of Guinea from Fredrik V's Atlas.
The Danish National Library, Copenhagen
Back / jacket flaps: Photos by Leif Svalesen and Tove Storsveen 1: flap: Allan Iversen

Printed in Portugal

This book has been published with the support of UNESCO under the
cultural program 'The Slave Route' and the Norwegian Association of
Non-Fiction Writers and Translators.

Library of Congress Cataloging-in-Publication Data
A catalog record for this book is available from the Library of Congress
ISBN 0-253-33777-1

1 2 3 4 5   05 04 03 02 01 00

PICTURE CREDITS
Aust-Agder Archives, Arendal, p. 44, 98 top, 102, 103, 131, 161, 198, 199, 228
Aust-Agder Museum, Arendal, p. 10, 162
Bergen Maritime Museum, p. 57
British Museum, London, p. 61, 96-97
Drawings by Christian Bogø, Denmark, p. 44, 109, 156 (photo: Aust-Agder Archives)
Karsten Bundegaard, Copenhagen, p. 174, 175, 176
Danish National Library, Copenhagen, p. 14, 46-47, 64-65, 66, 67, 69, 71, 72,
    78-79, 98 bottom, 126, 127, 129, 135, 136, 139, 188, 200 both, 201, 204
    top, 206, 207, 208, 209, 210, 225 bottom
The Royal Society of Sciences and Letters, Trondheim, p. 47 bottom (photo:
    Thor Nielsen)
The Danish Museum of Natural History, Frederiksborg, Denmark, p. 194
The Royal Danish Administration of Navigation and Hydrography, Map and
    Land Registry Office, Copenhagen, p. 157
The Danish Maritime Museum, Kronborg, Denmark, p. 25, 26 (drawing: Erik
    Gøbel), 40-41, 56, 62, 91, 95, 104 bottom, 106, 123, 128, 134, 138, 143,
    196, 197, 203, 204 bottom, 232 (photo: Henning Henningsen)
Allan Iversen, Oslo, p. 17, 18, 19
John Murray Publishers Ltd, London, p. 68
The Copenhagen City Museum, p. 168
Lange Nilsen Fotodesign, Arendal, p. 49, 172, 177, 178 bottom, 179 both, 180
    both, 181 both, 182 both, 183, 184, 185 both, 186 both
Lausant Collection, Paris, p. 58 (photo: Explorer)
Drawings by Ants Lepson, Arendal, p. 28-29, 144, 146, 154, 169, 100 bottom
Modern Photo Co. Ltd., Accra p. 229 bottom
Norwegian Maritime Museum, Oslo, p. 178 top (photo: Pål Abrahamsen
    large picture and Pål Thome)
Danish National Archives, Copenhagen, p. 21, 22, 23, 30, 34, 38, 39, 42, 43, 55, 76-77, 82, 86, 92, 100 top, 104-
    105, 111, 113, 120, 122, 124, 152, 167, 171, 195, 222, 223
Drawings by Mads Stage, Rode, Denmark, p. 15, 27, 32, 33, 132, 140, 149, 150
Tove Storsveen, Oslo, p. 218 top
Leif Svalesen, Arendal, p. 48, 50, 99 bottom, 159, 164, 166, 190-191, 198 top, 202 bottom, 205 both, 212, 213
    both, 214, 215, 216, 217, 218 both, 219, 220, 221, 222 top, 225 top, 226, 227 both, 229 top, 230, 231,
    232 bottom, 233, 234
The Free Library of Philadelphia, p. 202 top
Verdens Gang, Oslo, Pedro's drawing, p. 20
Drawing by Ann-Carin Wessel, Horten, p. 193
Roland Nimako, p. 237

# Contents

# *Prologue*

T HE SILENCE WHICH LONG SURROUNDED the transatlantic slave trade is the result of both the oblivion into which its physical symbols and sites of remembrance have fallen and the general lack of knowledge about them. It is the radical rethinking of these issues that has given great significance to the manner in which Norway has dealt with the wreck of *Fredensborg*. Indeed, to bring a slave ship up from the dark and silent depths of the sea is to shine the torch-light of history onto the very instrument of this tragedy. More than the amazing technical feat of underwater archaeology, to display the slave ship and the human context of its history brings an ethical dimension to the project by a country confronting the more obscure aspects of its history.

Yet Norway has decided to follow these two directions. And, as often in the course of history, the initial act was an individual one, in this case that of Leif Svalesen, who, against all odds and with a great deal of determination, has managed to glean exact information from the historical archives, and, together with underwater archaeologists from the Norwegian Maritime Museum, investigated the remains of the *Fredensborg* wreck. Through the publication of the *Fredensborg*'s history and the display of the objects found on board, the Norwegian authorities have confirmed their decision not only for Norway to assume its role in the history of the slave trade, but more importantly, for it to renew contacts with the countries which were the victims of this trade, in particular Ghana and the U.S. Virgin Islands. This is an excellent illustration of the aims and objectives of the UNESCO Slave Route project. UNESCO, through multidisciplinary approach which brings together all the partners historically involved, has decided to link knowledge of the slave trade tragedy with the knowledge of all the interactions it has generated, in order to make better known the intercultural dialogue that has taken place between Europe, Africa and Americas.

The Slave Route project in itself is a kind of path towards the future. People are assuming past responsibilities in order to build a constructive future together. UNESCO is thus introducing a new dimension into the dialogue between cultures, peoples and civilizations which goes beyond knowing one another to bringing to light the interactions which history, through its long memory even of tragic events, has created between peoples.

D. Diène
Director, Division of Intercultural Projects
UNESCO, Paris

# Foreword

THIS BOOK PRESENTS A FASCINATING CHAPTER in the history of the slave trade – a true, detailed, account of a Danish slave ship, the *Fredensborg*. In 1767–68 the *Fredensborg* sailed the triangular trade route from Copenhagen to the Gold Coast in Africa, then onward to the Danish West Indies with a cargo of black slaves, and finally home over the north Atlantic toward Denmark. In the hard autumn weather, it went aground on southern Norway's inhospitable rocky coast. It was there, in 1974, that the diver Leif Svalesen, along with his brother and two friends, found the wreckage of the ship. Since then he has devoted much time and effort to explaining the nature of the Danish slave trade in general, and to telling the story of the *Fredensborg* in particular. Svalesen provides a spellbinding narrative about the ship and its trip, about finding the wreck, and about his explorations in Africa and the West Indies.

After the wreck of the *Fredensborg* was located and identified, one of the main tasks was to research the extensive written materials preserved in Danish and Norwegian archives pertaining to the ship's journey and stranding. These texts, together with the items that were retrieved from the wreck – from exotic goods such as elephant tusks and dyewood to the crew's tobacco cans and shoes with fine buckles – constitute perhaps the most thorough documentation of a slave ship found as a wreck anywhere in the world.

By the 1600s, Denmark was already fully integrated into the international economy, including overseas shipping and trade. Christian IV created the East India Company in 1616, which quickly established a trading post in Trankebar on India's east coast. In the mid-1600s, ships flying the Danish flag occasionally began to sail to the Gold Coast in Africa, where headquarters were established at Fort Christiansborg and at Fort Fredensborg, from which the slave ship took its name. The Danes colonized the island of St. Thomas in the West Indies around 1670, adding the neighboring islands of St. John and St. Croix after the turn of the century. Thus the Danish king in the 1700s ruled over a worldwide Lilliputian empire. Denmark-Norway never became a colonial power of international importance. The possessions in Asia and Africa were only small trading posts, operating on the basis of rental and trading agreements with the local authorities. Only the three West Indian islands were real colonies, and they were of the most modest size. They were sold to the United States in 1917 and are now called the U.S. Virgin Islands. The

Danish trading posts in India and on the Gold Coast were sold to England in 1845 and 1850, respectively.

Denmark's possessions in Asia, Africa and America were to some extent linked economically. Danish ships brought home to Copenhagen large quantities of textiles and small white cowrie shells from India, used as currency on the Gold Coast. These goods were then sent from Copenhagen to the Gold Coast, where they were traded for slaves. The slaves were carried over the Atlantic to the plantations in the West Indies. From there, it was primarily raw brown sugar that was sent home to Copenhagen, where it was refined into fine white sugar – one of the largest industries of the time, and an important source of income for the capital's great merchants.

In the Atlantic trade between 1670 and 1807, the vast majority of voyages (approximately 3,000 in number) went directly back and forth between Denmark and the West Indian islands. About 260 ships, however, received passes to sail the triangular route from Denmark to the Danish West Indies. There were also some 80 trips made by vessels with their origins in the Danish West Indies, which sailed back and forth directly between the islands and Africa. Altogether the Danish-Norwegian ships carried approximately 85,000 African slaves over the Atlantic, while the Danish forts on the Gold Coast sold another 15,000 slaves who were transported on other nations' ships. The trip from Africa's coast to the West Indies took approximately three months, while the entire triangular trip normally took one and a half years.

The slaves endured inhumane conditions during their transport in the so-called middle passage across the Atlantic from the Gold Coast to the West Indies. The heat along the equator was stifling, the calculated space per slave was about the size of a coffin, and the provisions on board were frugal and foreign. The slaves were often chained and separated from loved ones as they sailed into an unknown future.

The death rates on these voyages were particularly high. In the 1770s and 1780s, 15 percent of the slaves carried by Danish ships died during the trip across the Atlantic. On the *Fredensborg* eleven percent of the slave cargo, which consisted of 265 individuals, died. Death rates were high for the crews as well, normally reaching 33 percent. Of the *Fredensborg*'s original crew, 38 percent died during the triangular voyage – most during the stay on Africa's coast, where they succumbed to foreign infections and tropical diseases.

It has been calculated that in the period from 1450 to 1870, between 12 and 15 million African slaves were shipped on European and American vessels. Of these, nearly half were sent to the various West Indian islands, while the rest were sold to plantation owners in South America or North America. The conditions on these ships were every bit as bad as those on the *Fredensborg*.

The Danish slave trade left a number of tangible artifacts. Many of the original plantation buildings are still standing on what are now the U.S. Virgin Islands, including the current museum at Estate Whim on St Croix, along with the sugar mills, forts, churches and other public buildings, all built by slaves. The large and impressive Fort Christiansborg can still be seen in Ghana, and a part of Henrich Richter's large merchant quarters in Accra has been preserved.

*The slave ship* The King of Assianthe *was named after one of the African rulers and trading partners from the Gold Coast. The ship made three voyages in the triangular trade, the last one in 1802, shortly before the slave trade came to an end. Shipowner Isaac Leth in Arendal later purchased the ship, which is shown here at anchor in the Marseilles roadstead in 1806.*

Denmark possesses many artifacts and documents connected with the *Fredensborg*, the Guinea Company (which owned the vessels and financed the trade), and the period's large shippers and merchants. From the *Fredensborg* itself there are documents housed in the Danish National Archives in the form of journals, correspondence and accounts from this particular voyage and from the company's directors in Copenhagen. In addition, there are buildings such as the elegant Yellow Palace at 18 Amalie Street, where the Guinea Company was located. It was here that Henning Frederik Bargum, the first director of the company, had his residence. At one point Bargum had earned a large amount of money in the slave trade; however, he quickly squandered all of his capital and had to flee the country bankrupt.

The Schimmelmanns were one of the richest families during this period, and among those most involved in the triangular economic cycle in the Atlantic. Heinrich Carl Schimmelmann came to Denmark from Germany in 1761 to help the government with its economic policies. Almost immediately he bought the estates of Ahrensburg and Wandsbek in Holstein, along with the Berckentin Palace (now the Odd Fellows Palace) in Broadstreet in the capital, which was used for ceremonies and as a winter residence. In addition there was the county seat at Sølyst in Klampenborg. The family also acquired the estates of Lindenborg and Gudumholm in the Danish countryside.

As early as 1763, Schimmelmann purchased from the king the four largest plantations on St. Croix, along with the largest sugar refinery in Copenhagen. Five years later he completed his economic empire by establishing the Hellebæk munitions factory in Northern Zealand. By then he was prepared to participate in the triangular trade in a way that would ensure him an optimal profit. Under the neutral Danish flag, the slave trade enjoyed a boom period up until Schimmelmann's death in 1782.

Schimmelmann's initiatives led to an effective integrated economic system. From his estates came various foodstuffs, brandy and spun cotton textiles for the plantations in the West Indies. His munitions factory, which had a Danish monopoly, provided weapons for use in the slave trade in Africa, along with cutlasses and other iron implements for the plantations in the West Indies. The plantations produced raw cotton for the estates and sugar for the refinery in Copenhagen, which dominated the Danish market. Slaves were purchased on Africa's coast, then transported to his plantations on the other side of the Atlantic ocean. Through this complicated exchange of money and goods, Schimmelmann was able to earn a handsome profit.

Ernst Schimmelmann, Heinrich Carl's son, took over some of his father's government positions and the whole business empire in 1782. At that point he was one of Denmark's richest men. As an estate owner he controlled many hundred serfs; as a manufacturer he had several hundred workers dependent on him; and, as the largest plantation owner in the Danish West Indies he owned about 1,000 slaves.

Under the intellectual pressures of the times, however, Ernst Schimmelmann became an opponent of slavery. With his central place in the state's structure, he succeeded in 1792 – for both humane and economic reasons – in having the transatlantic export of slaves from the Danish part of the Gold Coast and import in the Danish West Indies abolished, through an edict from the king that took effect in 1803. Denmark was thus the first state in the world to forbid the transatlantic trade in slaves; however, slavery was allowed to continue in the Danish West Indies all the way up to 1848, long after other nations had ended the practice.

The following account of the slave ship *Fredensborg* is as exciting as a novel – but it is the truth.

Erik Gøbel
The National Archives, Copenhagen

# The Discovery of the Wreck

T HE AUTUMN STORM RAGES IN THE LITTLE OUTPORT. It is dark and the rain drums against the windows. The sound of the storm from the sea is intense, and the gusts of wind tear the leaves off the trees and send them whirling in among the old buildings. This is shipwreck weather and the vessels in the harbour cling to anchor ropes and moorings. A stooping figure in a dark cape defies the elements. Through rain-drenched panes it is difficult to see the stocky man clearly. He appears to be searching for something, as he scurries away towards the southeast. The mysterious figure disappears between two houses and crops up again between juniper bushes and stunted firs on the rocks out by the sea. With cape flapping he heads into the storm. Soon he is swallowed up by the darkness. But not even on this night does the slave trader find his gold and his belongings.

The outports along the Skagerrak off the North Sea, abound with exciting tales from the days of the sailing ships. They were favourably situated where the fjord meets the sea, and could provide safe anchorage when storms and contrary winds made the voyage difficult. The people who inhabited these outposts were often visited by ships from other lands, and were in touch with the outside world in a very special way. Seafarers came here from the West Indies and East Indian traders, men-of-war and timber vessels. But in spite of the outports and the skilled pilots, the dangerous coast took a heavy toll and many a ship went down. In these instances the outports also came in handy, and could provide salvage assistance and lodgings for the unfortunate seamen. Or, at worst, a grave.

The outport of Narestø is situated near the east side of Tromøy, not far from Arendal. On 1 November, 1745 the local inhabitants were unexpectedly brought into contact with a very special form of commerce, the slave trade. The Dutch vessel *Het Vergulde Lam* was on her way to Copenhagen. Among those on board was the Danish slave trader Ludevig Ferdinand Rømer. He had come from the Gold Coast in Guinea where the kingdom of Denmark-Norway was trading in slaves, ivory and gold. Even though he had fallen into disfavour and had to go home,

*Ludevig Ferdinand Rømer*

*forhen værende Oberkiøbmand paa Küsten Guinea*

*Malet af Fuchs*    *stukket af Baurenfeind*

*Slave trader and merchant Ludevig Ferdinand Rømer.*

there is every reason to believe that he had been successful, and that he had not a little gold dust in his chest.

After a long and arduous voyage, to their dismay, the journey of Ludevig Ferdinand Rømer and Captain Pieter Godbers comes to an end off the dangerous boulder-strewn island of Målen a little east of Tromøy. Everyone is saved by the skin of his teeth, but Rømer has to leave his valuables on board. They spend the night in Narestø and the next morning, when the wind has subsided, several members of the crew go back on board the wreck. When they return Rømer learns that his chest has been forced open and his valuables are gone. All he has left are "a few parrots".

It is likely that Rømer's valuables consisted of gold, and news of this had spread to Narestø. Plundering of wrecks was not unusual along the coast, and in this case a legend later arose about the slave trader who is searching for his gold. The legend also tells of a family in the outport who had considerable financial difficulties at the time, but had suddenly become prosperous after the wreck. Eventually Rømer obtained a passage to Copenhagen where he cleared his name, returned to the Gold Coast as a slave trader and later became a successful merchant in Copenhagen. He also wrote a book in which he described the conditions on the Gold Coast.

Rømer left behind his gold and a legend in Narestø. But twenty-three years later, in 1768, the little outport was again brought into contact with the Danish-Norwegian slave trade. This time the inhabitants had to help two slaves and the entire crew of a slave ship that went down just off the east side of Tromøy.

The sea traffic along the extensive and dangerous coast of southern Norway has been heavy for hundreds of years. But when the storms were raging, and the skerries were white with foam, anything could happen. With the forces of nature as an adversary, ships and crews were tiny counters in the great game of chance. Proud vessels were crushed and sank, and hopes and lives came to an end.

Records of accidents in the past were to be found in the archives, and Tromøy (outside of Arendal where I grew up) was well represented in the documents of the maritime courts of inquiry. We had a boat, and I became familiar with the sea at an early age.

Great Skottholmen, which is in the approach to Arendal, was the first goal of our youthful expeditions. The islet was just beyond our landing, and here in many ways we came into close contact with the sailing vessels of bygone days, and the maritime cultural landscape. One little beach consisted of ballast stones brought there by huge vessels, and it happened that we found one or two ship's spikes.

Here and there on the islet were many special mooring poles. Most of them were made of parts of old anchors.

A few hundred metres further along the fjord lay Smith-Sørensen's old shipyard. If we were really lucky we were allowed to come ashore and look at some of the strange objects that had been on board the sailing ships and steamers. In their day many wooden ships had been built at the shipyard, and the old saw was still there, along with the enormous steam engine. What a place for a young boy! It was not at all strange that my interest in sailing ships and history increased with every visit. I will never forget my first encounter with the diver at Smith-Sørensen's quay. He was standing on a raft in his impressive diving gear, with a big helmet on his head. Then he screwed shut a round window with bars in front of it, climbed slowly down a ladder and disappeared in a cloud of bubbles, with a rope and a hose in tow. We sat speechless with admiration. Imagine being able to dive and explore the bottom of the sea!

As long as people have travelled beside and on the sea, the desire to penetrate the unknown has been present. Diving was even carried out in antiquity, and when Alexander the Great conquered the ancient city of Tyre in Lebanon in the year 333 B.C., he used divers to penetrate the harbour blockades. The development of diving equipment proceeded slowly: Leonardo da Vinci advanced his theories and others continued the work. As early as the seventeenth century in Sweden, several cannons from the *Wasa* and the *Kronan* were saved with the help of a primitive diving bell. August Siebe's diving helmet began to be used in the nineteenth century. The great turning-point was the development of modern compressed air equipment by the Frenchmen, Jacques Yves Cousteau and Emile Gagnan, during the Second World War. I devoured Cousteau's book *The Silent World*. The diver had eliminated the hoses up to the surface, and carried the supply of compressed air in cylinders on his back. Jules Vernes' "Mobilis in Mobili" – mobility in the mobile – had become a reality!

With the mass production of diving equipment, "the silent world" was within reach of more and more people. I, too, was bitten by the diving bug, and the same was true of my younger brother Tore and our friend Odd Keilom Osmundsen. We bought a fjord cruiser, the 54-foot smuggler *Capri*, which we converted into a diving boat. The three of us were interested in coastal culture and the history of ships, and we were aware of the opportunities that were in store for us, right outside our parlour door, so to speak. But how were we going to locate the right places?

With the heavy traffic in and out of the Skagerrak there have been many shipwrecks. The sailing ships were difficult to manoeuvre, and with the crude navigation equipment of the day there were often problems in determining the position. Many of the shipwrecks occurred at night, and usually during the dark time of the year. Gales, with easterly winds, were especially bad along the coast of southern Norway. This resulted in heavy seas and strong currents that moved towards shore. Some places stood out as being especially dangerous, like Målen, the ship's graveyard where Rømer's ship went down.

After the vessels sank to the bottom, things began to happen. The insidious shipworm, *Teredo navalis*, soon turned up on board with its smaller colleagues and began gnawing on the ship's timber. As a rule, after a few years on the seabed in our waters, there is not much wood left. Most often, only parts of the hull are intact, while cargo and other objects that were on board may be buried in layers of sand and mud. Sometimes these wrecks are easy to find. The remains of ship's timber, large anchors or cannons may be a good sign as they are easy to catch sight of. At other times there could be a load of bricks, stone slabs, tiles, special kinds of wood etc., which reveal that something has happened. In some instances the wreckage may be almost completely hidden, so it pays to be on the lookout for the tiny details that are often decisive for the discovery of a wreck.

As a rule, most of the thousands of wrecks that lie along the Norwegian coast are cargo vessels. The Middle Ages are represented, but there are few written sources to go by from that period. There are many wrecks from both the eighteenth and nineteenth centuries, most often ordinary toilers from the heyday of the sailing ships. They rarely offer great treasures, but may contain objects and cargoes of interest. Some wrecks have exciting tales to tell. These might be company ships on their way to or from exotic waters, naval vessels, or ships from expeditions. There is also an example of one brown-eyed and dark-haired family in Arendal that may be traced back to a shipwrecked Spanish vessel called the *Sagrado Nacimiento* in 1785. The frigate *Charitas*, which went down off the Hesnes Islands outside of Grimstad in 1797 with skipper Henrick Ibsen on board, may be closely identified with Henrik Ibsen the dramatist. His grandfather's shipwreck and death in Terje Vigen's waters is the true drama in the Ibsen family history. Other wrecks may come as a pleasant surprise to the finders, like the *Akerendam* at Runde, with its great hoard of gold and silver, and the *Samson*, with all its silver coins, in Homborsund.

My first encounter with the slave ship *Fredensborg* occurred when I read *Slavenes Skip (The Slave Ship)*, by the Danish author Thorkild Hansen. Through his trilogy *Slavenes Kyst (The Slave Coast)*, *Slavenes Skib (The Slave Ship)* and *Slavenes Øyer (Islands of the Slaves)*, we gained an insight into a part of Danish-Norwegian history that was unknown to us. In our school books there was no mention of the slave trade in those days. In his book *Skipsforlis på Sørlandskysten (Shipwrecks along the Coast of Southern Norway)*, Hartvig W. Dannevig wrote about the *Fredensborg* that went down off Tromøy. But it was Thorkild Hansen who turned the merchant vessel into a slave ship that sank with, among other things, ivory on board. It cannot be denied that the interest in the *Fredensborg* greatly increased after this. Several divers tried to find her, but the closest they came was the discovery of a rib from a whale. The diver, whose heart nearly stopped beating, received a dressing-down from a furious fisherman while he clung to a salmon net with the heavy whalebone which he thought resembled an elephant's tusk!

Tore and I were living at Galtesund on the western side of Tromøy. The *Capri* was usually stationed at Kilsund a little further to the east. Both coming and going, we passed Gitmertangen where the *Fredensborg* went down. And almost always I thought about the slave ship and the exciting history from the eighteenth century. It didn't take long before we began a closer examination of the circumstances around the shipwreck of the *Fredensborg*.

*Final planning in the pilot house of the Capri before the dive. From the left: Leif Svalesen, Odd K. Osmundsen, Tore Svalesen and Hartvig W. Dannevig.*

Our little team was expanded with yet another member, the coastal historian Hartvig W. Dannevig. He was not a diver, but had a thorough knowledge of the cultural history of the coast. In collaboration with the Aust-Agder Museum he has carried out significant pioneering work with studies in archives and development of the working method – from document to wreck.

After a shipwreck the local judge usually held a maritime court of inquiry. This "extraordinary court" was most often held in the vicinity of the site of the shipwreck, and the captain and several members of the crew on board had to give statements about the course of events. All this was meticulously entered in the records. The documents covering our part of the coast were waiting for us in the National Archives in Kristiansand.

With the records of the inquiry as a point of departure, we began the task of locating the exact site of the wreck. As was so often the case with the inquiries, the information as to the whereabouts of the wreck was very vague. Gitmertangen was large, and each of those who gave evidence, which was recorded in the journal in December 1768, "knew exactly" where the *Fredensborg* had gone down. Against this background the area was very large. It would take a considerable length of time and an infinite number of dives to carry out the search. This made us decide not to start diving for the wreck too soon. First we drew our own, large-scale map of the entire area in question. On board the *Capri* we had a good depth finder. When we had a complete picture of the conditions on the seabed, we continued with studies

*17*

of the winds and currents at the site. We also received assistance from an oceanographer, and his information confirmed what the local fishermen had told us. We asked the fishermen whether they had found wreckage in their nets, but no one had brought up anything that could put us on the right track.

One Sunday, late in the autumn of 1973, a gale blew up from the southeast. There were towering waves, and all along the outer side of Gitmertangen the sea was boiling. This is what it must have been like when the *Fredensborg* went down, I thought as I stood watching the white foam from the breakers, where the strong current split up along both sides of Tromøy. While the rain was lashing my face, I truly wished I could have turned back the clock to 1 December 1768. A brief look would have been enough to let us know where the wreck lay.

Throughout the spring and summer of 1974 we continued to work on our map of the shipwreck. Again and again we examined the details in the inquiry, and, along with the other material we had collected, a plan began to take shape. The most likely spot for the wreck was marked on the map, and we were ready for the next phase in the search for the slave ship *Fredensborg*.

The visibility in the water was good when we started diving on Sunday 18 August 1974. The *Capri* was anchored at Kjørvika on the inner side of Tromøy. This was where the *Fredensborg* was said to have sought shelter from the storm. We made our way out to the planned position in the pram and began the dive in relatively shallow water. From here we followed an undersea fissure down into the depths. The bottom was covered with sand and the contours of the rock rose up on both sides. There was no trace of the wreckage, and it grew darker and darker as we went deeper. As we rounded the outer edge of the rock, which turned to the east, the depth gauge registered 28 metres. Suddenly we caught sight of some dark contours against the white sand. There were wooden logs, four altogether, and the longest was lying up against the steep rock. We took a few samples of the logs and

*The first elephant tusk comes to the surface 205 years after the shipwreck. From the left: Odd K. Osmundsen, Leif Svalesen and Tore Svalesen.*

*The task of documenting and bringing up the ivory is in full swing at the exposed spot where the Fredensborg went down. At the top centre of the picture there is a glimpse of Målen where Rømer's ship was wrecked.*

sent a marker flag up to the surface to enable us to localize the spot. On the ledge above the fissure we found a small, worn, solid wheel.

Back on board the *Capri* we held a ship's council in the pilot house. The samples we had taken turned out to be mahogany and dyewood. We marked our finds on the map. We all had a definite impression that these finds had some connection with the slave ship. We agreed to get in touch with the Danish National Archives in Copenhagen and received a quick and friendly reply. After only a few hours they were able to inform us that the *Fredensborg* was carrying both dyewood and mahogany on board when she went down.

The following Sunday we were back at Gitmertangen. When the dive was completed, our yellow markers were bobbing on the surface, revealing even more discoveries of "foreign types of wood". We had not yet found the wreck itself, even though several smaller details of wood and iron had been found at depths of 20–40 metres. A special pattern was beginning to take shape on our map. We were now convinced that the *Fredensborg* had been "standing with her port side facing land", somewhat further inside the bay than we had first thought.

Three weeks were to pass before the weather was favourable enough for us to continue diving. On Sunday, 15 September, we were back in place out in the bay. The plan was clear: we would begin our examination of the seabed all the way inside the bay, and work our way out. The visibility in the water was good that day. The sun brightened up the white sandy bottom and searching conditions were perfect. On the western side of the bay there was a large rockfall, and another on the eastern side a few metres further out. It was shallow where we were searching, only 7–8 metres deep, and everything, except the sandy bottom halfway between the rockfalls, was covered by a carpet of seaweed and kelp. After a short time on the seabed we discovered the first signs. Upon closer examination a black "stone", well

PEDRO

*After a front-page story in the newspaper* Dagbladet, *about a "Cultural-historical world sensation", "Pedro's" amusing cartoon appeared in* Verdens Gang *with the following caption: "It's high time Norwegian culture had a chance to show its teeth!"*

camouflaged by seaweed and patches of red limestone, turned out to be a piece of ship's timber! Soon we found another, in addition to a log of dye-wood. When we removed the seaweed and the sand was blown away, several other things emerged: rusty iron, bits of wood and glass. A slightly curved, reddish brown surface under a large blade of sweet tangle turned into a cannon.

Lying here, beneath the seaweed, sand and stones, was a wreck. But was it the *Fredensborg*? At this depth we had plenty of time at our disposal. As we continued our examination there were more and more traces of the shipwreck that had occurred here. Suddenly we spotted a curved, yellowish-white object partly buried under the sand and stones, only four or five metres away from the cannon. Soon we could make out the contours of the first elephant tusk! Among the stones lay several tusks of various different sizes: elephant and hippopotamus tusks. Now we had no doubts that we had found the *Fredensborg!*

That same evening we got in touch with Director Svein Molaug of the Norwegian Maritime Museum in Oslo, and gave him an oral report. A written, well-documented report was sent the following day. Even though the tusks on the seabed had been concealed under stones and seaweed, we were uneasy. The idea that unwelcome visitors could have seen what we were doing was disturbing. We were afraid that other divers would ruin our discovery before it had been properly investigated. The ivory did not belong to us. After the discovery of the Runde treasure, the Law for Protection of Cultural Heritage had been expanded to include the cargo on board sunken ships. The change had been made only a few months before we found the tusks, which now belonged to the State.

Straight away, the Norwegian Maritime Museum sent people to advise and instruct us. After the ivory had been duly documented on the seabed, it was carefully taken up. When news about the discovery of the wreck reached the media we had even more to cope with. The discovery of the *Fredensborg* hit the headlines, and we posed again and again, and displayed the tusks on TV, for the newspapers and the weekly magazines.

After being registered, the ivory was taken to the Norwegian Maritime Museum. Some time later we were given half the tusks as a reward.

For my part, after the discovery, I became even more interested in the *Fredensborg* and the history of the slave ship. The desire to learn more was considerable, and when I received a survey of the material that was to be found in the Danish National Archives, I ordered more than 2,000 pages of ship's logs, construction details, inventories, etc. Since then there have been even more. These documents form the basis of the history which now follows.

# *The Slave Ship Fredensborg*

# PART I

# Dag - Journal

ved

Det Kongel. Octroyerede Danske Westindis. & Guineis. Compag.

## Nye Ladning

## No. 2.

Begynds dend 21 Martij 1752 og Endt dend med Septbr. 1753.

Ladet

## Fregatten Cron Printz Christian

# CHAPTER I

# The "Cron Prindz Christian" and the Company Trade

T HE 5TH OF FEBRUARY 1753 WAS A RED-LETTER DAY at the shipyard of the Royal Chartered Danish West India & Guinea Company in Copenhagen. The Company's "New Construction No. 2" was ready for launching, all decked out with flags. The Directors were present in all their finery, along with Master Shipwright Ole Gad, who had been in charge of the construction, and Master Smith Møller and Christian Irgens, the Company's Director of Stores. They watched excitedly when the signal was given. The 100-foot long frigate was christened *Cron Prindz Christian*, after the little prince who would later become King Christian VII, and then she was launched "to the accompaniment of Cannons and Trumpets".

The construction, which had begun in March 1752, had taken about ten-and-a-half months. After the launching followed the time-consuming work with the fittings, rigging and accoutrements. There was a considerable amount of equipment and provisions that had to be stowed away before the frigate was ready to sail. With the crew well on board, and the hold full of provisions and supplies for Fort Christiansborg on the African Gold Coast, they weighed anchor in September 1753. Then the *Cron Prindz Christian*, which was rechristened the *Fredensborg* a few years later, set out on her first voyage in the triangular trade.

We do not know very much about this first voyage, which was extra long. The ship's logs have not been preserved and other important documents have later been lost. However, in his book *Dansk Vestindiene 1661–1917 (The Danish West Indies 1661–1917)*, published in Copenhagen in 1928, Kay Larsen writes that the frigate "suffered a cruel fate" after it sailed from Copenhagen. On the Gold Coast the chief officer and several other members of the crew became sick and died, and soon after leaving the Coast, Captain Ole Reinholdt also died. Christopher Juul, who had signed on in Africa, had to assume command. When the *Cron Prindz Christian* finally arrived at St. Thomas in the West Indies in 1755, there was a surplus of slaves and the ship was sent further west in search of a better market.

*Opposite page:*
*The* Cron Prindz Christian, *which was later rechristened the* Fredensborg, *was built at the Company's own shipyard in Copenhagen, as "New Construction No. 2".*

*The original seal of the Danish West India Company.*

It took a long time before anything was heard from the vessel, but in February 1756 there came a report from St. Thomas that the long overdue Company ship had arrived at St. Louis under suspicious circumstances. This city was situated on the northern coast of the French colony of Saint-Dominique. It was decided to send a royal squadron to investigate the matter. When the squadron sailed into the harbour of St. Louis they found the *Cron Prindz Christian* riding at anchor with the Danish flag waving in the stern.

It turned out that the sale of the slaves had brought in only 26,000 rixdaler, which was far less than had been anticipated. Upon their arrival only 200 of the original "slave cargo" of 600 had survived, and these were in a deplorable state of health. Captain Juul had been so upset by all the adversity that he died, and for the young chief officer who had assumed command, the situation was completely out of hand: "Every man on board helped himself to the provisions, the money and the supplies," writes Kay Larsen.

Commander Fisher, who was in charge of the squadron, called for an investigation. As a result, four of the mutineers "were placed as prisoners on board the naval vessels" and replaced by sailors. The *Cron Prindz Christian* was "then sent to St. Thomas to fetch a cargo of sugar and sailed with this for Copenhagen."

This account of the first voyage of the *Cron Prindz Christian* is the only reference we have. The period of waiting for the Company and the families of the crew must have been long. They must certainly have believed the worst had happened: a shipwreck, a hijacking or complete mutiny. Not until November 1756 did the *Cron Prindz Christian* come back to Copenhagen with its load of sugar, under the command of Captain Michael Jacob Rønne. The chief officer was named Giønge, and it is his testimony during the maritime inquiry on which Kay Larsen bases his account. This appears to be reliable, and individual details may be documented. But 600 slaves seems to be a very large number for a ship the size of the *Cron Prindz Christian*. Since only 200 slaves were sold, the loss in this case amounted to 400, which constituted two-thirds of the slave cargo. From Christiansborg on the Gold Coast there is documentation of the purchase of 125 slaves, but we know nothing about the loading further down along the coast. Nonetheless, the first voyage in the triangular trade must have been a nightmare for the slaves as well as for the crew on board.

When the *Cron Prindz Christian* returned from her dramatic maiden voyage after three years, several changes had taken place in Copenhagen. The West India and Guinea Company had been taken over by the Crown as early as 1754, and the *Cron Prindz Christian* was now put into the West Indian trade. There was a constant demand for supplies from the three Danish-Norwegian possessions, St. Croix, St. Thomas and St. Jan, while important colonial products were to go back to Copenhagen. The first direct voyage to the West Indies – with Rønne still as captain – lasted from December 1757 until September 1758. The return cargo consisted largely of sugar. The following March, Captain Rønne set out on a new voyage to the West Indies, where he was replaced by Captain Cordt Gylve Orm. On the homeward journey, the West Indiaman came into Mandal in mid-December, and remained there until spring. In April they were finally back home in Copenhagen after a voyage that had lasted for more than a year. The third voyage to the West

Indies, which was begun in August 1760, took even longer. On the return trip, with the hold full of sugar, they came to Arendal in December of the following year. Here they were laid-up for the winter, and did not arrive in Copenhagen until May 1762.

Captain Orm must have enjoyed staying in Arendal. In December he was back again, this time on the outward voyage. It was hazardous to set sail in northerly waters in December, and the *Cron Prindz Christian* remained at anchor throughout the winter at the outport of Merdø, outside of Arendal. Not until April did Captain Orm find the wind conditions favourable enough for him to set sail for the West Indies. In December 1763 he delivered yet another load of sugar in Copenhagen. On the frigate's fifth voyage to the West Indies, from August 1764 until July 1765, Captain Orm was relieved of having to spend the winter in Norway. After coming home the *Cron Prindz Christian* was handed over to Master Shipwright Ole Gad. He made the necessary repairs, including sheathing and caulking, and prepared the ship for new duties. During the five voyages to the West Indies we see that the *Cron Prindz Christian* spent three winters in Norway. This gives an idea of the significance of the Norwegian outports and coastal cities to the sailing ship trade.

Denmark-Norway started early with long and demanding voyages. Two great companies found in Copenhagen based their navigation on two different sailing systems which utilized the monsoon and trade winds. A highly-developed shipbuilding technique and an abundant supply of ship's timber kept the shipyards busy in both Denmark and Norway. And, as a rule, there were plenty of experienced seamen to man the ships.

As early as 1616 an East India Company had been established which acquired the rights to the trade in the Orient. The Company's major shareholder was King Christian IV, who invested 16,000 rixdaler in the enterprise. The first expedition to the Orient in 1618 was headed by the royal chancellor's secretary, nobleman Ove Gjedde, who was only 24 years old.

Despite the fact that extremely large numbers of the crew died, they succeeded in reaching an agreement with the "Naik" of Tanjore in India. Fort Dansborg was built in the coastal town of Tarangambadi, which was called "Trankebar". The site is

*Copenhagen was an active trading centre which had the highest qualifications for building ships and carrying out long, demanding voyages.*

25

20 miles south of today's Madras. For some 200 years the fort on the Coromandel coast was a Danish-Norwegian possession and an outpost for trading in the East. From a commercial point of view there were both good and bad years; the bad years were the result of shipwrecks and other problems. In 1643 the old company ceased its activities, but in 1688, after several inactive years, a new company was in operation. At this time Admiral Cort Adeler was a prominent figure, and he organized regular voyages to Trankebar, where a Danish-Norwegian governor still remained. The outbreak of the great Nordic war, combined with shipwrecks and a lack of capital, curtailed the activities and once again, in 1729, the trading was discontinued.

However, the voyages to the East were not abandoned. The first Danish–Norwegian expedition to China took place in 1730, in a little Swedish frigate that had been captured by Tordenskjold at Marstrand. As early as 1732 Frederik IV gave a charter to a newly established company, and the Asiatic Company was given the exclusive rights to carry on trade with both India and China. They took over the city of Trankebar and Fort Dansborg and started regular voyages to the Orient. This was a long journey, a total of 30,000 nautical miles round trip. The voyage ended in Canton in China, the only place where the Emperor accepted the Europeans who in China were called *fan-kwae* – "the sea devils". As a rule the ships set out from Denmark around New Year's. This time of departure was adapted to the southwest monsoon in the Indian Ocean which could be crossed in three months. The homeward journey, after a stay of about three months in China, was adapted to the northwest

*The regular routes from Denmark to China and India in the Eighteenth century are shown by broken lines, the return voyage by unbroken lines. The natural limits of the voyages imply that all the northern European nations followed the same routes.*

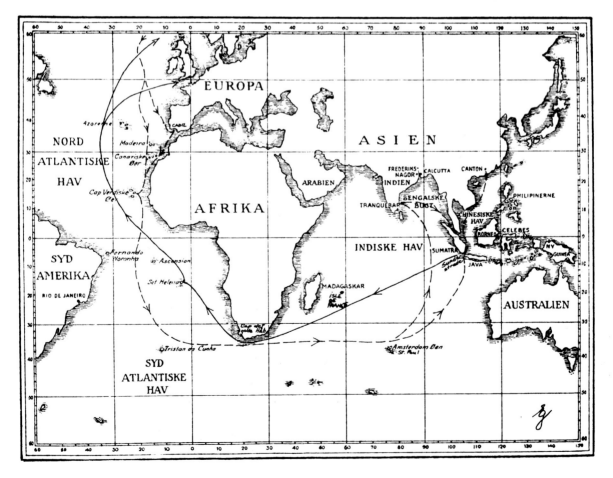

monsoon, which provided fair winds back to the Cape of Good Hope. From there to home they largely followed the same route as on the outward voyage.

The death-rate on board was considerable. An average of eight percent of the crew died, while even more became seriously ill. Even so, this was regarded as a relatively good result for the overseas trade. In spite of everything, the travellers to China were gone for a year-and-a-half or more, and some of the provisions crossed the equator four times! They mostly brought silver Spanish coins that could be traded with the Chinese, who had little use for European goods. On the homeward voyage the cargo consisted largely of tea, in addition to porcelain, silk, lacquerwork and spices. The ships of the Asiatic Company were large and the captains enjoyed a high social status. The ships required large crews and most of the seamen came from Jutland and Norway.

The other great Danish-Norwegian company was the Royal Chartered West India and Guinea Company, also with headquarters in Copenhagen. In 1671 a West India Company was established which later, in 1674, was given a monopoly on all Danish-Norwegian trade and shipping to the West Indies and Guinea. St. Thomas was colonized in 1672, and in 1718 they took possession of the neighbouring island of St. Jan.

In 1733 France sold St. Croix to the kingdom of Denmark-Norway. As the largest of the three colonial islands, and with a favourable topography, it was extra well-suited to the operation of plantations. Now the triangular trade really gained momentum because of the growing need for slaves on the plantations. In Copenhagen the Company was managed from a representative office building on Strandgaden, in Christianshavn, and there was increased activity both here and in the "sugar refinery". When a separate warehouse was built by the harbour, the flow of goods was even greater. But even after a reorganization, and a later increase in share capital, the operations of the West India and Guinea Company were unsatisfactory. While the *Cron Prindz Christian* was on her maiden voyage in the triangular trade, the Crown redeemed all the company shares. The shipyard in Copenhagen passed into private hands, while the sugar refinery in the same city was retained. This was later sold to the Minister of Finance, Heinrich Carl Schimmelmann, along with several plantations in the West Indies.

When we look at the map it is easy to understand why the route followed by the *Cron Prindz Christian* and the other company ships was called "the triangular trade". From a sailing point of view, this was an ingenious route which made the most of the winds and currents. The beginning and end of the journey – in and out of the Kattegat, the Skagerrak and the North Sea – were normally the most dangerous when it came to accidents and shipwrecks. In the first part of the triangular trade, the ships took advantage of the favourable currents at Portugal and the Canary Is-

*The ships that traded along the triangular route utilized the favourable winds and currents provided by nature.*

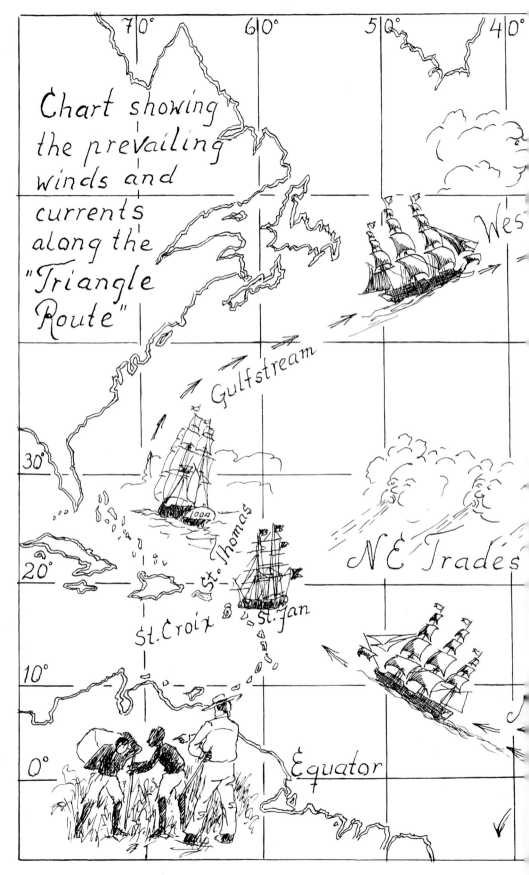

Chart showing the prevailing winds and currents along the "Triangle Route"

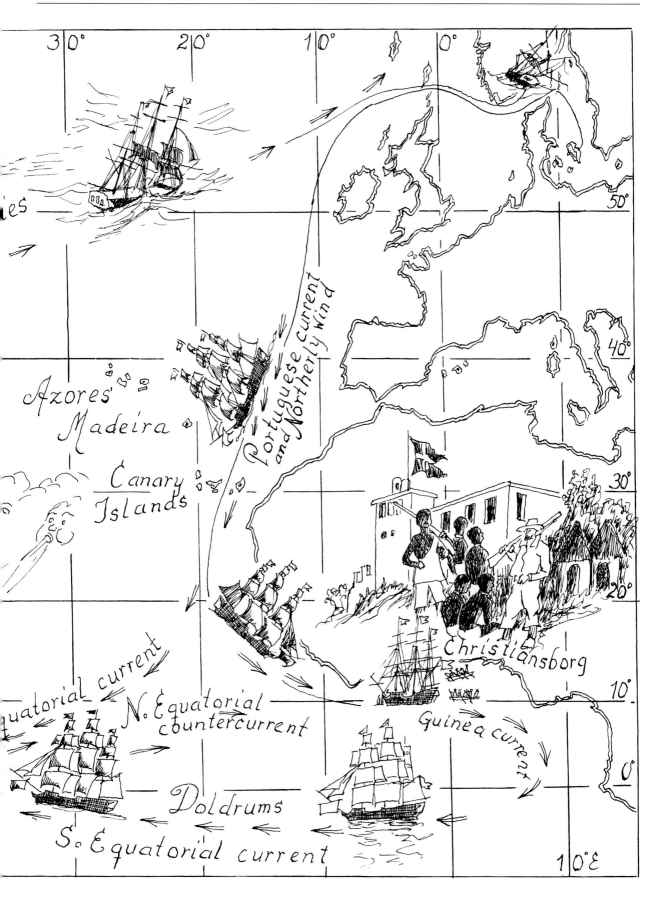

Azores

Madeira

Canary
Islands

Portuguese current
and Northerly wind

Christiansborg

quatorial current

N. Equatorial
countercurrent

Guinea current

Doldrums

S. Equatorial current

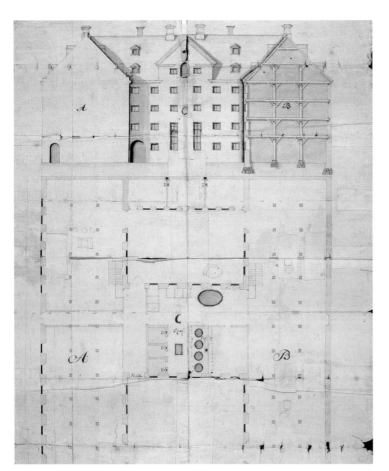

*A drawing of the West India Guinea Company's sugar refinery at Torvegade in Christianshavn, in Copenhagen 1732. Great quantities of raw sugar from the West Indies were refined behind the tall windows in the centre building.*
*The building was later sold to H.C. Schimmelmann.*

lands. The Portuguese northerly wind also helped along the way. When the ships rounded West Africa on their way into the Gulf of Guinea they followed the Guinea current until they could drop anchor off one of the many fortified trading stations along the Guinea coast. Here the provisions and all the important supplies were brought ashore and stored in the storehouses of the fort.

After a sojourn along the Gold Coast they could embark on the so-called "middle passage", with a cargo of slaves, ivory and gold in the hold. This was a difficult part of the voyage. Normally, many of the crew members died of tropical diseases during their stay in Africa, and with a load of slaves who had to be fed and guarded, there was a great deal of extra hard work for those who were left. The fear of a rebellion on board was always present. The slave captains utilized the tail end of the Guinea current before they turned west at São Tomé. Now they had to rely on the southerly equatorial current and the trade winds. There was always great rejoicing when the dreaded "Doldrums" had been passed, and after two or three months at sea they were able to drop anchor in the West Indies and rid themselves of the troublesome cargo.

After the slaves had been sold and the hold had been emptied and cleaned, colonial products that were the result of slave labour on the plantations were taken on board. The cargo in the last part of the triangular trade consisted largely of sugar, rum, dyewood and cotton. After they set their course for Europe, once again with a full hold, they had to take advantage of the Gulf Stream and the westerlies. The colonial products were greatly in demand in Europe and good prices were obtained. This was of considerable importance to the economic development in the seventeenth and eighteenth centuries. The great nations taking part in the transatlantic slave trade were England, France, the Netherlands and Portugal. But Denmark-Norway also had a hand in this very special form of shipping and profited greatly by human transport and slave labour.

The products that were brought home by the Asiatic Company and the West India Guinea Company turned Copenhagen into one of the most important trading centres in Northern Europe. Like the other countries that were engaged in the same traffic, this led to a great increase in prosperity.

# CHAPTER 2

# The "Fredensborg" Is Fitted Out for the Slave Trade

**W**HILE THE FRIGATE *CRON PRINDZ CHRISTIAN* was being repaired by Ship-wright Ole Gad, after her last voyage to the West Indies, the West India Guinea Company was undergoing considerable change. The economy of the Danish-Norwegian kingdom was in a terrible state, and the expenses in trading and shipping on the Gold Coast and in the West Indies had been greatly reduced. It was during this period that the successful merchant Henning Frederik Bargum submitted his plans that would enable the monarchy to dispose of the Guinea trade. Bargum was a partner in one of Copenhagen's great business firms, which was owned by a Widow Gustmeyer. As the widow's nephew, the well-travelled Bargum was in an advantageous position. He had a monopoly on the operations of a hat factory and a whalebone factory, and in 1760 had managed the extraordinary feat of acquiring complete control of the tobacco trade in Denmark. He was given the title "Tobacco Director-General", and had to pay a barrel of gold every year in duties to the State. Thus, by the eighteenth century the tobacco trade was already worth its weight in gold!

During his travels in England, France and the Netherlands Bargum had observed that the trade in slaves and sugar could yield good returns. On 18 March 1765 he was granted a royal charter for a new company, with the right to carry on trade for twenty years in Guinea and the West Indies. Later that year he also received a royal charter for the Christiansborg and Fredensborg forts, as well as for the smaller trading stations along the Gold Coast. This new company was given the name "The Royal Chartered Danish Guinea Company", but was better known as "The Bargum Trading Society" or "The Slave Trade Society". When the annual meeting was held on 19 February 1766, Henning Bargum was elected director. The other three members of the Board were Merchant Johan Frederich Reindorph, Chamberlain Carl Engmann and Sea Captain Jesper With. The Company had been granted special privileges, including exemption from a considerable number of duties, but it had to accept responsibility for the maintenance of the forts and trading stations in Guinea. Even though the share capital was not as great

as had been desired, the Company acquired a sugar refinery in Copenhagen.

In "The Yellow Palace", in Amaliegade in Copenhagen, plans were underway for lucrative voyages in the triangular trade with the sloop *Elonora*, and the frigates *Christiansborg* and *Cron Prindz Christian*. On 9 April 1767 Christian Tychsen, who was born in Tønder County, was appointed governor and chief merchant at a monthly wage of 66 rixdaler. Then he was off to Guinea on the *Christiansborg*. Here he found conditions in a sorry state, and he had his hands full in his new office. The *Elonora*, under the command of Captain Thadsen, was the second ship to sail for the Company. The *Cron Prindz Christian*, which was still being repaired, was rechristened the *Fredensborg* after the Company's fort in Guinea.

The *Fredensborg* had been bought at an auction for 5,225 rixdaler in 1766 and a royal deed of conveyance was made out for the ship. When the year was over, and Shipwright Ole Gad's bill for various repairs had been settled, the value of the ship had risen to 6,829 rixdaler. But there was still a great deal that remained to be done.

Throughout the winter and spring of 1767 there was feverish activity on board the *Fredensborg*. As the only member of the Board with seafaring experience, Captain Jesper With was busily equipping the ship in the best possible way. He had many years of experience behind him on sea-going vessels, and a total of five voyages as a "China Captain". It was this experience that earned him election to the Board as a co-director. The stalwart captain could hardly have been too pleased with the designation "Slave Trade Society". If anything, this had an unpleasant ring, even in those days. While Ole Gad's men were busy with their work, others were pouring up and down the gangplank. Some came on board to take measure-

ments. Others delivered their wares. The purchases were made from private individuals as well as firms in Copenhagen. Jacobine Brandt sewed red curtains for the
captain's cabin, while Bookbinder Graue delivered 12 prayerbooks and a book of
family sermons that had been rebound. Adjuster of Weights and Measures Nør-
gaard brought new, 4-pound weights for the "Bismer" balance (or steelyard).
Butcher Klyse drove up with a horse-drawn cart loaded with meat. Baker Ulstrup
delivered bread, while Candlemaker Niels Larsen delivered 300 pounds of candles.

Since the *Fredensborg* was to carry slaves from Africa to the West Indies, a great
deal of special equipment was needed. A "slave stove" was purchased for 175 rixdaler, and an extra amount of medicine was delivered from Mr. Place the apothe-
cary. Quantities of surgical instruments arrived from Monsieur Schienck, along
with a large supply of linen cloth for bandages. There were barrels of cheap clay
"slave or Negro pipes", while the Tobacco Shop delivered tobacco. In order to
keep the cargo of slaves under control they purchased foot irons and bolts. Pewter-
er Friderichsen was fortunate enough to receive an order for an enema syringe
with two tubes. Four half-pound cannons, called "swivel guns", were purchased
from Skipper Dahlstrøm for the slave bulkheads, while a  Mr. Hartmann repaired
the ship's drum and put on a new drumhead.

Many different professions were necessary in order to build and fit out a ship
like the *Fredensborg*. "Sculptor" Møller was there with his woodcarving tools. He was
probably carving a new nameplate after the *Fredensborg* had been rechristened. The
master glazier and the mirror maker were busy with their tasks, as well as the block
maker and the sailmaker. They performed their duties, delivered their wares and
presented their bills. The Guinea Company could dip into its share capital, and

*Copenhagen was a
favourable point of
departure for fitting
out ocean-going ships.*

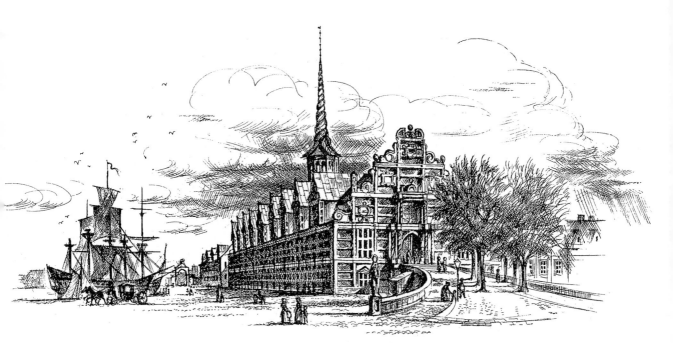

# Equipage Rulle

over det Kongl. Octroijerende Guineiske Compagnie Skib Fregatten Fredensborg undtagen og med Skibet indgaaende Mandskab, nemlig

| Charge | No | Navne | Maa. nedlig | Charge | No | Navne | Maa. nedlig |
|---|---|---|---|---|---|---|---|
| | | | Rdr | | | | Rdr |
| Capitain | 1 | Espen Kiönig | 24 | Matros | 24 | Transport | 105 |
| Øvr Styrm | 2 | Peder Christian Lundberg | 16 | | 24 | Jens Pedersen | 5 |
| Assistent | 3 | Christ. Andr. Henr. Hofmann | 10 | | 25 | Claus Larssen | 5 |
| Ober Mestr | 4 | Joch. Christopher Sixtus | 10 | | 26 | Jens Lebertsen | 5 |
| 2de Styrm | 5 | Johan Frantzen Ferentz | 10 | | 27 | Niels Matths. Fridsberg | 5 |
| undr Mestr | 6 | Carl Friderich Engmann | 7 | | 28 | Peter Stolm | 5 |
| 3de Styrm og Schribtel | 7 | Christ. Hanssen Beck | 9 | | 29 | Pet. Dieder. Grinberg | 5 |
| 4de Styrm og Bouelent | 8 | Andr. Siwertsen Gad | 8 | | 30 | Jochum Bollwandt | 5 |
| Baadsmand | 9 | Christoph. Christens. Rosenberg | 9 | | 31 | Frid. Jenss. Kruse | 5 |
| Øvr Tömm | 10 | Jacob Jacobsen Beck | 16 | Lds. Matr | 32 | Abraham Christophers | 4 |
| Koch | 11 | Nicolay Orgensen | 8 | Oploggr | 33 | Hans Anders. Skotman | 3½ |
| Quart. Mestr | 12 | Abraham Engmann | 7 | | 34 | Peder Mads. Skou | 4 |
| undr Tömm | 13 | Johan Jacob Koch | 12 | | 35 | Wogn Olsen | 3 |
| Bödker | 14 | Iwert Jacobsen | 8 | | 36 | Andreas Skaaning | 3½ |
| | 15 | John Andersen | 6 | | 37 | Aijl | 2½ |
| Baadsm. Mat | 16 | Peder Thoersen Nordbergen | 6½ | Drenge | 38 | Erich Anker | 2½ |
| Matroser | 17 | Thomas Greissen | 5½ | | 39 | Ole Erichsen | 2 |
| | 18 | Andr. Friderich Schlacke | 5½ | | 40 | Bendt Thamsen | 2 |
| | 19 | Hans Iwerstsen | 5½ | | | | |
| | 20 | Ragnal Nielsen | 5½ | | | pr Maaundlig | 272 |
| | 21 | Ole Nicolaisen | 5½ | | | og for Maaunder | 3 |
| | 22 | Anthonie Olsen | 5½ | | | | |
| | 23 | Peder Johnsen | 5½ | | | Summa | 816 |
| | | Lat. | 105 | | | | |

paid everything in cash. The signing on was in progress, and the crew list was completed. Since we are going to accompany the *Fredensborg* on a voyage in the triangular trade, it might be interesting to become acquainted with the crew on board and see what their monthly earnings were:

|  |  |  |  |  |
|---|---|---|---|---|
| 1 | *Captain Espen Kiønig* | 24 | *rixdaler* | *per month* |
| 2 | *Chief Officer Peder Christian Lundberg* | 16 | " | " |
| 3 | *Ship's Assistant Christian Andreas Hoffmann* | 10 | " | " |
| 4 | *Ship's Surgeon Joch. Christopher Sixtus* | 10 | " | " |
| 5 | *Second Mate Johan Frantzen Ferentz* | 10 | " | " |
| 6 | *Petty Officer Carl Friederich Engmann* | 7 | " | " |
| 7 | *Third Mate  Gunner Christian Beck* | 9 | " | " |
| 8 | *Fourth Mate and Steward Andreas S. Gadt* | 8 | " | " |
| 9 | *Boatswain Christopher Rosenberg* | 9 | " | " |
| 10 | *Chief Carpenter Jacob Jacobsen Beck* | 6 | " | " |
| 11 | *Cook Nicolay Ørgensen* | 8 | " | " |
| 12 | *Quartermaster Abraham Engmann* | 7 | " | " |
| 13 | *Carpenter Johan Jacob Kock* | 2 | " | " |
| 14 | *Cooper Ivert Jacobsen* | 8 | " | " |
| 15 | *Sailmaker  John Andersen* | 6 | " | " |
| 16 | *Boatswain's Mate Peder Thorsen Nordbergen* | 6 1/2 | " | " |
| 17 | *Able Seaman Thomas Greissen* | 5 1/2 | " | " |
| 18 | *Able Seaman Andr. Friderich Schlacke* | 5 1/2 | " | " |
| 19 | *Able Seaman Hans Ivertsen* | 5 1/2 | " | " |
| 20 | *Able Seaman Ragnal Nielsen* | 5 1/2 | " | " |
| 21 | *Able Seaman Ole Nicolaysen* | 5 1/2 | " | " |
| 22 | *Able Seaman Antoni Olsen* | 5 1/2 | " | " |
| 23 | *Able Seaman Peder Johnsen* | 5 1/2 | " | " |
| 24 | *Able Seaman Jens Pedersen* | 5 | " | " |
| 25 | *Able Seaman Claus Larsen* | 5 | " | " |
| 26 | *Able Seaman Jens Sivertsen* | 5 | " | " |
| 27 | *Able Seaman Niels Mathisen Fredsberg* | 5 | " | " |
| 28 | *Able Seaman Peder Holm* | 5 | " | " |
| 29 | *Able Seaman Peter Didrichsen Grønberg* | 5 | " | " |
| 30 | *Able Seaman Jochum Bollvardt* | 5 | " | " |
| 31 | *Able Seaman Friderich Jenssen Kruse* | 5 | " | " |
| 32 | *Cook's Mate Abraham Christophersen* | 4 | " | " |
| 33 | *Ordinary Seaman Hans Andersen Skoemager* | 3 1/2 | " | " |
| 34 | *Ordinary Seaman Peder Madsen Sckow* | 4 | " | " |
| 35 | *Ordinary Seaman Wogn Olsen* | 3 | " | " |
| 36 | *Ordinary Seaman  Andreas Skaaning* | 3 1/2 | " | " |
| 37 | *Ordinary Seaman Aye* | 2 | " | " |
| 38 | *Ship's Boy Erich Ancker* | 2 1/2 | " | " |
| 39 | *Ship's Boy Ole Erichsen* | 2 | " | " |
| 40 | *Ship's Boy Bendt Thomsen* | 2 | " | " |

Opposite page:

*Crew list before the departure from Copenhagen.*

Captain Kiønig was from Copenhagen and had considerable experience as a seaman. Ship's Surgeon Sixtus was the ship's doctor. He had an assistant named Carl F. Engmann who was the petty officer. In addition to his medical duties, it was the surgeon's job to barber the officers as often as they wished. The petty officer took care of the remaining crew members, who were supposed to be shaved every eighth day. Erich Ancker from Christiania is listed as a ship's boy, but soon after their departure he was promoted to ordinary seaman. Aye was an African. It cost the Company a total of 272 rixdaler a month in wages, as long as everyone remained alive. But this did not last long!

As has been mentioned, a considerable amount of special equipment, tools and materials were needed for a ship like the *Fredensborg*. Several of the key people on board signed receipts for long lists of items in which the minutest detail was listed. These included the boatswain, the ship's carpenter, the cook, the cooper, the sailmaker, the steward, the gunner, the ship's surgeon and the chief officer. The total crew consisted of 40 men. Several supported a family, having a wife and young children back home. Others were young adventurers who were undoubtedly looking forward to a long voyage in foreign waters. However, it could be dangerous to be on the crew list of a slave ship. During a voyage in the triangular trade as many as one-third of the crew could usually count on dying. How many of those who signed on were aware of this? The seamen may have talked among themselves on the wharves and in the taverns, so they must have known something. But, like most seamen, they were accustomed to dangers on stormy seas and sailed in order to provide for themselves and their families.

The upper deck of the *Fredensborg*, which ran the entire length of the ship, was usually called the gun deck. This was where the ten four-pound cannons stood, five on each side. From the mainmast and all the way astern lay the quarterdeck, which was a raised deck built up over the gun deck. The wheel and the binnacle were placed here. This was usually where the officers stayed when they were on deck and had to keep an eye on the ship and the navigation. Underneath the quarterdeck, all the way aft, was Captain Kiønig's cabin. The ship's Council met in the cabin, which served as the ship's office and the officers' mess, and where the table was set for daily meals and special occasions. The cabin was the most luxurious room on the ship, with elegant furnishings and curtained windows in the stern. Captain Kiønig had his own bedroom, and he also had a toilet. Chief Officer Lundberg's cabin was next door to the captain's. The mizzen mast was the sternmost of the ship's three masts.

The forecastle deck was higher. The large anchors were located here, as well as the foremast. Under the forecastle was the galley where Ørgensen, the cook, prepared the meals for the crew. Running along the starboard and port sides, between the forecastle and the quarterdeck, were two narrow gangways that were called "catwalks". The open gun deck between the forecastle and the quarterdeck, where the male slaves were aired, was usually called "the pit".

On the gun deck there were three hatches leading down to the 'tween-deck. Under the middle hatch were the seamen's quarters, where they kept their sea chests and slept in hammocks. The large hold in front of the cabin was used for storing cargo. With a cargo of slaves, this was where the males were packed together. The boatswain and the carpenter shared a cabin almost all the way forward. Here too were stowed the reserve supplies of sails, ropes, blocks, etc. The quarters for the mates, the ship's assistant, the ship's surgeon and possible passengers were located in the aftermost part of the 'tween-deck. This is also where the provisions, sail locker and bread-room were to be found. It was in this part of the vessel that the female slaves and the children were kept. Nearest the stern was the gunner's storeroom, which contained the important arsenal of weapons and equipment for the cannons. The hold in the bottom of the ship, below the 'tween-deck, was used for storing cargo as well as large water barrels, cases of provisions and other supplies. Here are some of the *Fredensborg*'s vital measurements: the length from stem to stern was 100 feet (31.4 metres); the greatest beam was 28 feet (8.8 metres), while the height between the decks on the 'tween-deck was 6 feet (1.88 metres). The draught was 16 feet (5 metres).

The supplies of food and drink were especially important, and great quantities were needed in order to carry out a long voyage. In addition to their own provisions, they also had to take along most of the food for the slaves during the middle passage. The list was extensive and included the following items, some of which have been converted and rounded off to present day weights and measures. Only the largest quantities have been listed.

| | | | | | |
|---|---|---|---|---|---|
| *White rice* | *3,400 kg* | *Pork* | *4 barrels* | | |
| *Red rice* | *1,000 kg* | *Hams* | *60 whole* | | |
| *Horse Beans* | *9,320 litres* | *Beef* | *44 barrels* | | |
| *Peas* | *10,200 l* | *Lamb* | *Fish oil* | | |
| *Ship's bread* | *5,800 kg* | *Dutch Cheese* | *Rye meal* | | |
| *Soft bread* | *450 kg* | *Stockfish* | *Red wine* | | |
| *Butter* | *2,055 kg* | *Klip-fish* | *Old wine* | | |
| *Brandy* | *64,265 lbs* | *Pickled herring* | *New wine* | | |
| *of which for* | | *Salt cod* | *Rhine wine* | | |
| *use on board* | *3,872 lbs* | *Oats* | *Wheat flour* | | |
| *Beer for officers* | | | | | |
| *and cabin* | *9,530 lbs* | | | | |
| *Barley groats* | *200 barrels* | | | | |

The rice had been purchased from the East Asiatic Company. It is worth remembering that during the voyages to the East, commodities were purchased that were to be used during the other great sailing system, the triangular trade. The horse beans that were ordinarily used as animal fodder were an important part of the diet of the slaves. Fort Christiansborg was to receive most of the brandy and some of the other provisions. Let us take a look at what else they had on board:

| | | |
|---|---|---|
| *French brandy* | *Wine vinegar* | *Prussian beer* |
| *Pearl barley* | *Prunes* | *Raisins* |
| *Tapioca* | *Currants* | *Pepper* |
| *Dried cherries* | *Ginger* | *Cinnamon* |
| *English mustard* | *Saffron* | *Cloves* |

| Coffee beans | Nutmeg | Cardamom |
| Brown sugar | Rock candy | Granulated sugar |
| Congo tea | Green tea | Bohea (black) tea |

As we can see, they took along a variety of spices and other delicacies. Not even saffron was lacking, and the quantity was 3 *lodd,* or 46.5 grams. In those days it was customary to take along live provisions. On board the *Fredensborg* there could be heard grunting and quacking and cackling. They had brought 8 live pigs, 10 ducks, 10 chickens and 2 geese. The winged provisions were well installed in five stationary and two movable chicken coops on the quarterdeck. For the poultry they had brought four barrels of chicken feed. And to be on the safe side, in case the egg laying should stagnate during the voyage, they had brought 400 eggs. The list ended with "a large quantity of vegetable seeds for planting during the voyage". With two kilos of seeds on board it was clear that vegetables and other greens were to be grown on the *Fredensborg*! And now we come to the vital water. Great quantities were needed for the crew and the animals on board, as

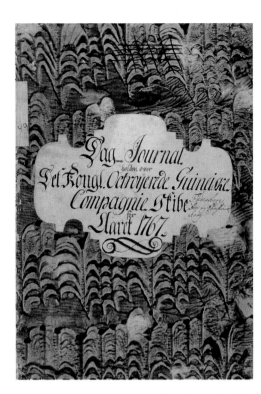

*The Company's Director of Stores kept an accurate and daily ledger of expenditures for the* Fredensborg *and the other slave ships. The ledger was concluded with itemized lists of payments and accounts.*

well as for the slaves. The water from Copenhagen was renowned for its purity. Rømer claims it became stagnant only once during a voyage, unlike poorer water which had become polluted a total of four times. 160 large water casks were securely stowed along with the other supplies.

After Ole Gad had finished the repairs and the caulking, the *Fredensborg* was anchored off Castelpynten on the evening of 5 June 1767. They spent the next several days loading supplies and finishing other tasks on board. Beck, the third mate and gunner, who was responsible for the weapons, took along four men and rowed to the gunpowder factory. They returned with eight barrels containing 300 pounds of gunpowder. Vintner Zinn delivered 11 cases of wine for Fort Christiansborg, and on the following day he returned with the ship's own supply of wine. The ship was bustling with activity as the final preparations were being made for the visit by the Board of Directors on Friday 12 June. The decks were scoured, trial shots were fired by the cannons and the brass mountings were polished until they shone.

The great day arrives. At 3 o'clock in the morning the crew is already putting the finishing touches on the preparations for the visit by the Board. At 9 o'clock the launch is sent ashore and returns with "the Trumpeters and Kettledrums". At precisely 10 o'clock the Directors arrive in the longboat. The six rowers are dressed in white shirts and white canvas trousers. On their heads they are wearing velvet caps, with red tassels and a tin badge engraved with the letters "DGC" – the Company's initials. Chief Officer Lundberg, who is in command of the longboat, is wearing a hat adorned with silver galloon, or braid, and red plumes. Hanging from a chain around his neck is a silver-plated badge with a whistle. The Directors of The Royal Chartered Guinea Company are wearing their finest attire, and no doubt attract attention on their way out to the *Fredensborg*. The newly refurbished black frigate is an impressive sight with all her decorations. There is a northerly wind and Company flags and jacks are fluttering in the breeze. The ten cannons have been loaded and rolled out of the gun ports, ready to fire. Then the illustrious visitors go up the gangway, holding onto the red rope that has been threaded through iron stanchions topped with polished brass knobs. First comes Director Bargum, followed by Chamberlain Engmann and Merchant Reindorph, and finally, "China Captain" Jesper With.

"To the accompaniment of trumpets and kettledrums" they come on board and are received by Captain Espen Kiønig in his best attire. He is wearing "a black dress coat with a silk embroidered vest", knee breeches with silver buckles, white silk stockings and new shoes, also with silver buckles. On his head he wears a white, powdered wig and a gold-braided hat which is slightly worn. On his finger he wears a gold ring with a white stone, and he is sporting his gold watch.

After a 9-gun salute the inspection begins. The forty-man crew stand on the deck, side by side, while the Ship's Articles are read aloud, paragraph by paragraph. Some look older and more experienced, others are only young boys. Then

*The "Exalted" Board of Directors" have signed the Captain's journal.*

*This picture from 1785 shows the* Fredensborg's *successor. She was also called the "Fredensborg", and was named after the fort in Ningo. There is every reason to believe that the two ships were quite similar; the tonnage of one was 278 tons, the other 276. Both had been built to sail in the triangular trade. The number of gun ports was the same and both were three-masted frigates.*

Fregatten Fredensborgs

Dragtighed 130 Commerce Læster.

Prima Plan, 10 Skland

Adimeret med 10 ℔ Att 4 ℔ ½ tt Canoner

Dyb gaaende

Fer 14¼ Fod

Agter 16 Fod

Læsrens begyndelse.

Læsrens Ende.

Til alt min reyse giøre Gud den aller høyeste Naade
Lyrke og Velsignelse, saa det maar Hans Gud til den
det Høy Kongel. Octroyerede Geunische Compagnieds Gavn
bedste og mig til deig velfærde og Velbehag.

a. Været Lad mig i din vellærdighed for min
Siuueker flyd og Kiel din vey for mig;

each member – with finger upraised in the air – takes an oath to remain loyal to King and country, and observe the strict regulations on board:

"…but above all we promise to obey the Captain, the Chief Officer and the other officers, who have been charged by the Company to command us, in every instance, at every time and in every place, wherever and whenever something is to be done in the service of the Company, and see to it that it is carried out, dutifully and obediently in every way, without showing or feigning idleness, whether on land or at sea, on board or ashore; and to this end be duty-bound to risk life, property and blood, the way faithful subjects and Company servants can and should do…..SO HELP US GOD AND HIS HOLY WORD."

After the inspection the Directors dine in the captain's cabin in the stern. It has recently been renovated, with red silk curtains tied back with silken bands and decorated with mohair tassels and tin-plated screws. The cabin has been scrubbed with green soap, and the four windows in the stern are sparkling and clear. Around the table, which is covered with a white cotton cloth and white napkins, the guests and officers are sitting in brown leather chairs. The captain rings his bell and the serving begins. They dine on light grey Staffordshire ware, and elegant wine glasses are raised. They drink toasts to everything of importance and significance of the day, and, most certainly, also to a successful voyage and return. They drink coffee from blue-patterned porcelain cups from China, and the ladle is frequently dipped into the punch bowl. Chamberlain Engmann is in high spirits. He orders even more salutes and the cannons thunder on deck. A total of 125 shots are fired before the Directors choose to leave the ship at 8 o'clock in the evening.

In the days that followed the final preparations for the departure were made. Several empty water casks were filled, and the finishing touches were put on the rigging and on the deck. The most dangerous cargo taken on board was the large supply of gunpowder that was intended for Guinea. On Monday 15 June the *Fredensborg* was more or less transformed into a floating bomb when two boats under the command of Chief Office Lundberg and Third Mate Beck fetched the gunpowder from the factory. A total of 8,695 kilos of gunpowder for Fort Christiansborg was carefully stowed below. In addition to the ship's own supply, which consisted of 420 kg cannon-powder and 10.5 kg gunpowder, there were more than nine tons of explosives on the ship, enough to blow the *Fredensborg* to smithereens! After the gunpowder was on board, the captain was not allowed to remain on land at night except for "extremely pressing circumstances".

The most important part of the cargo to Guinea was spirits and gunpowder. They also took along 40 cases of muskets, 32,000 gun-flints, iron bars, cartridge paper, shoes, textiles and chests of West Indian coral necklaces. Box after box was carried on board, marked with numbers and "DGC". Many of these were articles for barter, to be converted into slaves, ivory and gold, to fill the hold once more.

Just before the departure two passengers came on board. These were the "Assistants" Wrisberg and

*Opposite page:*
*Page 2 of Captain Kiønig's journal, which describes the frigate's tonnage, crew, armament and draught fore and aft. Kiønig continues: "May the Lord Almighty aid us in our venture and grant me a pleasant and prosperous voyage, by the grace of God, to the benefit of the Royal Chartered Danish West India and Guinea Company, and to my own eternal welfare and salvation. Lord, in Thy righteousness, do justice to my enemies and show me the way."*

*The seal of "The Slave Trade Society", the Company of the* Fredensborg.

*The Captain and the Board of Directors partake of their meal in the cabin astern, and drink a toast to a successful voyage and return home.*

Grathorn. They were going to serve on the Guinea Coast, which ordinarily was simply called "The Coast". Captain Kiønig went ashore to fetch the expedition's chest which was necessary for the voyage. Among other things, it contained the ship's papers, the crew list, an Algerian and a Latin sea pass, various letters and instructions. The *Fredensborg* was ready for her second voyage in the triangular trade. The first voyage had been very problematic, but the next was to be even worse!

In "The Yellow Palace" the Board of Directors breathed a sigh of relief. In less than a year they had dispatched two ships, and the third was ready to sail. The final entry in the *Fredensborg*'s accounts was for 10 rixdaler for the pilot who was to accompany her to Elsinore. With a total of 19,606 rixdaler, the accounts were closed. This was the cost of a fully-equipped slave ship, including the crew's wages for the first three months. In addition there was the value of the cargo. They weighed anchor on 19 June, and the *Fredensborg* headed for Elsinore in the capable hands of Pilot Christopher Pedersen. For the Board of Directors an anxious period of waiting had begun. Would the ships return with their holds full of colonial products that could fill the coffers with hard cash?

CHAPTER 3

# To Africa by Way of Southern Norway

AFTER A SHORT RUN FROM COPENHAGEN the *Fredensborg* arrives at Elsinore late in the afternoon and drops anchor at a depth of 6 1/2 fathoms. The guard boat fires a 9-gun salute, which is returned with a 3-gun salute. Chief Officer Lundberg and Ship's Assistant Hoffmann are sent ashore to fetch the final papers and return with the ship's Øresund Pass and a letter of credit from Norway. During the four days they are riding at anchor at Elsinore, the captain takes the opportunity to fill up several barrels of water and secure an extra supply of wine and rum for himself. A letter forwarded by Mr. Bargum is brought by a pilot boat. Thursday 23 June there is considerable activity at Kronborg Castle. Flags and jacks are run up on all the anchored ships, and 27-gun salutes are fired from the watch boats and citadels. Kiønig notes that "Our Hereditary Queen has graciously consented to dine at Cronbourg and thereafter subject everything to a close inspection".

Kronborg Castle at Elsinore was begun in 1574 by the Danish royal house in order to consolidate control of the narrow approach to Øresund. The castle was built on the ruins of the even older fortification, "Krogen" ("The Hook"), which was begun as early as 1429 by Erik of Pomerania. From 1429, with Danish forts on both sides of the Sound, it was possible to demand "Sound Dues" from every ship that passed through. In the course of time it was only natural that the Sound Dues became very unpopular with the great seafaring nations like the Netherlands and England. But despite many protests from the seafarers and their homelands, the collection continued – bringing hard cash into the State Treasury and the king's private coffers. Up to 1587 the Sound Dues amounted to two-thirds of the national revenues.

In the course of time a number of special treaties were negotiated in order to avoid serious conflicts with various nations. But the Sound Dues were maintained, and were even increased fourfold by Christian IV for certain kinds of goods. After American protests and refusals to pay, the treaty abolishing the Sound Dues was signed at a meeting with the seafaring nations in 1857. The total compensation amounted to 32,158,000 rixdaler.

For more than 400 years the Sound Dues were collected from some two mil-

*Elsinore, with Kron-borg Castle and the old Customs House, around 1582. For centuries the Sound Dues paid by the ships were an impor-tant source of revenue for Denmark.*

*Elsinore, with Kron-borg Castle and the old Customs House, around 1582. For centuries the Sound Dues paid by the ships were an impor-tant source of revenue for Denmark.*

lion vessels, all of which were painstakingly recorded in the customs records. In addition there were all the Danish-Norwegian and Swedish ships that were exempt from duty. This could amount to several thousand a year. This gives us an idea of the extent of the traffic in and out of the Skagerrak/Kattegat, to and from the Baltic, which was the most important trade route in Northern Europe.

On Wednesday 24 June 1767 the *Fredensborg* weighs anchor for the last time in Danish waters. A 9-gun salute is returned by a single salute from Kronborg and two from Elsinore. At full sail they head out of the Kattegat. Late in the afternoon they take a bearing on Kulen north of Höganäs, and Kiønig records in his journal that they have sighted sixty other vessels. He concludes the day's entry with, "May the Lord Jesus continue to be my companion in the name of the Lord."

The distance between southern Norway and Jutland is short, in some places only 60-70 nautical miles. For a sailing ship with limited manoeuvrability and crude navigation instruments, the Skagerrak was a dreaded area. They were dependent on favourable winds and good weather for a safe voyage. If they were becalmed this could cause problems: the current could carry the vessel into shallow waters where she could run aground. If the wind increased from the wrong direction, it was best to put into a safe port and wait until conditions improved. It paid to give Jutland's coast a wide berth, as there were no ports. A name like "The Bay of Tears" spoke for itself. The Norwegian coast was preferable, despite dangerous waters with holms and treacherous skerries. Several outports cropped up which, in addition to safe anchorage, could provide a number of services. The outports were frequently used by seafarers who, in addition to cargoes, brought cultural influences from the outside world. Indeed, the Norwegian outports have been of far greater economic significance to the North and the Baltic countries

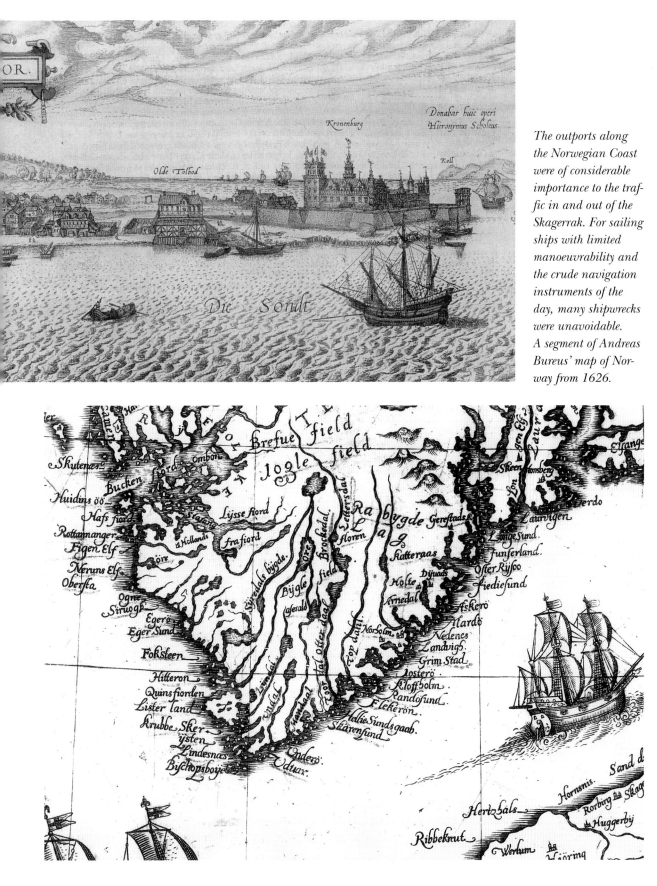

*The outports along the Norwegian Coast were of considerable importance to the traffic in and out of the Skagerrak. For sailing ships with limited manoeuvrability and the crude navigation instruments of the day, many shipwrecks were unavoidable. A segment of Andreas Bureus' map of Norway from 1626.*

*This model of the East-Indiaman* Queen of Denmark *is hanging in Tromøy Church. The model was built by carpenter Jens Marstrand and was a gift to the church from Parson Jens Boye, who was the ship's chaplain under the command of Captain Zacharias Allewelt.*

than has generally been realized. For the *Fredensborg*, which was engaged in overseas trade, the voyage in and out of the Skagerrak was the most dangerous part of the journey.

Saturday, 27 June, a pilot boat from Portør comes out to the *Fredensborg*, but there is no need for a pilot on board and they continue on their way.

Later in the day they sight Jomfruland to the northwest, and two days later they take a bearing on the Tromlings. The wind is rising from the southwest. It becomes hazy and overcast, and at 12 o'clock the captain summons the Ship's Council to a meeting in his cabin. The wind is unfavourable for a ship as heavily laden as the *Fredensborg*, and they decide to put into port. They head for the coast outside Arendal, and the Merdø pilots do not fail them. At 3 o'clock the pilot comes on board and two hours later the port anchor touches bottom at a depth of 6 1/2 fathoms. They let out two bights of cable and secure the new stern cable to a mooring pole on a little holm. The sails are furled, the skiff is put out and the two passengers go for a walk on Merdø. In the letter which Captain Kiønig writes to the Board of Directors the following day, he includes a report about the voyage thus far. Gales from west to southwest, along with heavy seas, have caused minor damage to the sails and rigging. The best course of action for the ship, cargo and lives has been to put into port and wait for better weather. Two men are sick; one of these is Able Seaman Ragnal Nielsen.

Merdø had all the qualities for a good outport. The anchorage was safe and sheltered from winds from every direction, and the approach to and from the open sea was short. Merdø was mentioned as a port as early as 1524. "West of Tromoe is the celebrated Harbour of Mardøe…", wrote Peder Clausson Friis in 1613. On Merdø one could quench one's thirst in one of the taverns, or from the spring that never ran dry. The pilots kept watch from Valen, the highest point on the island. By 1645 a compass rose had been carved in the rock, where the pilots could take a quick bearing before they set out. In common with many of the outports there was often a little "Seafarer's Graveyard", where sailors were buried who had either died of an illness or were so-called "shore-washers" – dead bodies washed ashore from wrecked ships. Merdø's graveyard, which was simply called "The Graves", was on the west side of the island. On Merdø there was a shipyard and a store. Seamen, fishermen and pilots lived here, and it was also possible to make minor repairs. Arendal, with its active trading and shipbuilding milieu, was located a little farther down the fjord. At the Næs Ironworks, a few miles outside of town, high-grade iron was produced that was used, among other things, for anchors, bolts and fittings in connection with the shipbuilding and repairs. A ropeworks at Tangen, on Hisøy, provided supplies of rope. It was not without reason that Captain Kiønig preferred to go into Merdø of all places.

While the *Fredensborg* is anchored in Merdø harbour, they take the opportunity of replenishing the water supply. A watchful captain always saw to it that the water barrels were filled with fresh water whenever the opportunity arose. Second Mate Ferentz takes five men and fetches five cords of birchwood and several spruce logs, which he buys from Toldorph, who lives on Gjessøya and has a store in Merdø harbour. There is still a fresh breeze, but not bad enough to prevent them from tarring both sides of the ship. Every day the men are summoned to prayers in accordance with the instructions of the "High Honourable Company" for its slave ships: "The Captain shall strictly and earnestly see to it that the fear of God is upheld on board the ship, and that prayers are said and hymns are sung every day, and that the Captain or the Ship's Assistant or one of the officers, on Sundays and holidays, shall read the day's gospel with an explanation of the sermon. Whereupon a hymn shall be sung before and after, and prayers shall be said every day."

On Annunciation Day there is a service in Tromøy Church. A number of the "men", or ordinary seamen on board, as well as the passengers and officers receive permission to attend church. Tromøy Church was an old navigational marker that had been used for centuries. There was a saying among seafarers: "When Tromøy Church on water stands, you are now three miles from land." In earlier times it was called "The Church on Mardø". The oldest part of the church is from the 12th century; the last time it was rebuilt and decorated was in 1758. The group from the *Fredensborg* has seen the white, south wall from the sea as they sailed past. Now they enter by the church vestibule and sit quietly on the benches at the back. Above the entrance to the choir they can see two angels flanking two lions that are holding King Frederik V's monogram and his motto: PRUDENTIA ET CONSTANTIA ("Wisdom and Perseverance"). Even inside the beautiful church the seamen are reminded of their profession: They listen to The Word while sitting in a navigational marker, looking up at the church ship, a model of the frigate *Queen of Denmark,* which belonged to the Asiatic Company in Copenhagen.

Jens Boye, the parson himself, has presented the model to the church. Boye, who is Danish, was the ship's chaplain on board the frigate during two voyages to Canton in China, before he became the parson on Tromøy. The captain during both voyages was Zacharias Allewelt who was born in Bergen. Allewelt had also been the

*Captain Zacharias Allewelt and Chief Officer Lewis Lawson who sailed to China on the* Queen of Denmark. *The clay figures are housed in the Aust-Agder Museum and were probably made in Canton in 1741.*

*The Captains Zacharias Allewelt and Jesper With also owned the property "Merdøgaard" on Merdø outside of Arendal. The boathouse is on the left, while the stall and the barn are hidden behind the main building. The combination of farming with sailing was practical in these coastal communities. Merdøgaard is now a museum and represents a traditional old skipper's residence.*

captain of a slave ship. In 1727 he took the galleon *The Young Maiden* on a voyage in the triangular trade. At Fort Christiansborg in Guinea he loaded 51 slaves, of whom 19 died during the passage to the West Indies.

Zacharias Allewelt had also owned a house on Merdø. From the deck of the *Fredensborg* one could see all the way over to the large two-storey house off the port bow. Allewelt was married to a girl from the Arendal district, and they had four children. He had sold the house to another China Captain, Jesper With, who was on the Board of Directors of the Guinea Company and had sent the *Fredensborg* on its way. Jesper With had also found a wife in Arendal, and they had a son named Mouritz. Little Mouritz sailed bark boats by the sandy shore just below the house on Merdø. Later he would be given larger vessels to sail. After several voyages to the East, Mouritz With also became a famous captain. He and his father each went on six voyages with the great Chinafarers, and the three captains from Merdø and Arendal carried out a total of 16 voyages as China Captains. This is no out-of-the-way cranny where the *Fredensborg* is lying at anchor on her way to Guinea, but an active and extrovert society with strong links with both Copenhagen and the wider world.

Able Seaman Ragnal Nielsen becomes worse. Doctor Sextus' medicines are ineffective and Nielsen asks to be permitted to disembark. The seaman has a brother who lives in Sandvigen, on Hisøy, not far from Merdø. He is taken there in the afternoon. Before Captain Kiønig will discharge him, there are financial problems that must be settled. The seaman owes two months' wages in advance and ten rixdaler to the captain. Nielsen says he will repay this as soon as he is well and finds employment. His diagnosis and credit must have been poor because Captain Kiønig will not accept this. He insists upon a guarantee. This is arranged when Naval Lieutenant Abo, who is Ragnal Nielsen's naval superior, is called in. Against a guarantee that Nielsen's brother, who is on his way from Lisbon, will repay the debt of 21 rixdaler, everything is settled. The brother is unaware of the debt he has incurred, but his wife agrees in order to solve the problem. Ragnal Nielsen's sea chest, which is still on board, is opened and the contents itemized before it is sent ashore with Abo. In order that all the formalities are taken care of, Sixtus writes out a doctor's certificate as a voucher for the ship's journal.

The vacant berth of seaman on board the *Fredensborg* has to be filled. Captain Kiønig goes in to Arendal and on the same day that Ragnal Nielsen is crossed off the crew list, a new name is written in. This is Christian Runge from Arendal who on 4 July 1767 boards the frigate at Merdøfjord, at a wage of 5 1/2 rixdaler a month. He receives an advance of 16 1/2 rixdaler in exchange for a receipt, which Kiønig locks in the ship's chest. Back in Arendal his father, Customs Examiner Conrad Runge, and his mother, Mette Marie, are undoubtedly worried about their son's forthcoming voyage in the triangular trade.

The watches on board the *Fredensborg* are divided into two so-called "quarters": The *King's Quarter* and the *Queen's Quarter*. Christian Runge replaces Ragnal Nielsen and joins Chief Officer Lundberg and Third Mate Beck in the Queen's Quarter. The day is divided into six watches. For measuring time an hourglass is used, in which the sand runs out every half hour. At the beginning of the watch the hourglass is turned, and when it is empty the helmsman rings the bell that hangs by the wheel. The blow, which is called a "strike", is a double blow with a slight pause between each two strikes. The forward watch repeats the blows on the big ship's bell. At eight bells, four hours have elapsed. The watch from midnight until 4 a.m. was called "The Dog-Watch", and was considered to be the worst.

The following days are spent on necessary tasks on board. Boatswain Rosenberg takes four men and rows over to Tromøy where they cut birch twigs for new brooms, while Gunner Beck inspects and oils the ship's small arms. Beck, who is fond of weapons, undoubtedly enjoys this task. On a slave ship weapons are an important part of the equipment. There is always the danger of a slave rebellion on board, and every weapon has to function properly. There is also the possibility of attacks from enemy men-of-war and pirates during the long voyage, and according to the instructions they "shall always be prepared for and capable of defense". Beck has a list of everything he is responsible for, and on this list we find:

## THE GUNNER'S INVENTORY

| | |
|---|---|
| 10 *four-pound cannons* | 1 *tailor's thimble* |
| 10 *gun carriages* | 6 *1/2 alen heavy cloth* |
| 10 *breechings for ditto* | (1 alen = 62.81 cm) |
| 20 *gun tackles* | 24 *tampions* |
| 40 *blocks* | 8 *firing pins* |
| 10 *lead plates* | 14 *lbs wicks* |
| 5 *spare wheels* | 60 *lbs red ochre* |
| 4 *half-pound swivel guns with* | 30 *lbs anchor yellow* |
| *appropriate gun-mounts* | 40 *lbs white lead* |
| 4 *lead plates for ditto* | 3 *lbs cinnabar* |

1 drum with 2 drumsticks

1 extra drumhead for ditto

2 cannon worms

1 small ditto

40 gun-flints

8 cleaning rods

2 lambskins for ditto

839 lbs gunpowder

21 lbs fine priming powder

1 wooden plug and tallow

2 lead plates soldered together to
cover slave stove and opening
to powder magazine

114 x 4 lb ordinary and 1 bar-shot

9 x 1 lb lead ditto


23 small arms

4 blunderbusses with flintlocks

9 pistols

10 swords

2 copper calipers

7 powderhorns

2 iron linstoks


10 fuse casks

4 gun nails

1 hammer

9 padlocks

1 painter's grinding stone

50 linchpins

10 gun lanterns

2 hand ditto

2 lbs thick steel wire

30 lamp brackets

1 cabin chest with lock

150 foot bolts


300 foot irons

300 netting nails

3 lbs minium

1 lb brick red

109 potts boiled linseed oil
(1 pott = ca. 0.966 l)

28 assorted brushes

3 lbs cartridge thread

2 doz cartridge pins

2 cartouche cases

1 roll lead

1 clump lead

1 copper sheet

2 copper spikes

20 ditto small

6 iron crowbars

6 cartridge pouches

6 grappling hooks

1 armchest with lock and key

2 bullet-moulds for flint-lock
muskets and pistols

1 vice

2 cartouche plates

6 wooden linstoks

2 wooden powder measures

10 gun nails

1 pincers

2 gun bits

16 lead flintlock bullets

4 lbs thin white twine


1 file

8 axes

1/2 ream cartridge paper

2 hatch lanterns

1 casting stone

1 cabin lock and key

4 wooden half-cannons

30 wrist irons

15 ditto bolts


They have brought surprisingly few cannon balls. The supply would not last very long during a serious skirmish. There is only a little musket and pistol shot, but they have the equipment and lead for casting more along the way. The most intriguing items on the list must be the four wooden half-cannons. These are fake cannons that can be placed in the empty gun ports in the event of the approach of a possible enemy. Then the *Fredensborg* would appear to be more dangerous than she really is.

The ship's supplies of irons, bolts and nails are intended for the cargo of slaves. It is obvious that they were counting on enough foot irons for 300 slaves. The large supply of gunpowder on board creates a considerable security risk, not only for the ship and the crew but also for nearby ships and buildings and the inhabitants of the outports. It is not without reason that the instructions are especially strict on this point: "In the event there is a large amount of gunpowder in the cargo during the outward journey, the Captain shall see to it that absolutely no one comes anywhere near the powder chamber or is permitted to smoke tobacco. And if anyone does smoke tobacco this must take place out on deck, and there must always be a lid on the bowl of the pipe."

It is important that the powder kegs are turned at regular intervals in order to prevent the gunpowder from caking. Such an operation is carried out on 8 July. Gunner Beck and Ship's Assistant Hoffmann take four seamen with them for this dangerous task. According to the instructions: "...when entering the powder chamber one should proceed with the utmost caution, and see to it that fire and wicks are thoroughly extinguished and, in other respects, that it is treated correctly".

The weather is still bad, with plenty of rain, and the sails have to be loosened frequently in order to dry. Ever since Captain Kiønig went to Arendal he has stopped writing in his journal. The reason is not given, but there is every indication that he has a partiality for strong spirits. The Captain's failure to use the quill is no disaster, because Ship's Assistant Hoffmann writes all the more assiduously in his own journal. He is the Company's general controller and accountant on board the ship, and in accordance with the 22-page, 31-point list of Instructions, he is supposed to see to it that everything is done properly. It is inevitable that conflicts will arise between the officers, and a niggling ship's assistant who writes everything down. All sorts of things can happen during a long voyage, which the Company need not know about. If, for example, Captain Kiønig were to give the order to fire an imprudent little cannon salute in European waters in honour of one of the Company's servants, this would cost him a whole month's wages if it were recorded.

On 13 July it appears as if the wind is favourable enough to continue the voyage: "...in order to find out about the direction of the wind at sea, the Captain goes up to one of the highest cliffs near the water and observes the wind there, but finds it to be westerly at sea." Captain Kiønig has been up on Valen at Merdø, where the pilots have their lookout post, and they warn him against setting out in such conditions. But finally the wind veers east. The *Fredensborg* weighs anchor and sets sail, but encounters a strong current that stands inshore when they sail out. The pilots take no chances. They head towards shore, and the frigate remains anchored at Sandvigen until the following day. On 16 July 1767 the ship finally heads out to sea, and Hoffmann writes:

"Today, in the name of God, we have weighed anchor from Sandvig harbour and are heading into the North Sea, after we have been anchored here from 29 June until today, accordingly nearly 17 days. May God continue to be with us and show us His blessing in our undertaking". The good captain sets his course for the English Channel, the shortest way to Africa.

The octant and the compass were not the only navigational instruments that were used. The chief officer was responsible for four lead lines and four leads that weighed 60, 30, 12 and 8 pounds respectively. If the speed and depth were great, the heaviest lead had to be used in order for it to sink quickly. At the end of each lead there was a hollow filled with grease. The lead had two functions. It enabled them to take soundings of the depth, and samples of the condition of the seabed. Experienced captains and mates could often determine the position of the ship with the help of the samples from the bottom which were picked up with the lead. And on the *Fredensborg* the leads were frequently used.

Wednesday 29 July. "End of watch, took soundings, depth 27 fathoms, fine yellowish sand. 2 bells. Furled staysail. 4 bells. Took in topsails and main topmast staysail at end of watch, depth 25 fathoms, red coarse sand, pumped dry. During watch sighted lighthouse ahead. Ostend sighted at 8 bells. Sounding 22 fathoms, yellowish sand…"

Five days later they had sighted the White Cliffs of Dover, followed by the Isle of Wight where they were becalmed for four days.

Like other ships the *Fredensborg* was a self-sufficient society out on the great oceans. Those on board were more or less dependent on each other's knowledge. The captain and the other officers, the carpenter, the sailmaker, the cooper, the cook and the seamen were all necessary in order to ensure a safe voyage. The youngest, who were the nimblest, functioned best high up in a swaying mast.

Strict discipline was absolutely necessary on board if everything was to function. The Ship's Articles were the law that everyone had to obey. The punishment for breaking these laws was severe on land as well as at sea. The degree of punishment was not always in keeping with the general sense of justice, even according to the premises of the period.

However, quarrels were unavoidable on board a ship the size of the *Fredensborg*, where everyone lived in such close quarters. One day there was a more serious episode. Quartermaster Abraham Engmann was not very popular. He was arrogant and thought he was better than everyone else because he was related to Chamberlain Engmann on the Board of Directors. In addition, he was the petty officer's brother and thought he could take liberties on board, which irritated both the officers and the crew. On deck there were two beer barrels where everyone could help himself when he was thirsty. According to regulations they were supposed to drink from a pitcher that hung beside the barrel. It was forbidden to fill bottles. Engmann paid little attention to this, and one day, when he had come to fill some bottles, a fight broke out. During the King's Quarter, several of the crew members had received their porridge from the cook, and sat eating out on deck when the quartermaster from the Queen's Quarter turned up. Since Able Seaman Ole Nicolaysen was greatly involved, we will let him tell.

"…how, a moment ago, I was disgracefully attacked and badly beaten up by Abraham Engmann. The reason for this is as follows: He wanted to fill up his bottles, despite the fact that this is forbidden. I saw this and asked if he couldn't drink from the pitcher like everybody else, whereupon, I must confess, I called him a 'German lout'. I leave it up to my Captain to decide whether or not he deserves this name. But regardless of the outcome, I hope he will say that Abraham Engmann does not have the right to mistreat me in such a foul manner. Because, after he had heard these words, he rushed at me, threw me down on the deck, and hit me on the head with a bottle so everything went black, and it broke into bits, of which many fell into a bowl of porridge so the men were unable to eat more of it. I can bear witness to this and even more. The fact that this mistreatment could easily have cost me my life is so clear, that I have nothing more to add. I appeal to my lord Captain's just verdict, as to the punishment such behaviour deserves. I shall constantly see to it that I behave in such a way that my eminent Captain shall be satisfied with me."

*Captain Kiønig pronounces judgement on Abraham Engmann and Ole Nicolaysen after the fight by the beer barrel.*

Ole named several witnesses, and the Ship's Council was summoned aft to Captain Kiønig's cabin. One by one the witnesses were called in, and their evidence was largely in keeping with Ole's letter. We learn that it was the sailmaker's porridge that had been spoiled by bits of glass, and that Engmann had called Ole a "Norwegian blockhead". Then the case against Engmann was ready for judgement.

Ship's Carpenter Beck felt that Engmann ought to receive 150 lashes with the cat-o'-nine-tails and, in addition, lose a month's wages. Boatswain Rosenberg went in for 81 lashes and a month's wages. Second Mate Ferentz maintained that Engmann had never done anything for the benefit of the Company, but had always behaved as he pleased without the interference of any of the other officers. Several times previously Engmann had uttered curses and otherwise behaved improperly, so that in Ferentz' opinion he ought to be punished with half-a-hundred lashes, as a warning both to himself and to others. For the same reason, Nicolaysen ought to receive several lashes.

Chief Officer Lundberg pointed out that Engmann had been guilty of disobeying point 40 in the Ship's Articles, and had been insubordinate to all the members of the Ship's Council. He felt that a crime such as this, and bad behaviour, deserved 50 lashes with the cat-o'-nine-tails. In addition, Nicolaysen should receive some for having called Engmann a "German lout".

After this Captain Kiønig pronounced the following judgement: The accused, Abraham Engmann, was to receive 50 lashes with the cat-o'-nine-tails. The boatswain and the boatswain's mate were to see to it that the sentence was carried out at once. This was to take place inside the cabin. And for his cursing, Ole Nicolaysen was to receive several lashes. The number was left up to the captain. These were to be delivered out on deck in full view of everyone.

*Algerian Sea Pass from the 18th century. The top part was sent to the Barbary States. The corsairs did not understand Danish, but the practical solution was a wavy line as identification.*

When Engmann's punishment was administered in the cabin, it ended with his being reprieved after 30 lashes. Poor Ole, who had a bloodstained rag around his head, suffered the most. After 47 blows out on the deck Captain Kiønig decided that justice had been done, and dismissed it with a wave of his hand.

According to point 40 of the Ship's Articles, severe punishment could be expected for certain offences on board. Abraham Engmann and Ole Nicolaysen could be thankful that neither of them had pulled a knife on the other. When tempers flared, it was easy to resort to a knife, which most seamen carried as a necessary tool of their trade. Thus, strict regulations were necessary concerning the use of a knife: "Whoever on board the ship pulls a knife in a temper to harm his neighbour or defend himself, even

though no harm is done, then the hand of the one with a knife shall be pinned to the mast by the same knife, and he shall remain standing until he draws the knife from his hand, and, in addition, forfeit two months' wages!" There is reason to believe that the strict Ship's Articles from the time of Christian IV, for "Merchant ships that sailed to the West Indies, Guinea, as well as the Mediterranean" were not fully carried out. On a long voyage every man on board was needed. This was especially true of the triangular trade.

The *Fredensborg* carried a Latin and an Algerian Sea Pass. The Latin Sea Pass was proof that the ship was Danish property. It was written in Danish, English and French, in Latin letters – hence the name. The Algerian Sea Pass was more unusual and an important part of the ship's papers. This was a permit of safe passage through pirate waters!

The North African countries of Algeria, Tunisia, Morocco and Tripolitania were known as "The Barbary Coast". For centuries the "barbarians" were a considerable threat to shipping off North Africa. In their swift vessels, often rowed by galley slaves, they usually struck during a calm. They demanded exorbitant sums in order to release ships and crews who had been captured. Many Danish-Norwegian ships had been seized by the pirates. The seamen were made slaves and lived under terrible conditions in foreign lands. Some of the captors were very brutal, like Mulai Ismail in Morocco.

In Norway as well as Denmark there was considerable sympathy for the poor seamen who were slaves under barbaric conditions. For this reason, with royal permission, collections were taken up in the Danish-Norwegian churches in order to ransom the seamen. Twice a year the collection was taken for the "Prisoners in Turkey", or "the Slave Treasury" as it was later called. In the churches the collections were made on Christmas Day and on Candlemas Day – 2 February. Sometimes the names of the prisoners were read aloud, as during the collection in Arendal Church in 1713 when the money was intended for Anders Fridericssøn from

*New Construction no 1, The Country's Desire from Copenhagen, was captured and brought to Algeria in 1769. This was only two years after the Fredensborg had sailed past on her way to the Gold Coast. Christian Børs from Bergen was one of the crew members who had been taken prisoner. He ended up serving coffee as a slave for the Dey of Algiers until peace was restored in May 1772.*

*57*

*The prison for Christian slaves in Algeria, rendered by an unknown artist in the 18th century.*

Bergen and Ellef Larssøn from Arendal. The result was 106 rixdaler, which was far more than usual, but then of course this was a local boy. Skipper Larssøn had been on his way to Spain in 1712 when the ship was captured and the entire crew taken prisoner. Jørgen Andersøn was also among the unfortunates. He was released from captivity after four years, the skipper somewhat earlier. It is apparent that Larssøn, who died a few years later, had been ruined by this experience. In spite of the collection, his widow had to struggle for many years in order to repay the rest of the ransom which had probably been borrowed. During the period from 1713 to 1758 around 650 rixdaler had been collected for the Slave Treasury in Arendal Church. There were many churches in the country so that considerable sums were collected for this special purpose. In 1756 the directors of the Slave Treasury were able to report to the king that "God in this way has blessed this good work, so that, up to now, one hundred and sixty-three people have been released, and not a single one of your Royal Majesty's subjects remains as a slave in Algeria". It had cost around 1000 rixdaler for every slave whose freedom had been purchased, a considerable sum at that time.

Paradoxically it sometimes happened that the entire crew of a slave ship, on their way to West Africa to transport Africans to the West Indies, ended up themselves as slaves among the barbarians. Most of those who were captured were from ordinary merchant ships on peaceful errands. A few of the prisoners escaped slavery by allowing themselves to be converted and become a part of the society. When women were captured, it was a short trip to the Arab harems. For this reason several of Europe's leading seafaring nations found it necessary to enter into treaties with the barbarians. The payment for a safe voyage was largely made in luxury items, cannons and gunpowder.

After lengthy negotiations, Denmark-Norway succeeded in working out an agreement with the Dey of Algiers in 1746. His corsairs were to respect the Danish-Norwegian flags and property, and the seamen were to be neither sold nor mistreated. The parties were to live in eternal peace and friendship, and were not supposed to molest one another's ships. A similar treaty was signed with Tunis in 1751, with Tripolitania the following year, and with Morocco in 1753. After a decree of 1 May 1747 every Danish-Norwegian ship that sailed further south than Cape Finisterre in northwestern Spain had to carry a special Sea Pass, which they had to show if they were attacked by pirates.

The top part of the Sea Pass had been clipped away in a wavy line, and was to be found on board the Algerian pirate ships. The main part, containing the name of the ship, etc., was on board the Danish-Norwegian vessel. If the wavy lines matched, they were allowed to sail on.

Slowly and steadily the *Fredensborg* sailed south without having to use the Algerian Sea Pass, which cost around 52 rixdaler in Copenhagen. She was greatly assisted by the Portuguese Current and later by the Canary Current. It became warmer and warmer with every passing day. And during the beautiful sunsets, when it began to be cool out on the quarterdeck, it sometimes happened that Captain Kiønig and Fourth Mate Gadt took out their violins. Someone else on board played the flute. Out on the great ocean familiar melodies stirred up feelings of homesickness, even among the toughest men on board. The youngest thought about their mothers and fathers, others about their wives and children – while Able Seaman Niels Mathiesen thought about death. He had been sick ever since he signed on in Copenhagen, and his condition had worsened during the voyage. Considering the health standards of the time, one could count on the fact that among 40 men there were some who had serious ailments.

On Friday 28 August they were sailing between Madeira and the Canary Islands. The sails were set and the carpenter was making new oars for the rowboat. Six bells and the sands had run out in Niels Mathiesen's hourglass. He was dead and was immediately brought up on deck, where the sailmaker received orders to sew him into his own hammock. His hands were folded on his chest, and the sailmaker started sewing. Since the supply of cannon balls was so small, there is reason to believe that coal was used as a weight at his feet. According to custom, the final stitch was sewn through the nose of the deceased to ensure that he was dead and not unconscious. Then the sailmaker made a few holes by the side of his head to let out the air. When the corpse had been sewn in, the flag was lowered to half-mast and the deceased was placed on a plank lying on two trestles by the gangway port. It was a hard and fast rule that when a body was committed to the deep, it had to be done from the starboard side. They had no ship's chaplain, so Captain Kiønig officiated and said a few appropriate words about the deceased. They sang a hymn and recited The Lord's Prayer, while the crew stared at the unmistakable shape that was ready to be given up to the sea. At a signal from the captain the plank was tilted so the body slid down into the water. "Farewell Niels! May the Lord have mercy on your soul". His shipmates stared at the bubbles that came up from the deep and vanished in its wake.

The following morning the dead seaman's worldly goods were brought out on deck, evaluated and sold at auction. Ship's Assistant Hoffmann recorded everything in his journal:

| | |
|---|---|
| *1 knife with sheath* | *1 saucepan* |
| *1 ditto* | *1 bunk pillow* |
| *1 hammer* | *1 paper bag containing a little tea* |
| *1 pair worn slippers* | *2 pairs woolen gloves* |
| *A few small possessions in a white canvas bag* | *4 pairs old woolen stockings* |
| | *1 pair old boots* |
| *2 pairs new shoes* | *1 down coverlet with sheet* |
| *1 pair pewter shoe buckles* | *1 pillow* |
| *1 Danish prayerbook* | *1 blue greatcoat* |
| *2 white and 1 blue-chequered shirt* | *1 hat* |
| *1 old greatcoat* | *1 cap with visor* |
| *2 blue kerchiefs* | *1 wallet with 2 compartments* |
| *1 pair wide pants* | *1 fishing line* |
| *1 pair white underpants* | *1 canvas greatcoat* |
| *1 brown woolen wrap* | *1 old bag with lengths of cloth* |
| *1 pair flannel pants* | *1 pair duck pants* |
| *1 dish* | *2 knitted vests* |

A seaman did not bring many belongings with him on a long voyage. Perhaps this was everything Niels Mathiesen owned here on earth. There is no mention of money. Even though he had a wallet with two compartments it was empty. His possessions, which were evaluated at 8 rixdaler, were sold for about 19 rixdaler. The hammock that was used for the burial belonged to the Company. It was estimated at 1 rixdaler, which was deducted from his effects. This was the same amount that Ordinary Seaman Peder Madsen paid for a white shirt during the auction.

Day after day they continued south. After a while the *Fredensborg* headed in a more easterly direction and set her course for the Gulf of Guinea. The Guinea Current was of considerable help because it also moved in the "right" direction. Captain Kiønig had not recovered the desire to write after the stop at Merdø. If the ink used decreased only slightly, the supply of potables at his disposal decreased all the more. He only made a few notes in his journal during the voyage to the Gold Coast. The Company's instructions to the captain were clear enough. According to point 39 in the Ship's Articles he was supposed to write in his journal every day.

One day the men were assembled on deck and the Ship's Articles were read aloud. It was best to have a reminder before they arrived in Guinea. In addition, according to the instructions, this was supposed to be carried out at regular intervals. Christian Runge, who had taken over as Able Seaman after Ragnal Nielsen, had to swear an oath to the King and the Company under a broiling tropical sun.

Between 11 a.m. and 12 noon on 20 September they sighted land and stood in towards the coast. When the *Fredensborg* passed the Dutch Fort Elmina, and later the

Opposite page:
*A 17th century map of West Africa with an inset of the Gold Coast. The many forts and trading stations marked with flags reveal the predominance of forts along the Gold Coast. The development continued after the map had been drawn.*

*When the* Fredensborg *arrived at the Gold Coast, Fort Christiansborg must have looked something like this.*

English Cape Coast Castle, they fired a 9-gun salute in accordance with the instructions of the Company. They were outraged when the English returned a salute of only 5 guns. As they sailed along the coast they saw many vessels – French, English and Dutch. They anchored at Fort Anomabu, where a large canoe with ten Africans and an English boatswain came paddling out to the *Fredensborg*. Later in the day Second Mate Ferentz, along with Able Seamen Antoni Olsen and Ole Nicolaysen, rowed over to an English ship. They wanted to find out about the state of things at Fort Christiansborg, and learned that all was well. A total of eight English ships was lying at anchor in the roadstead at Anomabu. Most were undoubtedly slave ships that were waiting for cargoes. When Captain Kiønig gave orders to weigh anchor, the *Fredensborg* was in difficulty. Both flukes and the stock on the stream anchor broke, and they lost an anchor buoy and some rope. Later in the day they passed the English Fort James and the Dutch Fort Crevecour, which were not far from Christiansborg. A 7-gun salute was returned in full. Soon they could see Fort Christiansborg off the port bow, where the Danish flag was waving in the breeze, and the cannons were reloaded. They greeted the main Danish-Norwegian fort on the Gold Coast with a 9-gun salute. The fort answered with the same number, while the *Fredensborg* turned against the wind and dropped anchor. The Company ship, the snow *Elonora* with Captain Thadsen in command, fired a 5-gun salute which was returned. A total of 28 salutes had been fired by the time the *Fredensborg* dropped anchor in Christianborg roadstead on 1 October 1767, after a voyage that had taken 103 days.

Chapter 4

# Slaves, Ivory and Gold

The arrival of a ship from Copenhagen was an important event at Fort Christiansborg, which had been built in 1661. To the white personnel at the fort any sign of life from home was a great encouragement. Most of them were clearly marked by their stay on the Gold Coast, which was very demanding both physically and mentally. Letters from family and friends, and news from home were rare luxuries. The death-rate was high and the arrival of a ship usually meant new personnel. Others had an opportunity to return home.

If the *Elonora*'s cargo had been welcome, the *Fredensborg*'s cargo was even more valuable. With her 139 tons, the *Fredensborg* carried considerably more than a snow, and the products that were brought to the Coast were the key to the entire trading system. The white man was in Africa to barter for slaves, ivory and gold. To the west lay the Ivory Coast; the Slave Coast lay to the east. But this was the enticing Gold Coast! With imposing bastions and menacing cannons, the forts were lined up like pearls on a string.

The whites were spared the troubled hunting for slaves in the bush. They only had to sit and wait. On their own two feet, the slaves walked in through the gates of the fort, brutally driven by African merchants who would reap the rewards of the well-filled storehouse of the fort. The vicious circle was well underway. A state of dependency had soon arisen that was of mutual advantage to both the Whites and the Africans. European goods were in great demand. Spirits flowed and trade flourished.

It all started in 1492 when Christopher Columbus re-discovered America, which was called "the New World" or the "West Indies". On his second voyage in 1493 he brought along two blacks, who were put ashore in Hispaniola in the Caribbean, where the first Spanish settlement was established. There is no reason to believe that there were plans to use Africans as manpower at that time. As the need for labourers gradually arose, they first tried the natives who were called "Indians". It soon turned out that the Indians were unable to withstand the hard work and the European diseases. Many succumbed. As a result there was an acute

*A map of Guinea. In this version from Frederik V's Atlas we see:*
*A – Dwelling,*
*B – Kitchen,*
*C – Grainery,*
*D – Trading House,*
*E – Veranda,*
*F – Public Area,*
*H-G – Royal personages. Notice the piles and measuring of the elephant tusks. The Fredensborg had almost a ton of ivory on board when she went down.*

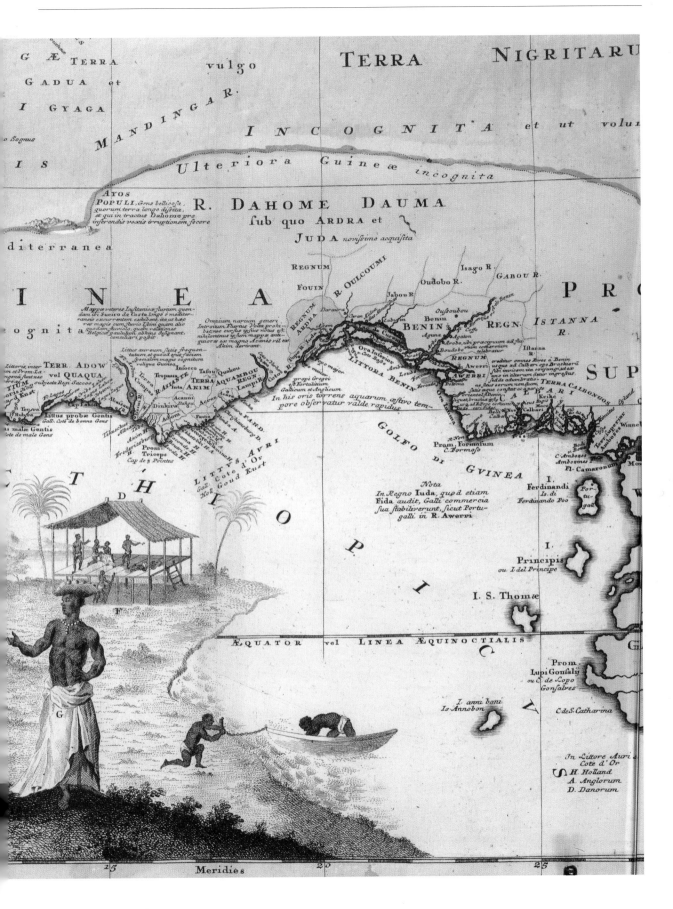

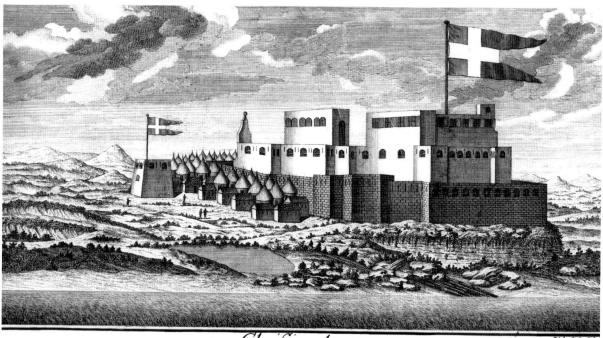

Christiansborg
ved accra
paa Cuften Guinea naar man feer det i N:O.

*A view of Fort Christiansborg from the sea around the middle of the 18th century. The little fortification with its own flag was called Prøvestenen ("The Touchstone").*

demand for manpower, both on the plantations that cultivated sugar, cotton and tobacco, and in the mines. Slavery spread to South America, especially to Brazil, the islands in the Caribbean and several places around the Gulf of Mexico. It spread to several nations that had established colonies in "the New World", and among the actors were Portugal, Spain, England, France, the Netherlands – and Denmark-Norway.

As early as 1482 Fort São Jorge da Mina, later called "Elmina", was built by the Portuguese. They had discovered that this part of the coast was rich in gold, giving rise to names like "Elmina" – which means "the Mine" – and "the Gold Coast".

The Portuguese were also responsible for the oldest slave trade by ship along the Gold Coast. In the 1480s they purchased slaves in the Niger Delta and sold them to the Africans at Fort Elmina. Some of these slaves were probably used as manpower in the gold mines in the interior. A few years later the transatlantic slave trade had begun in earnest. Along a relatively short stretch of coast, one fort after another had been built in order to organize the flow of coastal commodities. They learned from one another and developed the ingenious sailing pattern which was called "the triangular trade". Millions of slaves had already been transported across the ocean when the *Fredensborg* arrived at the Gold Coast in 1767.

Fort Christiansborg stood on a little promontory that jutted into the sea. There was no harbour or quay that could be used for the unloading of supplies and slaves. In towards land the waters became very shallow with long stretches of sandy beaches and foaming breakers. Both the *Fredensborg* and the *Elonora* were anchored some distance out in the roadstead, a spot with sharp sunken rocks that were dangerous to the hawsers. Among the Africans were the so-called "remidors", or rowers, who were specialists at mastering the sea and the dangerous breakers with their canoes. The canoes had been hollowed-out from huge tree trunks and managed the passage through the breakers surprisingly well. The longboats on board the European ships were far less suited to this.

On board the *Fredensborg* there is a surge of activity after they drop anchor. The sails have to be furled and preparations made for unloading the cargo from Copenhagen.

A canoe slices through the breakers with a white man on board. This is Mr. Reimers from the fort, who has come to pay a courtesy and welcoming call. Reimers remains on board until the following day, and goes back with Captain Kiønig and the two passengers, Wrisberg and Grathorn, who are to serve at the fort. What they must be thinking as they plunge through the breakers, we do not know. A stay on the Coast may lead to prosperity and a quick career, but one may also contract a serious illness. There is every chance of being bitten by a malaria mosquito. The ensuing fever is called "climate fever" and, as a rule, results in death. Those who survive may hold out for a few years along the Coast, but it rarely happens that anyone returns home safe and sound. Dysentery, yellow fever, heatstroke, smallpox and the Guinea worm are other common afflictions. The deathrate is high and the life expectancy is alarmingly brief among the Europeans. It is said that entering the service along the Gold Coast means saying "Goodbye" to one's old age. In his book *Tilforladelig Efterretning om Kysten Guinea (A Reliable Account of the Guinea Coast)*, which was published in Copenhagen in 1760, Ludevig

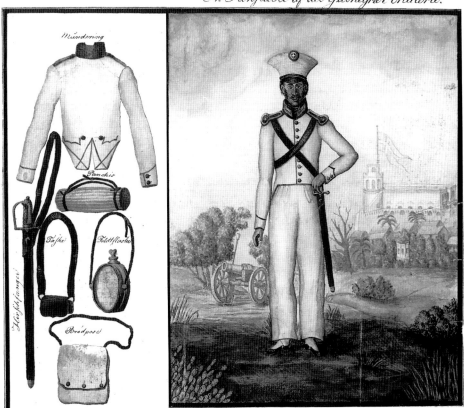

*A uniform and equipment used at the Danish-Norwegian forts in Guinea.*

*The Europeans encountered a long-established culture on the Gold Coast. At a yam feast in Asante around 1817 guests from several nations are present with their flags, including "Dannebrog", the Danish flag.*

Ferdinand Rømer – the man who, according to legend, haunts Narrestø – described conditions as follows:

"Arriving in this land is like arriving in a different world, where one sees different objects, different people and a different way of life. Everything is strange to us; we are grieved, we would rather beg for our daily bread from door to door than come to such an unpleasant land!"

Fort Christiansborg is a typical tropical fort with massive bastions and high whitewashed walls. Lined up on the walls are rows of black cannons as defence against attack from both land and sea. Around the courtyard are the storerooms, the fort's chapel and the notorious dungeons where the slaves are kept. Two cisterns provide the water supply. Governor Tychsen lives in the governor's quarters opposite the heavy main gate. The white personnel also live inside the walls. Rømer tells us that the fort is manned by "30 Europeans and 300 Negroes", but this could vary, of course. The Company usually saw to it that a doctor and a chaplain were among the white personnel.

The village of Osu, which is called "the Negeriet", is situated alongside the fort, and consists of a cluster of huts. Trees have been planted among the huts to provide shade from the blazing sun. One of the huts belongs to Asioke, an African woman who has had good contact with the fort and the ships in the roadstead. A redoubt called "Prøvesten" ("Touchstone") is just beyond the huts. Most of the people living in Osu have some connection with the fort which, having cannons, provides security and protection against enemy attack. The landing place for the canoes is on the eastern side of the fort not far from the main entrance.

Most of the whites prefer the security behind the thick walls of the fort. They are stationed in a troubled area where wars are raging among the Africans and life is worth only a pittance. The traditional religions, with their "fetishism" and mysticism, also create anxiety and apprehension. The feeling of security is greater with substantial supplies of bullets, gunpowder and provisions. Along the coast to the east are Fort Fredensborg and the trading lodges at Ada and Quitta (Keta), which are under the jurisdiction of Fort Christiansborg. In this way the Danish-Norwegian sphere of influence extends 150 kilometres along the Gold Coast. Both the fort and the trading lodges have been established through treaties with local rulers who are able to collect a substantial "lease".

Kiønig, who has brought several letters both private and from the Board of Directors, is ushered into Governor Tychsen's office at the fort. After a welcoming drink and a report about the ship's cargo, the governor brings Kiønig up to date about the problems he has had to cope with on the Coast during his year as governor. He arrived on the ship *Christiansborg,* and has already sent 245 slaves to the West Indies, thanks to the merchandise he brought with him as articles of trade. Tychsen has had a very busy period, since the fort and the buildings were in very poor condition when he arrived. With a large supply of old stock, the competition from the English, and not least the Dutch forts in the vicinity has been unpleasantly keen. For this reason it is necessary to unload the *Fredensborg* as quickly as possible in order to begin trading, because he now has two ships that must be filled with slaves.

When Captain Kiønig comes on board the following day, bad news awaits him. The fourth mate, the cooper, the quartermaster and an able seaman have already contracted the dreaded "climate fever". Kiønig writes to the governor and requests that the sick men receive the necessary treatment at the fort. The governor regrets that he has no room for the sick men in the overcrowded fort, and they must be placed in "the Negeriet".

*Qvoú, an African born close to Christiansborg in Osu, displaying his military attire and his talismans. This is how a prominent African warrior would appear when he went into battle.*

When the canoe plunges through the breakers in the afternoon of 6 October, there is a plain coffin on board. Sitting beside the coffin are Fourth Mate Gadt and Cooper Jacobsen, who were close to the deceased. With eyes dulled by fever they gaze at the coffin, probably wondering who will be next. The two, who have brought their own bedding, stagger up to Asioke's hut. Quartermaster Engmann is already lying there, bathed in sweat. He was brought ashore earlier in the day.

The first from the *Fredensborg* to die, poor Peder Jacobsen finds his final resting place in the large graveyard of the fort, where the whites are lying in row after row. A salute is fired for the seaman.

The cost of carrying on the trade on the Coast is measured not only in money. By all accounts, the life expectancy for whites at the fort was less than two years. In addition, in the fort's graveyard there is plenty of room for the seamen who will be laid to rest there.

Ship's Surgeon Sixtus has to take care of the sick men from the *Fredensborg*. He is assisted by Schnell, the surgeon at the fort, who has "come to lend a helping hand".

Let us see what Ship's Surgeon Sixtus has brought with him in order to mend injuries and fight illness on a voyage in the triangular trade:

1 bone saw with 3 blades

1 wrench

1 separator

1 tourniquet in 4 parts i.e.

1 red braid silk band 1 in. wide

1 cloth bandage, 1 wooden toggle and 1 piece of leather

1 Abbel's forceps

1 red cloth bag in which to place instrument cases

1 casserole

1 case with complete double dispensing scale

1 pewter syringe with 1 pewter and 1 bone tube

1 "uberwerf" with 3 hooks

1 brass syringe with 3 tubes

40 alen new canvas

1 tin shaving basin

2 linen bands 1 in. wide

4 sponges

1/4 lb. thread

4 white skins

1 lb. twine

20 assorted jars

100 large and small stoppers

12 ditto boxes

4 papers of pins

1 silver catheter

1 trochar with silver ring and instrument case

1 pair of forceps with

7 curved needles in case,

2 needles with setatium with ditto, 1 brass-bound case containing these instruments

1 copper tea cettlel

1 Dutch scale

1 smaller Nurnberg ditto

1 small dispensing scale

1 dental forceps

1 little ivory syringe

1 double spatula

32 pounds Russian soap

4 old canvas cheets

1 serpentine mortar with pestle

1 graduated glass

2 medium ditto with pestles

4 lbs. "tow"

6 ox bladders

2 books "capsales"

2 ditto ordinary

2 quires writing paper

20 bottles A'zii

40 ditto      "

20 ditto      "

20 ditto      "

1/4  lod silk

24 assorted needles

1 "enema syringe with 2 tubes"

*1 chest with mountings, lock and key, as well as a complete assortment of jars and medicine bottles, 4 locks – 1 cabin lock and 3 cupboard locks with appropriate keys.*

This list gives some idea of what a ship's surgeon had at his disposal for taking care of the crew and a large cargo of slaves. In addition, most ship's surgeons had their own private instruments. This is why Sixtus' list is lacking in certain items. The contents of the numerous jars are not specified. But at any rate there was no "cinchona bark" (now quinine), which could have saved many lives. It should be mentioned that in those days, doctors on Dutch ships usually took along 155 different kinds of medicines on a voyage to the Orient. The Europeans who came to Africa brought diseases with them, but they encountered far more for which they had no remedies. In many instances the traditional medicines of the Africans were more effective. The chaplains at the fort, Johannes Rask and H.C. Monrad, report that it was possible to cure many ailments with a mixture of Grains of Paradise, Spanish pepper, palm oil and lemons. Indeed, even dysentery could be effectively treated with "mealy dishes prepared of yams and corn mixed with a yellowish root".

The unloading of the *Fredensborg* is soon well underway. Captain Kiønig supervises everything – according to the instructions: "When unloading the ship the Captain shall pay close attention, and see to it that the goods are carefully taken off the ship, and that all the special gun cases leave the ship in one piece, and that the gunpowder is kept dry when being loaded into the boat or the canoes, and that it is carefully packed and covered to avoid the breakers near land."

In order to unload the cargo quickly they have also borrowed the *Elonora*'s longboat from Captain Thadsen. The two longboats bring the cargo up to the breakers, where it is transferred to the remidors' canoes and ferried through the foaming breakers to the landing place. The barrels of spirits are first brought up on deck, where they are checked and topped up. Leakage – for which there may be several reasons – is not unusual. Then they are carefully lowered into the longboats along with various kinds of barrels and cases. The gunpowder is treated with extra care. There are several tons that have to be taken ashore, and it must be kept dry. The fort's own slaves – the "inventory slaves" – are waiting at the landing place to receive the cargo. Under strict supervision they carry the supplies into the storerooms of the fort, which are then properly locked.

The Directors in Copenhagen are very particular about the keeping of accounts. Two of the Company's directors, Engmann and Reindorph, have experienced life on the Coast themselves and know how easily things can get out of hand.

*A view of Fort Christiansborg from the east at the landing place. Asioke's hut, where many of the crew were nursed for their illnesses, was in "the Negeriet" alongside the fort.*

det Kongeliche danske hoved Castell
*Christiansborg*
ved accra
paa Custen Guinea naar man seer det i S:W.

One of the cases marked "DGC" contains a double set of ledgers, cashbooks, wage lists, inventory lists, journals, etc. According to the instructions everything of the slightest importance shall be duly recorded for the information of the Directors. During Fort Christiansborg's long and turbulent history the journals and ledgers have not been kept as painstakingly as the new Company has planned.

A few days after their arrival the decision is made to send the longboat, under the command of Second Mate Ferentz, with goods to Fort Fredensborg at Ningo. On board they are carrying 200 Danish and 50 Dutch muskets, 1,500 lbs of gunpowder, 100 iron bars and two barrels of spirits. From Fort Christiansborg they have brought a chest of linen, a barrel of knives, a basket of mugs – and two chests of "pantjes". These are small or large lengths of cloth that can be used as loincloths, toga-like garments, etc. Later the boat is sent on another trip to Fort Fredensborg with three coffins, 3 barrels of spirits, 55 kegs of gunpowder and two barrels of pork.

Fort Fredensborg, which was built in 1736, was beautifully situated by a lagoon at Ningo about 75 km east of Christiansborg. This fort was smaller than Christiansborg, but it also had bastions, thick walls and cannons. When Rømer served at the fort there were ten Europeans in residence, in addition to the rest of the garrison who were from the Coast. Nor was a "Negeriet" lacking alongside the walls of the fort.

After the purchase of St. Croix in 1733 the need for slaves increased and Fort Fredensborg turned out to be a good supplier. This was also the fort after which "our" slave ship was named. A large amount of salt, an important item of trade among the Africans, was obtained from the lagoon by the fort. With regard to the

*Fort Fredensborg, after which the frigate* Fredensborg *was named, was beautifully situated by a lagoon at Old Ningo. This drawing from the middle of the eighteenth century was reproduced in Ludevig Ferdinand Rømer's book which came out in 1760. Here he gained some of his most valuable experience as a slave trader.*

*Freedensborg, ved Ningo*
*–paa Cuſten Guinea naar man ſeer det i N:O:*

Ph. Räder Reg D. Calc. fec. Haffs

arrival of ships, Fort Fredensborg was more favourably situated in that the breakers were rarely a hindrance to traffic.

The rainy season sets in and with it the "travats", or squalls, in the form of violent gusts of wind, thunder and lightning and cloudbursts. During a violent travat on Sunday evening, 8 November, it is necessary to drop a spare anchor in a hurry. While this is being done, Chief Officer Lundberg has the misfortune of slipping on the catwalk on the port side. He falls overboard, and the crew can hear desperate cries in the darkness. They throw out ropes, man the longboat and search in vain for the unfortunate man. Lundberg's cabin is then locked and the key delivered to the captain's cabin. On the following day they find the chief officer dead, entangled in the ropes they had thrown out. "His large jacket was over his head, which had probably choked him", Hoffmann writes. Lundberg is hauled up on deck, and in spite of sharks that infest the sea his body is found to be unharmed.

Later in the afternoon the carpenter has finished his coffin, and the body is placed inside, dressed in a white shirt and a few other old garments. An honorary 7-gun salute is fired as the coffin is taken ashore. Lundberg is buried in the graveyard of the fort.

Second Mate Ferentz now moves up as chief officer after Lundberg. He is well qualified for the position. Captain Kiønig is not the only one who has neglected to keep a journal. Lundberg has also been lax in this respect, and the final entry is dated 5 September. It appears as if both he and Kiønig have had a premonition that they will not be held responsible for their neglect. When Ferentz takes over the journal, he writes in a firm and determined hand:

"In this authorized journal, provided by the Royal Chartered Danish Guinea Company for the Second in Command, I the undersigned have continued to make entries from 8 November of this year...

J. Ferentz"

With flourishes and curliques ending in a vertical line, the introduction stops where, to his considerable irritation, he leaves behind a couple of ugly ink splotches from his quill. From now on the writing picks up. Ferentz was obviously a man who prided himself on his ability to write, and made it a point of honour to provide a full account. Thanks to him, and an even more conscientious Ship's Assistant Hoffmann, we are informed about most of what took place.

In the days that follow life continues on board the *Fredensborg* – but hardly as usual. Sickness wreaks havoc among the crew. The unloading of the cargo continues, and barrels of pit coal, spirits and iron bars plunge through the surf in the canoes of the remidors. The ship's carpenter has begun to plane the materials for the slave platforms, while the sailmaker repairs the sails that also have to be aired after the powerful cloudbursts. The men on board sometimes receive fresh supplies from land. This might be meat, vegetables or chickens for the sick. Let us see how Ferentz has experienced the next few days on board:

"Sunday 22 November: A.M...loosen sails, hold service. Both carpenters and Fourth Mate Gadt and Abraham Engmann sick. P.M...9:30. Had a travat SE and SSE, with near gale and rain. Hauled a bight of port hawser on deck. At the same moment our old hawser parted. 10:30 P.M. travat over, hauled in the hawser, found it had parted just by the kedge anchor…"

The anchoring conditions outside the main fort were very difficult. Sharp undersea rocks could cut the cables, so they had to be examined every day. A smaller rope connected to a buoy was fastened to the anchor, so it could be saved if the anchor cable parted. The cables were especially exposed during the frequent and violent travats.

Wednesday 25 November: "A.M. Tortoise meat sent by Capt. Thadsen for the cabin. The sick men are still very weak, and getting weaker. P.M. A canoe brings Quartermaster Engmann on board. An English brig anchored off Fort James. Third Mate Beck returned from Fort Fredensborg and dropped the grapnel by the ship, brought him and the other seamen on board. Capt. Thadsen's longboat brought a hogshead of tainted corn for our pigs…"

Thursday 26 November: "A.M. Still no improvement among the sick. P.M. Letters arrived and some cabbage sent by the Capt. as refreshment for the men. The aforementioned English brig passed us, and later went down. 8 P.M. Set the watch and at night continued burning candles by the sick and set a man to keep watch over them…"

Friday 27 November: "P.M. 1 o'clock. Capt. Thadsen and Doctor Schnell and our Capt. came on board from land. 7:30 Fourth Mate Gadt died. Placed him aft and sealed his chest and cabin, began to make a coffin for him."

Again the report of a death is sent ashore, and a fort slave has to dig yet another grave for a white man. On the following day a farewell salute of 3 guns is fired, and the coffin containing the deceased is brought ashore. Thereafter the boat brings the two sick carpenters and the quartermaster to be nursed on land. After the deaths of Chief Officer Lundberg and Fourth Mate Gadt their belongings are counted and recorded. A chief officer had considerably more possessions than a poor seaman, and the lists in Hoffmann's journal are long. This time it is necessary to divide the things into groups like "wearing apparel", "linen", "silk", "navigation aids", "silver", "small items", "bedding", "new apparel" and "gold dust".

As one of the highest-ranking officers on board, Lundberg had been given permission to bring along some tax-free goods which he was permitted to sell privately. However, it was strictly forbidden to deal in anything that could harm the Company's own commercial activities. The gold dust which Lundberg left behind, worth 32 rixdaler, may have been the result of a possible dubious transaction.

On 29 November preparations are made for an auction on board, and the belongings of the two dead men are brought up on deck. Among the crowd are many seamen from the *Elonora*. The terms are clear: the purchase price is to be paid in Danish "currency", and the newly purchased articles must not be resold anywhere along the Coast. Hoffmann is in complete charge of the proceedings. He goes by the valuation lists from the journal; the objects are held up and the bids are quickly made. The final result is a total of 378 rixdaler for Lundberg's and 124 rixdaler for Gadt's property.

Three Norwegian seamen, Erich Ancker, Christian Runge and Ole Nicolaysen, purchased the following items on board the *Fredensborg*:
Erich Ancker buys 1 blue kerchief, 1 blue vest and pants, 1 pair of scissors, some

thread, 1 hat and 1 pillow. Christian Runge buys 1 new drawing-book, 1 old journal, 1 bundle of quills, 2 Baltic charts, 1 ruler, 1 mariners' almanac, 8 charts, 2 pairs of compasses, 5 pairs new shoes, 1 blue linen cloak, 1 pair embroidered wristbands, 1 pair long, blue knitted pants, 1 blue cotton undergarment, 1 prayer-book. Ole Nicolaysen buys 5 blue kerchiefs, 1 pair new shoes, 1 pair steel buckles and 1 old wig.

Ancker, Runge and Nicolaysen do not pay cash for their purchases. The amounts are carefully recorded in the ledger and deducted from accrued earnings. For the first two, this amounts to approximately three months' wages. Christian Runge from Arendal has made plans for the future. He knows how to write and already has a position of trust on board. Since Gadt became sick, Runge has kept his accounts with considerable skill and precision. At the auction he has purchased Gadt's nautical charts and compasses; he is staking on a mariner's career, and that he shall survive.

While the auction is in progress, the two ship's carpenters are dying in Asioke's hut in the Negeriet. Both Doctor Sixtus and Doctor Schnell from the fort have given up hope. Nothing works. Now, all they can do is wait. Not even Asioke's herbs help this time. Ship's Carpenter Beck dies during the night of 1 December, quite prepared for death. While still able to do so, he wrote a letter to his wife. He had a total of eight edifying books in his possession, including a Bible, Brockmann's *Book of Family Sermons,* Heydmann's *Prayerbook,* a church hymnal and a book of questions: *What Do I Comprehend?* On the following day Carpenter Kock follows his superior. Assistant Wrisberg, a passenger from Copenhagen, also dies, making this a triple burial. Not only did the two carpenters work together, they also brought a joint supply of delicacies like snuff, tea, rock candy, lemon juice and spirits.

On board the *Fredensborg* there are now problems. Without carpenters they are unable to make coffins. This time the fort carpenter is given the job. Even worse, however, is the fact that the considerable job of converting the *Fredensborg* into a slave ship remains. Captain Kiønig writes a letter to Captain Thadsen. The carpentry on board the *Elonora* will soon be completed, and Kiønig requests "on behalf of the Company" to be allowed to take over Thadsen's carpenter. Captain Thadsen obliges and lets him have the assistant carpenter, Axel Anthonisen Hæglund. As a little gratuity Captain Thadsen receives some materials for building a privy, or "water closet", for the slaves.

Since the *Elonora* is just about to depart, Captain Kiønig finds the time is ripe for a little get-together on board the *Fredensborg.* Along with Captain Thadsen and the Messrs Aarestrup and Biørn, and Doctor Schnell from the fort, they dine in the cabin. Normally such a party would last until the "wee hours", but as the host, Captain Kiønig, is not feeling well. They break up and retire around 5:30 p.m. With his experience from the Coast Dr. Schnell stares thoughtfully at Kiønig as he goes down the gangway to the waiting boat. He has seen the symptoms many times before.

Kiønig pulls himself together and that same evening, after a "pick-me-up", he sits down and writes a report to the Board of Directors to be sent with the *Elonora.* He describes the voyage from Merdø to Guinea and reports that the unloading has nearly been completed, with the exception of a few kegs of spirits. He regrets that several corals in cases no. 3 and 4 are spoiled and unfit as articles of trade. It is even worse with some mouldy textiles for which Warehouse Keeper Aarestrup has given him the blame. The 22 bolts of cloth are lying in a box that did not come from the *Fredensborg*, and both the chief officer and the ship's assistant have refused to sign for the damage. Nor can Kiønig understand how the threads of some West Indian corals could have rotted on board, as "on the ship no water has come to that place". At the end of the letter he mentions the state of the crew on board:

"Up to now we have already lost 6 men, a loss which is of even greater significance to us, as we have only been provided with the barest minimum of a crew, and we all have more than enough hard work to keep us busy with the necessary duties while we are under sail. Should Death visit us further, as it has up to now, then things will look bad for us. I therefore have even greater cause to burden myself with the fear that, by all accounts, we will not be leaving here for 6 to 8 months. The snow is now leaving with 170 slaves, and there will be none left for us. In addition, the traffic is bad. If in future I should have the opportunity, I shall not fail to report our condition to the Worthy Gentlemen. Except for Albert Engmann, we are all still well, God be Praised. May the Lord allow this to continue for a long time."

Then he signs the letter and puts away both ink and quill. At the end of the letter he is not being completely honest with himself when he writes that he is well, because Second Mate Ferentz has recorded the opposite in the journal. In addition, Erich Ancker from Christiania is ill and has been sent ashore to be nursed in Asioke's hut.

On the following day Captain Kiønig leaves the ship for the last time. He staggers in through the gate of the fort and collapses in a fit of fever. Ancker, however, is improving. The days on land have provided him with a glimpse of an alien world. The tiny fire on the floor of the hut is not intended for warmth, but for the

*The Danish-Norwegian Fort Christiansborg received considerable competition from the nearby Dutch Fort Crevecour and the English Fort James.*

smoke to keep poisonous snakes off the roof. After a week under expert care Erich is back on board again, while Kiønig's condition is becoming increasingly worse.

Monday 7 December the *Elonora* sets sail with 171 slaves in the hold. There are many on the *Fredensborg* who would like to be on board with Captain Thadsen, even though he is only in command of a simple little snow. In other respects, Captain Thadsen and his men do a good job for the Company because only 12 slaves die during the passage.

The *Fredensborg* lies anchored in the roadstead, while the slave dungeons inside Fort Christiansborg remain quite empty. The unloading of the heavily laden *Fredensborg* has taken a long time. Along with some of the last cases of merchandise they send an order to the fort blacksmith for 12 pairs of hinges for the slave doors on board. The barrels of spirits constantly have to be topped up before they can be brought ashore. The iron bars are also a part of the cargo – 658 of these, which probably come from the Norwegian ironworks, are carried ashore in four trips. It pays to keep a sharp look-out when the costly spirits are to be brought ashore. The remidors know a trick or two when it comes to obtaining an extra drop. Ferentz writes:

"12 o'clock Third Mate Beck rowed to the breakers from the ship in order to unload the longboat. In addition to the rowers, an extra man went back and forth in the canoes when they took the spirits ashore, in order to see to it that the remidors did not deceive us…"

No doubt Second Mate Ferentz is tense. The possibility of assuming command of the *Fredensborg* is considerable now that Captain Kiønig is dying inside the fort. Early in the morning Ferentz sends the petty officer as far as the breakers in the longboat in order to find out about the captain's condition. Halfway there they meet the big canoe with Hoffmann on board. "He brought with him the sorrowful tidings that Captain Kiønig went to rest in the Lord between 11 p.m. and midnight." Hoffmann and Ferentz seal the cabin doors, both cabinets,

*Christians- Borg.*

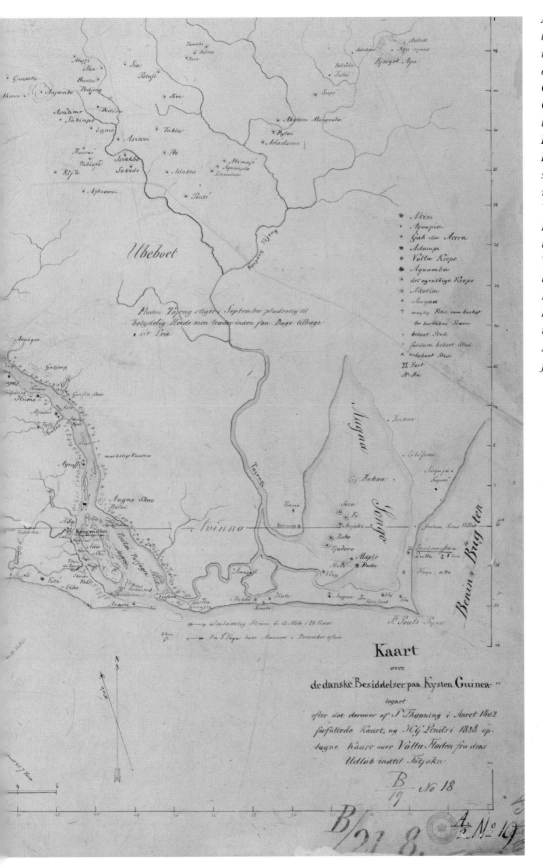

At the bottom left of the map of "the Danish possessions" along the Guinea Coast we can see Fort Christiansborg. To the east at Ningo lies Fort Fredensborg. Fort Kongensteen is situated by the mouth of the River Volta, while Fort Prindsensteen is farthest to the east. The Akwamu are located inland at the River Volta, north of Fort Fredensborg, in the villages of Aqvambu (Akwamufie) and Adome.

Kiønig's sea chest and the expedition chest. Thereafter, Hoffmann and the carpenter go ashore with 7 "planks from Westerwig", 96 three-inch and 20 four-inch nails for making the coffin. On board the *Fredensborg* the flags and jacks are lowered to half-mast, as has already been done at the forts. At Fort Christiansborg a salute is fired every hour on the hour, from 6 a.m. until the body is taken out of the hall.

"At 1 o'clock I take Second Mate Ferentz and Petty Officer Engmann to the breakers in the longboat, accompanied by 6 longboat rowers in full uniform, who go ashore to carry the body. At 2:30 there was a travat from NE and E, with a fresh breeze and rain. At 3:30 it was over. At 4:30 the body was placed in its final resting place. When he was put into the ground 13 minute guns were fired, which were answered by 13 salutes by the 4-pounders from the frigate *Fredensborg*, and later answered with 5 salutes. And then all the flags were hoisted."

Everything that had been used for nursing the sick was meticulously entered in the account book by Mr. Aarestrup at the fort. Before he died Kiønig had eaten and drunk for a little more than 3 rixdaler. In addition to this, they had used a length of white "salempuris" cotton for the shroud, 40 lbs of gunpowder, 1 dozen long pipes, 1 1/2 dozen ordinary pipes and 9 *potter* (1 *potte* = 0.9681 l) of Danish spirits.

Tuesday 22 December is a great day for Johan Frantzen Ferentz. He signed on the *Fredensborg* as second mate, but now – well assisted by a travat and bloodthirsty malaria mosquitoes – he is standing on the deck while his appointment as captain is being read aloud to the crew:

"…know all men by these presents that the decreed Governance of the Royal Chartered Danish Guinea Company, here on the Guinea Coast of Africa, at the main Danish Fort Christiansborg, has chosen herewith Second Mate J. Ferentz here on the ship *Fredensborg* to be commanding officer of this ship, and in the place of the deceased Captain Kiønig, to reside as captain of this ship, pending the approbation of the Worthy Board of Directors in Copenhagen, whereas he puts his trust in God in the Ship's incumbent officers, when like them may still be provided with a competent Chief Officer to bring the ship and its cargo to the West Indies, and from there to Copenhagen or to whichever port of unloading it might please the Worthy Board of Directors to dispatch the ship, and that in each and every way see to it that he will defend and be held responsible by the Worthy Directors in Copenhagen upon completion of the voyage."

At the same time, in the document signed by the Messrs Tychsen, Jessen, Aarestrup and Reimers, Christian Beck is appointed chief officer. It "is assumed that everyone on the ship, from the highest to the lowest, shows Captain Ferentz the proper respect and obedience, whether under orders or not, as their superior officer and Captain." After his appointment has been read aloud, along with the Ship's Articles, everyone takes the oath as usual.

Ferentz is no doubt proud as he watches flags and jacks being run up, while a 7-gun salute – which is answered from the fort – thunders over the roadstead to celebrate the solemn occasion. After the notables have left the ship, the Ship's Council meets at once in the captain's cabin. The Ship's Council, which now consists of Captain Ferentz, Chief Officer Beck, Boatswain Rosenberg and Ship's Carpenter

Axel Hæglund, shall elect a third mate and steward. A unanimous Council agrees that Christian Runge has diligently and conscientiously taken care of the Steward's duties, and that no one else on board is better qualified. Runge is summoned, accepts the job, and takes the oath that is special to the Ship's Council. Then he moves aft with the other officers. The seaman, who is able to write and has secured a bundle of quills during the auction of his predecessor Gadt's belongings, is now responsible among other things for the ship's supply of provisions and drinks, which requires extremely accurate bookkeeping.

Captain Ferentz installs himself as well as possible in Kiønig's former cabin. There is a great deal that has to be straightened out, but nothing to prevent him from assuming his duties as Captain on board. But there are new worries, because the newly hired Carpenter Axel Hæglund lies sick in the hold along with seamen Ole Nicolaysen, Peder Madsen and Hans Andersen, as well as Quartermaster Abraham Engmann. Like the conscientious man that he is, Ferentz concludes the journal of the Second Mate and takes out the one belonging to the Captain. Then he settles comfortably in one of the brown leather chairs, dips the quill in the ink and begins to write:

### IN THE NAME OF JESUS

I, Johan Frantzen Ferentz, Captain of the Royal Chartered Danish Guinea Company's Frigate called the *Fredensborg*, on 22 Dec. 1767, began to record in this Journal provided by the Worthy Board of Directors for the Captain.
Where this must be done, by the Grace and Mercy of God, for the Glory of God, for the benefit and advantage of the Worthy Royal Chartered Company, and my eternal Welfare and Salvation.

Johan Frantzen Ferentz begins his duties as captain of a slave ship "In the Name of Jesus"! In future it is easy to maintain that slavery and the slave trade were hardly compatible with Christian benevolence. Bishop Erik Pontoppidan in Bergen had his views about this in 1760: "...the Negro who is transported from there to the West Indies, in the event that he is not separated from wife and children, is far better off."

We must not forget that this was the middle of the eighteenth century, a time when much was different in the North, and in Europe as a whole, in comparison to modern criteria. To Ferentz this was first and foremost a job: he was a seaman and had set himself a goal of becoming a captain. The fact that his first command was on a slave ship was of little consequence to him.

Captain Kiønig's death resulted in considerable extra work. Ferentz, Beck, Hoffmann and Runge spent two days making an inventory of Kiønig's personal belongings, and the rest of the food and drink which the Captain had at his disposal. They started on 23 December, and Hoffmann filled page after page in the journal. It may be of interest to have a look at the clothing and other items that were brought by a Captain during a voyage in the triangular trade:

# J. Jesü=Naun:

Saauit Jeg Johan Frantzen Finack
samtt Capitein paa di høy=
Kongl. octroijende Compagnies
Fregat Sch: Fredensborg
Racht Legg: N:
d: 22.d Septbr: 767

Al d.D Steige ad den af den høy=
Direction mig Gives Fuldmalt
for Capiteinen

Hvor det Gives Guds haand Sy... Gehørighed
paa dit hnaae Stein BD die en
Det høye Kongel: octroijende
Compagnie Die Ganer
Og Sagter Og Jeg
die Kong: thr:
faat Og
Pally Sa..

## WEARING APPAREL

1 cerise cloth coat and vest
1 light blue broadcloth dresscoat,
    vest and pants already turned
1 black broadcloth dresscoat with
    silk embroidered vest and 1 pair
    German pants
1 blue cloth coat, vest and pants,
    vest without arms
1 pair black fustian pants
1 pair slightly old ditto
1 satin wool dressing gown and vest
1 brown cotton dressing gown
    swanskin (nappy, fine-twilled
    fabric for linings)
1 old red embroidered silk vest
1 green damask vest
1 cotton print dressing gown
1 white "sailor's coat somewhat
    damaged by the rats"

## LINEN

6 white nightshirts
10 white dress-shirts
1 ditto with embroidered
    wristbands
1 nightshirt
2 old ditto
1 blue-checked ditto
8 white towels
1 embroidered white vest
1 diagonally woven hemp
    or linen tablecloth
5 ditto napkins
2 tablecloths
12 ditto napkins
3 nightshirts with wristbands

1 half-worn sheet
1 red-checked pillowcase
1 pair red-checked underpants
1 pair blue-checked ditto
8 blue-checked kerchiefs
1 blue cotton ditto
12 white cotton caps
1 white linen kerchief
2 pair cotton thread hose

## SILK GOODS

2 pair white silk hose
1 pair silk hose
1 pair old black
1 old black silk kerchief

## WOOLEN GOODS

5 pair woolen hose
2 pair striped dishabille ditto
24 pairs Dutch ditto
1 old blue nightcap

## SHOES

2 pairs new shoes
2 pairs old ditto
1 pair old red slippers
1 pair black ditto
1 pair half-worn boots and
1 pair new ditto

## HATS AND WIGS

1 slightly worn gold-braided hat
1 ditto without braid
1 old ditto
1 old dress wig
3 ordinary ditto,
1 old clipped wig

A page from the Captain's journal.
Johan Frantzen Ferentz takes over as a slave captain – "In the Name of Jesus".

---

## GOLD AND SILVER

1 pair silver shoe and knee buckles
    with steel hearts and tongues
1 pair ditto shoe buckles
1 silver tablespoon with initials
    E.C.K.

1 silver tobacco jar engraved with the names
        Espen Christian Kiønig and Anne
        Marie Honing and various engravings
1 silver punch ladle
1 pair gold-plated silver cufflinks
1 gold ring with a white stone

In addition to this, there were "a number of small items" such as navigation equipment, bedding, 2 violins, a notebook, a pair of pistols with brass mountings, a couple of pistols in a case, 12 lb smoking tobacco, and the residue of some old rum in a barrel. Kiønig had probably counted on striking a good bargain over in the West Indies because he had a large stock of "negotiable goods". In addition to 44 bolts of assorted textiles, he had:

*14 single red and white silk kerchiefs*
*17 double ditto*
*6 half linen and half wool damask napkins*
*17 small blue-checked towels*
*1 ditto with larger checks*
*1 ditto red-checked*
*2 blue and white towels*
*3 blue and white cotton jackets*
*156 pairs assorted men's shoes*
*152 pairs Icelandic hose somewhat damaged by worms*

*9 dozen and 11 pairs men's gloves from Randers*
*1 chest with lock and key*
*1 gold watch*
*19 brass rings*
*2 red signets with compass*
*9 watchkeys*
*2 barrels flintstones*
*3 "barrels Negro pipes"*
*1 stoneware jug*
*1 mahogany tea-canister with silver teaspoons, sugar tongs and tins and 53 dl gold dust*

It appears as if Kiønig, who had gold dust worth 53 rixdaler, had been trading before he died.

The next thing they examine is the expedition's chest, which contains 47 different documents, receipts and instructions. Each document is numbered in the journal, and Hoffmann itemizes everything with his customary meticulousness. Among other things, they find Kiønig's master mariner's certificate, a package containing nine letters from men at the fort, and a power of attorney to Kiønig about collecting some money for Chamberlain Engmann. As captain, Ferentz has to assume responsibility for most of these papers, for which he duly signs. On Christmas Eve the four continue making the inventory. Now the contents of the cabin have to be checked, and this undoubtedly gives rise to many biting comments when it becomes apparent that, during Kiønig's relatively brief period as Captain, the following items have come up missing:

*1 prayerbook*
*7 pewter tablespoons*
*3 white diagonally woven hemp or linen napkins*
*1 fork*
*1 lb ink powder*
*3/4 lb sealing wax*
*1/2 ream paper*
*3 sheets notepaper*

*128 quills*
*5 coffee cups*
*3 saucers*
*1 porcelain plate*
*14 wine glasses*
*1 beer glass*
*1 brandy glass*
*3 slop basins*

The wine glasses may be accounted for – they knew the Captain's craving for strong drink. But then they are unable to understand how Kiønig managed to use up the entire stock of 1 lb ink powder and 128 quills! In addition, several objects are damaged, while the alms box with lock and key is intact and empty. When they start taking inventory of the provisions in the cabin, Ferentz pays even closer attention. The captain on board is entitled to a special selection of provisions. Kiønig must have been very fond of food and drink. In little more than half a year he had consumed:

| | |
|---|---|
| *4 casks of red wine* | *6 lodd cinnamon* |
| *5 casks old wine* | *5 ¹/₂ lodd mace* |
| *2 casks young wine* | *11 ¹/₄ lodd whole nutmeg* |
| *1 cask Rhine Wine* | *16 lb currants* |
| *4 casks French brandy* | *2 ¹/₄ lodd cloves* |
| *1 1/2 casks wine vinegar* | *1 lodd cardamom* |
| *1 keg Prussian beer* | *2 jars English mustard* |
| *300 lb prunes* | *16 lb coffee beans* |
| *12 lb dried cherries* | *100 lb brown sugar* |
| *16 lb raisins* | *3 lb Bohea (black) tea* |
| *¹/₂ lb pepper* | *4 lb Congo Tea* |
| *1 ¹/₂ lb ginger* | *4 barrels grain in hogsheads* |
| *7 ¹/₂ lb pearl sago* | *300 dried flounder* |
| *16 ¹/₂ lb pearl barley* | *50 lb granulated sugar* |
| *2 lodd saffron* | *50 lb rock candy* |

The supply of drinks that has been consumed amounts to about 600 litres. In addition, Kiønig had brought quite a bit at his own expense. There is no reason to believe that he consumed all of this by himself. The other officers were certainly the captain's guests on several occasions, and he also entertained guests on board before he died. But there is no doubt that Kiønig loved good food, and appreciated strong drink – a fact for which Ferentz will have to suffer until they come to St. Croix.

In the evening of Christmas Day, Axel Hæglund, who has been dying, draws his last breath. Once again the *Fredensborg* is without a carpenter. On the following day he is taken ashore in a coffin made by the cooper. Also in the boat are Ole Nicolaysen, Peder Madsen and Hans Andersen, all of whom are sick. Captain Ferentz is in a difficult situation. He is in command of a ship in which a considerable amount of carpentry work remains to be done before he can take in a cargo of slaves, and he has a constantly diminishing crew. In a letter to the Governor he must ask for qualified assistance from land, "as all of our carpenters have departed this life". Construction has not begun on the storm- or slave-bulwarks, nor on the slave platforms.

On land they have probably been prepared for the request, because the very next day the fort's two carpenters come aboard. They bring along two strapping slaves. In accordance with the captain's instructions, he is entitled to use slaves: "In order to ease the burden of the ship's crew the Captain shall select from the purchased slaves, or request from the governing body several days after their arrival at

Christiansborg, 4 to 6 of the fittest male slaves, among those who do not understand the language of the others, in order to use them as "Bombas" over the other slaves, at the same time as they can help with cleaning the ship, as well as with other jobs that should arise. In addition, to enable the crew to understand them, they may be taught a few Danish words; however Asante and Crepe slaves must not be taken for this. When these have come on board, they must not go ashore again unless they happen to become sick. These slaves shall now be fed the rations of a seaman on the ship. However, the crew shall be ordered not to entrust them with too much, but everyone shall behave properly, and at night allow them to remain below deck."

It appears as if most of the deck slaves manage reasonably well on board, even though they refuse to eat the probably rancid Danish butter. For this reason they are given palm oil and some Spanish pepper instead.

On New Year's Eve a pig is brought on board "as refreshment", but their situation at the end of the year is a source of considerable anxiety. Among a crew of 40 men, eight are already dead. Not long afterwards Ole Nicolaysen also dies.

The first half of January is dominated by the work of converting the *Fredensborg* into a slave ship. The carpenters from the fort and the six deck slaves largely do a good job on board. Nets made from rope yarn or marline are strung along the sides of the vessel to prevent slaves from leaping overboard.

*Fort Christiansborg in Guinea 1764.*

Ship's Assistant Hoffmann is constantly busy with his ledgers. Because of all the

confusion it is difficult for him to make the numbers tally. In a letter to the Ship's Council he writes that the first man who died, Niels Mathisen, has been debited with 1 rixdaler for the hammock in which he was buried. For all the other deaths the materials and nails were taken from the ship's supplies without this being entered into the accounts. "I am therefore requesting orders as to whether this shall be charged to the account of the deceased, and how much." The deaths of Captain Kiønig, Chief Officer Lundberg and Fourth Mate Gadt have occasioned a total of 28 salutes by the ship's cannons. "It is unknown to me whether the Company acknowledges such an expense, or whether the deceased themselves shall pay, and, if so, how much for each salute?" Hoffmann is critical of the treatment of figures and supplies by the deceased. He also questions the Ship's Council as to why the prescribed auctions have not yet been held after several deaths, as the clothing may easily rot "partly from the humidity, partly from the cockroaches".

It is quite apparent from the letter that a tense situation is brewing between Hoffmann and Ferentz. While the captain is concerned with the health of the crew and the conversion of the ship, Hoffmann irritates him with trifles about the accounts. But Hoffmann and Ferentz are not the only ones who are quarreling. On Epiphany, 6 January, Ferentz finds it necessary to repeat the Ship's Articles. He gathers all the men aft, and after the reading aloud – which is supposed to maintain discipline on board – everyone goes back to his work. But not long afterwards a nasty fight breaks out. The three Able Seamen Thomas Greissen, Peder Diedrichsen and Friderich Kruse have disagreed about something or other and come to blows. Discipline on board is important, and Ferentz has to make an example of them. The punishment is ten lashes for the offence; the same is meted out to Seaman Woye Olsen. He has had shore leave, and Hoffmann says without going into detail that he has succumbed to the temptation to break the Seventh Commandment.

Even though there are more important things to take care of, Hoffmann's letter must be answered. The Ship's Council declares that both the materials for the coffins and the gunpowder must be charged to the estates of the deceased. The Ship's Council emphasizes that it cannot be held responsible for the actions, or lack of such, of the deceased. A complete inventory has been made after the deaths, which Hoffmann must follow and keep an account of. In addition he is told to stop meddling in things which do not concern him. He should have set things straight while those responsible were still alive. It is Hoffmann's painful duty to enter the letter of reply in the protocol, for the information of the Board of Directors on their return home.

Hoffmann did not have an easy time of it. He was a zealous worker and was concerned first and foremost with the good of the Company. His instructions were clear but his relations were poor with the rest of the men on board. He was far too meticulous. On 11 January, however, Hoffmann had something of importance to record in his journal: "At 4:30 in the afternoon the flag at the Fort was flown at half-mast and a single gun was fired. Immediately afterwards the big canoe came to notify us of Governor Tychsen's death, with an invitation to accompany him to his final resting place. The Captain, the Petty Officer and I went ashore."

Tuesday 12 January: "In the morning 30 lb of gunpowder were sent to our ship in order to fire salutes for the Governor's funeral. In the afternoon the Governor was buried with the customary honours. Our ship fired 15 salutes as expected."

Things turned out for Tychsen the way they did for so many others before him. His term as governor did not last very long. Now a period of considerable activity began at the fort, and on 15 January Ferentz was summoned to a meeting in the great hall in Christiansborg. All the personnel at the fort were there, and they were informed about what had happened. Finally, everyone was asked if they had any objections to the appointment of Frantz Joachim Kuhberg as provisional governor or "Commander in Chief". All but two agreed to the nomination. When the oath was to be sworn to the new governor, the Messrs. Jessen and Aarestrup refused to do so.

The late Governor Tychsen had a great deal to straighten out when he arrived at the Coast. Many of the personnel at the fort had been so dissatisfied that they had tendered their resignations and gone home on the *Christiansborg*. The run-down buildings had to be repaired and new people hired. Tychsen left behind some extremely inaccurate accounts – if they could be called accounts; everything was in a complete muddle. The Board of Directors had already discovered this and established a committee of inquiry. The conclusion was clear: Tychsen had been incompetent! During his brief period as governor, slaves valued at 9,220 rixdaler had died, and he had left behind a total of seven keys to the fort's chest of gold. Only three keys were listed in the instructions, and the extra keys were a source of worry to the committee.

As captain, Ferentz gains an increasingly deeper insight into the situation. He reads through the different instructions and finds that "Ober Chirugus Sextus" is negligent when he fails to keep a record of the medicines used. Ferentz feels it is his duty to complain about this in writing:

"As I understand from the instructions which have been given to him, and of which I have a copy, then I should remind you about the same according to Point 11, that you will comply with this, as this no longer may or can be overlooked." Ferentz calls Sixtus' attention to the fact that he alone is responsible for the circumstances. If the Board of Directors charge him with neglect, "then he must not expect the slightest assistance from me, but must answer to this himself and alone."

The answer arrives at once, and Hoffmann has yet another letter to enter into his journal. Sixtus explains that it is absolutely impossible to comply with all the instructions about recording the patient's name, his illness and the date it was reported, whether restored to health or deceased, and all the medicines that were used in connection with the illness. He has committed himself to serving the Company faithfully, but has problems writing reports at night about medicines used every day, and gives an example: A man who has become sick is given drops or a powder, and continues his work. He is not sick for more than half or a whole day, and his condition is reported by word of mouth to the Captain or Commanding Officer on board, in the morning and the evening. This is what his predecessors had done when they were at sea. "I leave it up to the Worthy Board of Directors and other experienced men to judge whether or not it is possible to comply with Point 11."

On the following day they are given something new to think about. The Ship's Council has decided to auction off some of the late Captain Kiønig's belongings, and this brings in 232 rixdaler even though "some of his wearing apparel was very badly stained and torn, and some had been gnawed by rats". All of Kiønig's merchandise was saved for a later auction in the West Indies.

One day Ferentz receives a letter which is brought by canoe from the fort:

"Your Worshipful Lord Captain Ferentz
  and Honourable Ship's Council:

Owing to trouble on the road between Ningo and Ada, it is practically impossible to send the goods intended for the Quitta trading lodge by land because of bandits. It is imperative that the lodge be supplied with goods in order to obtain slaves for the ship's departure. As no opportunity for transporting the imported goods to Quitta has presented itself to date, I must hereby request your Worshipful Captain and Worthy Ship's Council for assistance in transporting the goods by the ship's longboat. Since this is the period of the harmattan wind, it should be possible for the boat to return again, although we do not know whether the instructions forbid sending the ship's longboat this far. We hope this will not raise objections, in that as soon as the goods have arrived at the Quitta trading lodge, it will be possible to obtain a quantity of 60 or more slaves within a short time. This is highly necessary in order to dispatch the ship, and should meet with the approval of the Board of Directors, as there are no alternatives of supplying the trading lodge. We request that the longboat comes as far as the breakers on 24 January in order to receive the goods for Fort Fredensborg, and, after its arrival, the goods will be loaded on board for further transport. In anticipation of your assistance, Worshipful Captain and Honourable Ship's Council, I remain your indebted and willing servant.
                     F. J. Kuhberg."

Ferentz writes a quick letter in reply, saying he will discuss the matter with the Ship's Council, and inform him of the decision as soon as it is made. Then he goes ashore to have a look at the three seamen who are ill. The cooper, who is in very poor condition, is in a room in the main fort, while Quartermaster Engmann, the petty officer's brother, is alone in the barracks. Both are being cared for by the fort's doctor. Ferentz also goes down to Osu to visit the men who seemed to be doing well: "Quartermaster Engmann appeared to be quite content to stay in Asioke's hut in the Negeriet, where he benefitted from all the attendance he could ask for."

Ferentz spends the night on land and goes out to the *Fredensborg* on the following day with 14 pairs of hinges for the slave doors, several barrels of water and six bottles of red wine for Ordinary Seamen Peder Madsen and Hans Andersen; they have "durchlauf" – diarrhoea – and Sixtus believes red wine will help. In the evening the Ship's Council meets in order to discuss the request from the fort. To be realistic, this is a difficult matter because common sense tells them they must not risk the already greatly reduced crew; they need every man on board the *Fredensborg*. In addition, they had to consider the well-known fact that along the coast, both the currents and the winds flow in an easterly direction. As a rule, it was almost impossible for vessels to return. But now, during the period of the harmattan, the chances of returning are much greater. The alternative is to wait even longer for a cargo of slaves. The Ship's Council decides to comply with the request from the fort, and on 24 January the longboat heads east under the command of Boatswain Rosenberg. He has taken along Seamen Anders Fredrichsen, Jens Jansen and Jochum Bollvardt, and they are armed with muskets and cutlasses. To be on the safe side they have taken enough provisions to last three weeks. "May God bless them and us, that this may be of advantage to the Company", Ferentz writes.

After a stay of nearly four months on the Coast, Ferentz believes he must have something definite to report. In a letter to the "Venerable and Worshipful Governor" he writes: "According to Point 37 of my instructions I hereby take the liberty of asking:

1. When do you propose to invite me to take my expedition away from here, and, in that event, with how many slaves?
2. If I may have as much water as is necessary for the ship from the fort's cisterns, and if not, where may I obtain the necessary water in the best possible manner, in order that I might plan this in time?"

While the longboat is on its way to Quitta, the cooper completes his passage through life inside the fort. When Hoffmann comes on board the following day, he finds that Third Mate Beck has sealed the cooper's sea chest. This has become a routine after the frequent deaths. Hoffmann goes over to a Portuguese ship that has cast anchor, and buys a little roll of tobacco which he shares with Runge. There is not much that escapes Hoffmann's keen eye or ear. He eagerly makes notes, and is happiest when there is something he can put his finger on:

Friday 29 January: "…early in the morning, muskets and cutlasses taken up to be cleaned. The Portuguese ship has set sail. A large canoe came to the ship, bringing the clothes the cooper had worn on land. The two black carpenters also came. The Captain bought two chickens and some eggs in exchange for spirits. That same day I happened to learn from Third Mate Runge that, from time to time, Captain Ferentz had sent a total of 57 *potter* of spirits ashore. In accordance with Point 8 of my instructions, I immediately questioned the Captain about the reason for this removal, but he became indignant and denied having anything removed from the ship, with the exception of 2 *potter* for himself and 1 *potte* for Third Mate Beck which they had given to the remidors on 22 December, as has been attested by the sheet.

C. A. Hoffmann"

On King Christian VII's birthday, that same day, the flags and jacks are hoisted. There have been two new auctions on board – of Carpenter Hægland and Ole Nicolaysen's belongings. Among other things, the carpenter owned two parrots, and these were sold for about 3 rixdaler to Peder Thorsen. The two black carpenters have completed the slave platforms on the starboard side and have

*This special drawing, which is a combination of a botanical design and a perspective, depicts the Danish-Norwegian trading station at Quitta. This was where Boatswain Rosenberg arrived in the longboat and delivered goods from the* Fredensborg. *The drawing was brought home on the frigate* Christiansborg, *to the widow of Captain Bernt Jensen Mørch, who died and was buried at the trading station in 1777.*

started work on the stanchions on the port side. The problems with illness and death never seem to end. When Ferentz goes ashore to receive assistance from Cooper Weis, he discovers that Quartermaster Engmann is in very poor condition. Ferentz looks after him for a while, "seeing that there was no one closer to him".

Communications among the competing forts along the Coast function well as long as this is mutually advantageous. A message arrives that an express messenger will be sent to Fort Elmina with letters for Europe. Ferentz believes the time has come to send home a detailed report to the Board of Directors, and starts to write. He tells about the conflicts in connection with the election of Kuhberg as the new governor, and gives the names of all the deceased. He ends the letter with a description of the last death: "Quartermaster Abraham Engmann died on 3 February, while his brother lies sick in the fort. And the present time we have 4 sick men on board, and great pains are being taken at the fort to expedite our departure, which, notwithstanding, shall take place by the middle of March, if not before that time."

Once again "planks from Westervig" and three-inch nails are sent ashore. The flag is lowered to half-mast, and Ferentz brings half a keg of spirits and two bottles of wine. This time the mourners include Engmann's brother, Captain Ferentz and several of the men at the fort.

A letter to Captain Kiønig from the Board of Directors in Copenhagen is brought to the ship, on the same day that Boatswain Rosenberg returns from Quitta in the longboat. Rosenberg has brought some materials that are taken ashore, and later in the day Captain Ferentz holds a service on board. The letter from the Board of Directors is a reaction to a report, which several members of the staff at the fort have sent home to Copenhagen. They have mentioned blameworthy conditions and conflicts at the fort, without going into detail. The Captain is told to investigate this more closely, without his or members of the crew becoming involved. Upon his departure from Guinea the Captain must see to it that he obtains letters of reply from both the financial officer and the governing body, who have also received letters, and have these forwarded as quickly as possible from the West Indies.

The slave platforms down in the hold consist of an extra shelf, which divides the 'tween-deck in half along both sides. The maximum height in the hold of the *Fredensborg* is approximately 1.90 metres, and this is divided in half in order to place the slaves in two layers, to make room for as many as possible. Solid supports from the deck up to the deck beams are an important part of the construction. The maximum height in the middle of the hold provides space for barrels for the excrement of the slaves. They have brought materials and plenty of nails from Copenhagen for all the extra work on board. After the slave platforms on the starboard and port sides have been completed, work begins on the slave- or storm bulwarks. These are solid partitions that extend from the deck, well above the quarterdeck. While the slaves are being aired on deck, a solid protection is important in order that the stern may be defended in case of a rebellion on board. Heavy doors are placed in the bulwarks with hinges made by the fort's blacksmith, and the four swivel guns are mounted on top of the bulwarks with the muzzles facing the airing deck. Behind these special preparations there is long experience with the transportation of slaves. A private "convenience" for the female slaves will also be perched on the outside of the port side of the quarterdeck, and will be well-cov-

*In 1784 Fort Prinsensten was built on the site of the old trading station in Quitta (Keta).*

ered for several reasons. The male slaves will be provided with a less complicated arrangement below the gangway on the starboard side. The gangway on the port side is taken down in order to make room for the slave stove.

In order to lay the bricks for the slave stove they are assisted by the fort's mason. As there is no mason on board, he brings the stones and mortar from land. The carpenter constructs a chimney hat on the top of the pipe. Cook Nicolay Ørgensen pays even closer attention to the work on the slave stove; he is the one who is responsible for the cooking utensils. In Copenhagen he has signed receipts for:

> *1 large iron slave stove with an iron door, 4 rings on*
> *the sides and 4 plates (or pads) on which the feet stand*
> *1 iron cauldron with 4 handles for ditto*
> *2 copper lids, 1 small and 1 large for the same*
> *22 iron grates for the same*

For practical reasons all the food for the slaves is to be prepared on the airing deck. The food is to be eaten with 100 wooden spoons from 12 platters. In the gunner's storeroom the carpenter is putting together bins for the millet, a variety of grain which was a local crop and was a part of the slave fare.

Ferentz keeps a careful eye on everything, both on board and on land. On 16 February he notes down the arrival at the fort of "Asante traders" with 14 slaves, at the same time as the auction of Governor Tychsen's belongings is taking place. Later he learns that 13 of the slaves have been purchased. The rejected slave must have been "an unsaleable defective slave".

The slave trade necessitated people with very special qualifications, for example, the ability to appraise a slave. One of these was the Danish slave trader and merchant Ludevig Ferdinand Rømer. He writes, "Preparatory to purchasing a slave, a Factor has his black attendants thoroughly examine the slave to find out whether he has been injured, is sick or has lost any teeth. The Negroes know how much the Factor is willing to pay, as well as the estimated price of each Black, which is usually based on the Christianborg price-list from 1749. The value of a male slave is given as 6 ounces of gold or 96 rixdaler. Therefore, one slave is valued at:

| | | |
|---|---|---|
| *2 flint-lock muskets à 6 rixdaler* | = | *12 Rdl* |
| *40 lb gunpowder* | = | *16 "* |
| *1 cask Danish brandy* | = | *7 "* |
| *1 piece of calico* | = | *10 "* |
| *1 piece of Indian "Callowaypoos" cotton* | = | *6 "* |
| *1 piece of Indian "Salempuris" cotton* | = | *10 "* |
| *2 pieces of gingham* | = | *10 "* |
| *2 iron bars* | = | *4 "* |
| *1 copper bar* | = | *1 "* |
| *4 pieces "plattilias" or linen cloth* | = | *8 "* |
| *1 "cabes" of coral* | = | *2 "* |
| *1 tin basin* | = | *2 "* |
| *20 lbs cowrie shells* | = | *8 "* |

*Total   96 Rdl*

Should one or two teeth be missing, 4 or 8 rixdaler would be deducted from this amount." Slaves from the Danish-Norwegian forts and trading stations were also sold to other nations. This could be to the so-called "interlopers", ships that operated along the coast, independent of companies and nations. Rømer has also experienced speculative buyers in this respect:

"It can be quite annoying when a Portuguese is to purchase slaves; we have the slaves on display everywhere, and have them rub themselves with palm oil when they are offered for sale, to make them look good before the captains see them; a Portuguese can spend four hours looking at one slave, he smells their throats, he feels them everywhere; the slaves have to caper about for him, laugh and sing for him. Finally he licks their chins to find out whether they have beards, and if a slave has the slightest scar on his body he rejects him. An Englishman is also particular, but not as unreasonable as a Portuguese. A Frenchman usually takes everything that is black."

In his book Rømer also describes the measures taken in order to prevent the slaves from escaping:

"When the slaves have not been stolen by the Negro who brings them to the coast, the black trader, at the place where he has purchased them, attaches the slave's arm with an iron clamp to a large block of wood, which the slave is barely able to lift; the slave has to carry this on his head or shoulders; the black trader does this to prevent the slave from running away along the way; he fastens the arm of a female, boy or girl slave to the waist."

Special security measures are also necessary for the deck slaves who are working on the *Fredensborg*. For the most part they behave themselves on board and do good work, but one day a slave is caught red-handed as he is breaking open a seaman's chest in order to steal. He receives a few lashes from the cat-o'-nine-tails, and thereafter sneaks over to the figurehead in order to jump overboard. This is discovered at the last moment, and a shackle is fastened around his foot with a chain secured to a ring bolt on the deck. Thereafter it becomes a regular routine to "put the slave in irons for the night" and release him in the morning. During the day he wears an ankle-ring that enables him to work.

It is easy to imagine Captain Ferentz' desperation when he loses yet another man on 9 March. This time Able Seaman Hans Ivertsen is debited for planks and nails for a plain coffin. Thus far, a total of 12 men are dead, and Ferentz is beginning to doubt whether he will ever sail the ship to the West Indies with a large cargo of slaves on board.

On 12 March Ferentz takes on board " 2 good slaves that I was thinking of using as deck slaves, as I can see that most of the men are growing weaker. And only a few who are taken ill may be cured. I would leave it to the worthy Board of Directors to investigate the cause of this, God willing, on our successful return home. For my part, I take great pains to look after them, and I am gratified if they are restored to health. I hope the worthy Directors will not blame me for violating the regulations, by taking more slaves on board than are permitted, but necessity has driven me to it".

During all this time the fort has been a hotbed of intrigues. Jessen and Aarestrup are embittered because neither of them has been chosen for the office of Governor after Tychsen, and Reimers finds himself in a vulnerable position. Ferentz keeps his eyes open and reports to the Board of Directors; he has heard that Financial Officer Quist has delivered a report to the Governor and the Privy Council. This time it concerns Reimers, and there are complaints about his bad behaviour towards the financial officer and the administration of the Quitta lodge. Reimers is summoned to attend a meeting of the Privy Council, but he refuses as they are unable to show a writ of summons. While the financial officer is writing the summons, Reimers and Aarestrup slip into the Negeriet, so there is no written notice that day. But they catch up with Reimers, and the Privy Council pronounces judgement on him in the form of a notice of dismissal. This is far from an honourable discharge, and he is advised to go back to Copenhagen on the *Fredensborg* and be brought to account for his sins.

Friday 18 March the Captain writes in his journal: "A.M. 2 men inspect and oil all the small arms, and load them with blanks and peas, except for four which are only loaded with blanks…Painted the cannons with necessary colours."

Four days later: "3 P.M. A canoe arrives with Able Seaman Jens Sivertsen, and Ordinary Seamen Erich Ancker and Woye Olsen, who were free of fever, but they looked miserable and were very weak. Andreas Fredriksen has recovered, but Peter Diedrichsen and Jochum Bollvardt are sick, as well as Third Mate Beck who is seriously ill and at times is delirious…"

Governor Tychsen had not only left everything in a mess, his white housekeeper, Mistress Anne Møller, was left behind without means, in an alien land where she was no longer wanted. There were few white women who tolerated life along the Coast; most of those who came there died or went home at the first opportunity. This did not create difficulties because the white officials at the Fort could pick and choose from among the local women. Rømer says:

"This is accepted by the authorities, because the Whites thereby become established as if native, and one sees that they are not as jealous, ill-humoured or as eager to escape the country as before. And once the native woman has presented the white man with a couple of mulatto children, he becomes just as fond of her and their children, as a man who has his real wife and children in Europe."

According to a dispensation granted by Bishop Worm, all the Danes and Norwegians at Christiansborg had been given per-

*The white officials at the forts and trading stations felt at home with their black women. These women from Accra appeared on the title page of Paul Erdmann Isert's book.*

Paul Erdmann Isert's,
ehemahl. königl. dänisch. Oberarzte an den Besitzungen
in Afrika,

**Reise nach Guinea**

und den
Caribäischen Inseln in Columbien,
in Briefen an seine Freunde beschrieben.

*Akraisches Frauenzimmer.*

*A British map from 1729 gives a good impression of the location of the different ethnic groups, or nations, along the Gold Coast. Many of these were fighting among themselves, which could result in changes in the balance of power among them.*

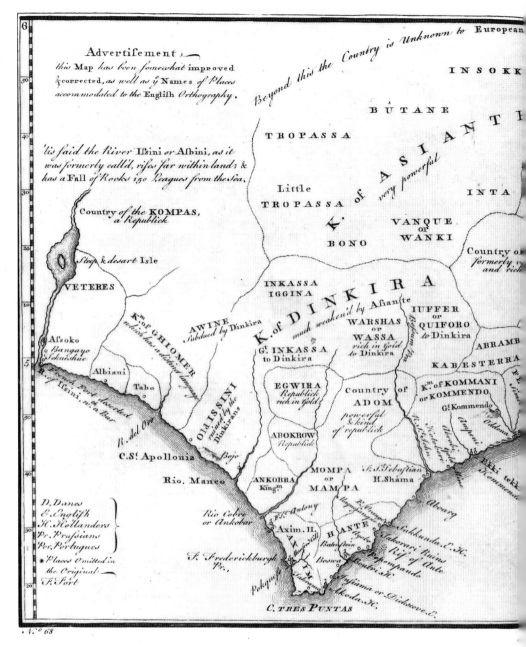

mission to "take unto themselves a black woman", but only one! The conditions were as follows:

1. The man had to promise to convert his heathen wife to Christianity.
2. When the man went to Europe, he should take her with him if she wanted to go.

Taking an African wife was called "cassare", which is a Portuguese word for marriage, and means "to take into one's house". The African women took good care of their white husbands, and with a safety net of local family connections the white men who "cassarerte" were better off socially and mentally than the rest. A wife obtained cheaper food, and her white husband had a much safer life in this alien

Plate LX. Vol. II. p. 565

land than was otherwise customary. In other words, "cassare" was a kind of life insurance, as the woman did her best to keep her husband alive; if he died mysteriously, she could risk being charged with having poisoned him.

Efforts were made to provide the numerous mulatto children, who were the inevitable result, with schooling, and bring them up in the Christian faith. The man who had an African wife had to pay into a special "mulatto fund" that was intended for the children's upbringing. As a rule, the boys entered the service as soldiers at the forts and trading stations, while the girls willingly followed in their mother's footsteps.

Mistress Møller was granted passage on board the *Fredensborg*, as they "wanted to get rid of her in a decent manner". Ferentz is able to promise her a cabin of her

*An African village is attacked by brutal slave raiders.*

own, and that she may dine in the captain's cabin. But Ferentz adds that facilities for a woman on board are poor. Reimers – who was dismissed in disgrace – needs more room on the ship. He has five private slaves whom he wishes to sell in the West Indies, and makes a deal with Ferentz. They agree on a freight charge of 35 rixdaler per head, which is the Company's minimum price.

*A stream of slaves flowed down to the coast from the interior.*

By April they have been at the Coast for half a year, and have had to contend with travats, the heat and illness. Even though there are still sick men on board, the health conditions are gradually improving.

Ferentz finds it is time to remind the fort about the letter he sent on 20 January, requesting an answer to his question about the departure date. In the reply from the fort, the excuse is that it has been quite impossible to determine when they can obtain enough slaves, but they hope everything will be arranged in about 14 days or so. The fort is now bustling with activity; slaves are constantly arriving from Ningo and Quitta. An inland conflict also has a positive influence on the supply; prisoners are sold in exchange for muskets and gunpowder and other enticing trading goods.

The branding of the slaves usually takes place in the Company's court-yard. The Guinea Company marks its slaves on the front of the right thigh. The Company's mark consist of an "S" inscribed in a heart. The "S" stands for "Slave", whether one speaks Danish or English.

On Monday 18 April, the Captain writes: "A canoe arrived with a case marked 'D.G.C. No. 2', containing 42 elephant tusks and 43 'crevells', or small elephant and hippopotamus tusks...The canoe departed for the fort immediately, taking the Cooper and some rope for tying the slaves together..."

*So that the slaves could be identified, they were branded. The mark was usually burned into different parts of the body. The Guinea Company preferred to use the right thigh.*

*Here we see a copy of the Company's own branding-iron.*

The next morning all the cannons are fired before the loading begins. The slaves are brought out to the *Fredensborg* in the fort's great canoe, and by the end of the day 136 male slaves have been safely stowed in the hold. The fort blacksmith has been busy shackling the slaves; "they were all secured by foot irons, two by two." From now on the crew have to be extra vigilant, and Ferentz orders a guard, armed with a cutlass, to be posted at each of the hatches.

The next few days there is feverish activity. First the adult female slaves are brought on board, then the girl and boy slaves. The passengers, Reimers and Mistress Møller, arrive along with 30 chickens and 3 goats. Several barrels of water are loaded on the ship, as well as other refreshments for the voyage. One of the male slaves is replaced. "He was a pawn from the King of Akwambo and was sent back to shore in the canoe."

*The record in the Captain's journal of the loading of the slaves in April 1768.*

The fort has kept its promise. Within a few days the *Fredensborg* has been filled with slaves, and when the remidors paddle back to shore on the evening of 21 April, they take with them two casks of brandy, as is the custom after they have brought an entire cargo of slaves on board.

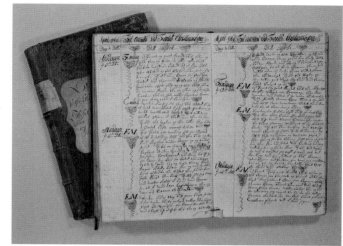

*After months of waiting the slave cargo is finally brought on board.*

The last days in the Christiansborg roadstead are occupied with the final preparations for the departure. Early in the morning Factor Dahl, from the fort, brings on board the gold they are to take with them. He also has two barrels of water and a cow for fresh meat. After he has left, Ferentz summons a meeting of the Ship's Council to determine whether they can undertake a voyage to the West Indies with their reduced crew. They agree that they should have two Mulattos as extra help, for which they send a request to land. The reply from the fort is quick and contains a scathing criticism of Ferentz for not asking about this earlier. None of the Mulattos are willing to go, but he can take along the fort's cooper, Mads Georg Weis, who is also a capable seaman. At 11 p.m., just before they weigh anchor, Cooper Weis signs on the *Fredensborg*.

A cargo of slaves is in the hold, one of the many contributions of the Danish-Norwegian dual monarchy to the history of the slave trade. For the second time the frigate from Copenhagen is about to set sail on the middle passage with its cargo of misery. In the West Indies, on the other side of "The Great Salt", they are waiting for new manpower.

# CHAPTER 5

# The Black Slave Ship

THE SLAVERS PREFERRED TO SET SAIL AT NIGHT when everything was quiet on board and the slaves were asleep. This was probably best because the slaves were fearful about what awaited them in their new existence. "The slaves who come from the hinterlands believe that we Europeans buy them to fatten them up like swine, and eat them when they have become fat. This fear can make them so desperate that they would try to kill us," wrote Rømer, who had experience and knew almost everything about the slave trade. Captain Ferentz was familiar with the proven formula of departing at night. Saturday 23 April: "At midnight we weighed anchor in the name of Jesus. By 1 o'clock the anchor was up and all sails were set."

The fort had sent wishes for a good journey in writing: "May God grant you a safe arrival at St. Croix, and we pray the Lord that you have a successful journey, and may God protect you." Captain Ferentz could use all the good wishes he could get, but he was in greater need of experienced seamen. Even though the instructions called for a maximum stay of four months at the Coast, they had been lying at anchor for 205 days, nearly seven months. A total of eleven men had been left behind in the fort's graveyard, in addition to Niels Mathisen, who had been buried at sea during the journey south. This was a frightening loss which showed that the slave transport took a heavy toll among the seamen, and was a source of grief and sorrow to those who were left behind in the Danish-Norwegian kingdom. Up to now the following had lost their lives:

| | |
|---|---|
| *28 Aug. 1767* | *Able Seaman Niels Mathisen* |
| *6 Oct.* | *Able Seaman Peder Johnsen* |
| *8 Nov.* | *Chief Officer Peder Christian Lundberg* |
| *27 Nov.* | *Fourth Mate Andreas Sivertsen Gadt* |
| *29 Nov.* | *Chief Carpenter Jacob Jacobsen Beck* |
| *30 Nov.* | *Carpenter Johan Jacob Kock* |
| *16 Dec.* | *Captain Espen Kiønig* |

Opposite page:
*Full utilization of cargo capacity was important on the slave ships, which is evident from the stowage plans of the English slave ship* Brookes. *Fig.4 shows a fully-loaded 'tween-deck. In Fig. 2 and 5 we see how the scant headroom in the hold is fully utilized. Thus, with extra slave platforms like those in the* Fredensborg, *there was room for even more slaves on board. The drawing is from Thomas Clarkson's book* The History of the Abolition of the African Slave Trade, *(1808).*

| | |
|---|---|
| *25 Dec.* | *Carpenter Axel Antoniussen Hæglund* |
| *4 Jan. 1768* | *Able Seaman Ole Nicolaysen* |
| *28 Jan.* | *Cooper Ivert Jacobsen* |
| *2 Feb. 1768* | *Quartermaster Abraham Engmann* |
| *8 Mar.* | *Able Seaman Hans Ivertsen* |

The slaves, who made up the live cargo, were burdened by grief and desperation. Many had probably been sold several times before ending up in the fort's barracoons, but their introduction to a large slave ship was even more terrifying than the journey to the coast and the fort. Hoffmann sharpens his quill and lists the cargo that has been brought on board:

| | |
|---:|---|
| *144* | *male slaves* |
| *78* | *female slaves* |
| *9* | *girl slaves* |
| *20* | *boy slaves* |
| *9* | *male deck slaves* |
| *260* | *slaves and 5 male slaves as cargo* |

It paid to carry as many slaves as possible. The slave platforms on board the *Fredensborg* had been constructed with this in mind. An estimated space of 180 x 40 x 70 cm for each slave was normal, which by comparison was slightly less than the space in a coffin. It has been said that there were two kinds of slave captains. The captains who were called "loose packers" believed that giving the slaves more room meant fewer deaths. The "tight packers" believed that as many slaves as possible on board yielded the greatest profits. The transport of slaves was a business. Ferentz took the slaves that had been brought to the forts and trading stations during their long stay. He had enough foot irons for 300 slaves, but there were only 265 on board. With less than two slaves per register ton, conditions were reasonably good for the slaves and the crew that had to take care of them, at least as far as space was concerned. The Company's instructions to the captain were clear, not least concerning the treatment of the slaves on board: "It is recommended to the Captain that the greatest importance is attached to the conservation of the slaves. He shall personally and frequently see to it that the officers ensure their proper treatment on board the ship, and that no member of the crew strikes or kicks them. The

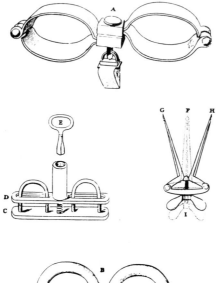

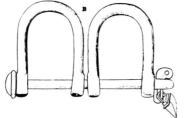

*In order to control the live cargo, the slavers usually had special equipment. A: Wrist irons. B: Foot irons, which were used on board the* Fredensborg *for securing the slaves two by two. C and E are thumb screws with a key, while the last "instrument" is a so-called "speculum oris", a mouth opener. This was used for force feeding when the slaves refused to take food.*

crew shall not mistreat them, but encourage them instead, and be careful when bringing them in and out of the hatches, etc."

In addition: "Once the slaves are on the ship, and during the passage, in order to prevent the stench and spread of sickness among so many people on board, one must take care that no part of the ship is allowed to be filled with excrement. Three times a day the ship must be washed down inside and out, and every morning, while the slaves are eating on deck, the hold where they sleep must be cleaned out. During the day funnels made of canvas, for providing fresh air below decks, are hung down in the hold. Three times a week the quarters are fumigated with juniper, which is to be brought from here for this purpose, occasionally with gunpowder, followed by a sprinkling of vinegar."

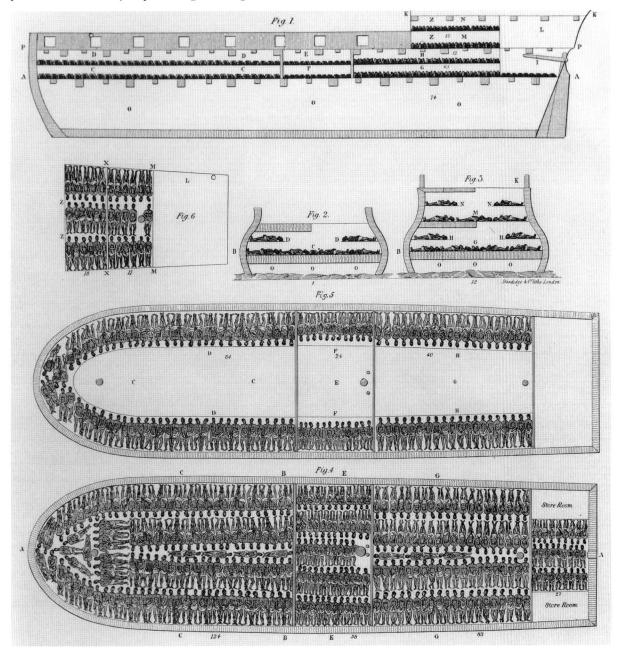

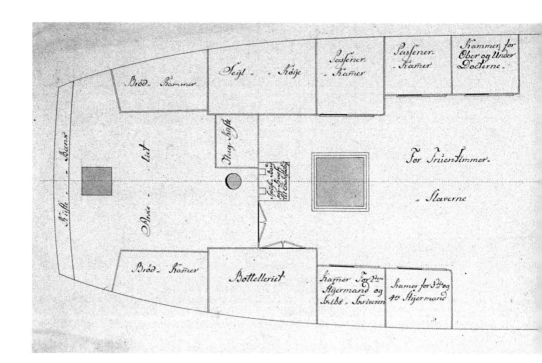

It is hardly worth speculating whether this formulation was prompted by humane or economic motives. In order to sail the frigate safely across the Atlantic, Ferentz had thirty seamen and nine deck slaves. At the time of her departure there was a total of 297 people on board the frigate, which was a little more than 31 metres long. The fear of a slave rebellion was always present, and the deck slaves also represented a security risk, even though they enjoyed a higher status. But Fer-

*The* Fredensborg II *heading for St. Croix with a cargo of slaves.*

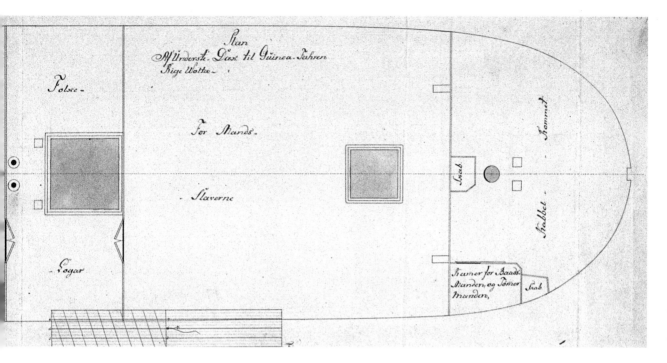

entz had no choice because several members of the crew were sick, and others were so weak that they were unable to climb the rigging. The adult male slaves were the most dangerous. They had been placed in the 'tween-deck, while the women and the girl slaves were kept aft with the children. Solid bulkheads with locking doors were put up betwen the holds for the men and the women. The seamen were kept on the alert around the clock in order to avoid a dangerous situation. The instructions for preventing a slave rebellion were clear:

"The Captain shall maintain strict discipline over the slaves in order that the female slaves are not given too much freedom, and are kept apart from the male slaves. Both the Captain and the crew are earnestly advised to keep them under constant supervision night and day, to prevent anyone from causing serious trouble. He shall therefore give strict orders to the carpenters, the cooper and the cook, along with the rest of the men who use iron and suchlike implements to keep this equipment under lock and key. When these are needed and used, great care must be taken to keep the slaves from getting hold of them. Likewise, and at all times, as long as the slaves are on deck, the gun lockers in which the muskets and ammunition are stored must remain closed, and kept on the quarterdeck where the male slaves must never be allowed. When these gun lockers are opened, no one – neither male nor female slaves, nor children – must be allowed on deck as long as these remain open."

There are few drawings of Danish-Norwegian slave ships under sail with slaves on board, but there is one of the *Fredensborg*'s successor which is very illustrative. It was also called the *Fredensborg,* and was named after the fort in Ningo. There is every reason to believe that the two ships were very similar; one displaced 278 tons, the other 276 tons. Both were constructed within an interval of a few years for the triangular trade. The number of gun ports was the same, and both were three-masted frigates. These slave frigates had some special equipment which distin-

*Draft of the Danish-Norwegian slave ship* Rio Volta *which completed five voyages in the triangular trade. Of a total of 1,591 slaves that were taken on board 1,357 survived the middle passage.*

*Like the other slave
ships, the* Fredens-
borg *was at the mercy
of the prevailing
winds and currents.
After sailing well into
the Gulf of Guinea
they changed course
and headed west,
passing to the south
of Prindzens Eyland,
also called Principe.
Then they set their
course for the West
Indies.*

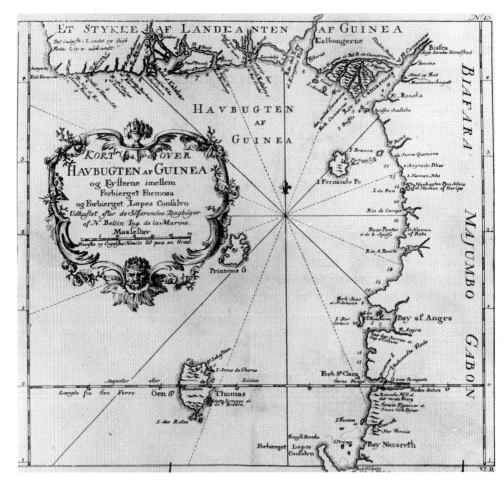

guished them from ordinary merchant vessels. First, there were the funnels (or so-called "windsails") with openings in the direction of the wind. They were made of canvas and their function was to funnel fresh air down to the slaves in the hold. The invention was probably Danish and saved the life of many a slave. The two forward funnels provided fresh air down to the male slaves, while the funnel closest to the stern sent air to the women and children. Every evening the funnels were hoisted up and the hatches closed and bolted for security reasons. The large storm- or "slave-bulwark" is just in front of the mainmast. It jutted out over both sides of the ship and extended well above the afterdeck. Cannons called "swivel guns" were placed along the top of the bulwarks. These could be turned in every direction and were usually loaded with peas to prevent serious injury to the slaves. In serious situations they could be loaded with a handful of musket shot. The front bulwark was just aft of the foremast. This was much smaller but afforded some protection to the seamen who were in the forecastle. Both bulwarks were constructed of heavy planks. A box-like construction was perched on the outside of the port side, in front of the longboat aft. This was the "toilet" for the female slaves. So-called "quarter-netting" was stretched along both sides of the ship to prevent the slaves from jumping overboard, and the empty gun ports were fitted with iron bars. The heads visible in the drawing between the slave-bulwarks are male slaves who are being aired. The guns on the large bulwark are manned, and the men standing there are also carrying muskets. On the quarterdeck we can see female slaves being aired, and just in front of the mizzen mast two women are grinding millet. The slave ship has started the middle passage, and all the sails are set except for the mainsail and the topmast staysail. During the days after the departure, Captain Ferentz notes in his journal:

Sunday 24 April. "Course S 1/2 W. Wind W to WSW with light breeze. Secured both bowers to railing. Stowed hawser in 'tween-decks midships. Slaves fed and given three rounds of water. Locked all provisions barrels. Pumped the bilges with 60 strokes. Pipes, tobacco and brandy for the slaves. Distance made good 14 1/4 miles. Meridian distance from Cook's Loaf 37 5/10 minutes. Observed position 4 degrees 25 minutes northerly breeze. Longitude 20 degrees 30 minutes."

Captain Ferentz is no longer as particular about recording the number of sick crewmen and slaves. He leaves this to Ship's Assistant Hoffmann. Now, he is first and foremost a seaman and navigator, who is going to sail his ship across a great ocean between two continents. He scrupulously enters information about the winds and weather, the course and distance covered. As usual Hoffmann is observant and notes all the other details. On the same day he records that Chief Officer Beck, three seamen, eleven male slaves and one female slave are sick. The following day the number of sick has increased to five among the crew and seventeen slaves.

The *Fredensborg* is heading east. The course followed by Ferentz is tried and true; it has been adapted to natural conditions and follows the Guinea current and the prevailing winds further into the Guinea Bay. There is gold on board, securely locked up in the expedition's chest in the captain's cabin. Ship's Assistant Hoffmann was there with Ferentz when it was handed over at the fort. 55 *lodd* gold (1 *lodd* = 15.5 grams) are packed inside a wooden capsule marked "D.G.C." To be on the safe side, it is sealed in five places with two of the Company's wax seals. 25 *lodd* gold are kept in a cylindrical glass, wrapped in paper and marked "D.G.C." This is sealed with 2 Company seals, while for safety's sake Captain Ferentz has placed his seal on both packages. The gold dust weighs a total of 1 1/4 kg.

To the southwest, on the port side, they can see Fort Fredensborg with Dannebrog waving in the breeze. In these waters, as captain of the slave ship *Christiansborg*, Ferentz will later wage a life-and-death struggle in a violent slave rebellion. For the time being, on board the *Fredensborg*, he has everything under control. The journals of the captain and the ship's assistant provide us with a good picture of what is taking place on board.

Monday 25 April: "All light sails secured. A travat blew up with near gale and rain. 10 slaves from the north loosened from irons. Smoked out 'tween-decks with tar and pitch. Scraped and scoured the slave holds fore and aft. Slaves fed. Chief Officer Beck and Seamen Friderich Kruse, Antoni Olsen, Peder Holm and Jens Pedersen sick. 15 male slaves, 1 female slave and 2 boy slaves sick. Course SSE. East meridian distance from Cook's Loaf 42 8/10 minutes."

Tuesday 26 April: "Smoked out slave holds with tar, juniper and gunpowder. Slaves fed. The men secured the stays on the bowsprit. The slaves picked a little oakum. Becalmed and drifted about until the wind rose. Slaves washed themselves. All sails set. 2 male slaves recovered. 13 male, 2 female and 2 boy slaves sick. Seaman Peder Holm recovered. Chief Officer Beck and Seamen Antoni Olsen,

Friderich Kruse, Jens Pedersen and Peter Diderichsen sick. Course SSE. Dist. 7 1/2 miles. East meridian dist. from Cook's Loaf 68 minutes."

Wednesday 27 April: "Sighted terns that followed us. Gathering travat clouds. Loosened starboard cable and payed down into the hold. Took out the late Captain Kiønig's woolen garments to be aired. Set all sails, ran before the wind. Today seventeen male, two female and two boy slaves with same sickness. Chief Officer Beck, Seamen Antoni Olsen, Friderich Kruse, Jens Pedersen sick. Course SE to S 1/2 E. Dist. 8 3/4 East meridian dist. from Cook's Loaf 100 minutes."

Thursday 28 April: "The female slaves enjoyed dancing their 'Negro Dances' on the quarterdeck. In the morning slaves also fed horse beans and salt meat. 2 slaves received lashes with cat-o'-nine tails for fighting. Two bells, a little travat blew up, tacked and headed east. Slaves fed, all light sails set. Bring up hogshead of grits from the hold. The Ship's Council affixed their signatures to the Bill for Refreshments from Christiansborg. Among the slaves: 3 male slaves recovered. Sick: 14 male, 2 female and 2 boy slaves. Otherwise sick: Chief Officer Beck, Cook Ørgensen, Antoni Olsen, Friderich Kruse, Jens Pedersen and Andreas Fredriksen. Course SE to S 3/4 E. Dist. 7 1/2 East meridian dist. from Cook's Loaf 129 minutes."

Friday 29 April: "Captain's instructions read to the crew in the morning. Many bonitos jumping around us. 7 bells. Reduced all light sails. 8 bells. All sails set again. Chief Officer Beck, Andreas Fredriksen and Cook Ørgensen recovered. Seamen Jens Pedersen, Antoni Olsen, Friderich Kruse and Ship's Boy Bendt Thomsen sick. Among the slaves 15 males, 4 females and 1 boy sick. Course SE last SW. Dist. 10 miles. East meridian dist. from Cook's Loaf 161 8/10 minutes."

Saturday 30 April: "Overcast calm, sails set according to weather conditions. Caught a little shark that was eaten by the crew. One of the deck slaves stole some bread from the crew and received several lashes with the 'cat'. Travat with heavy rain and near gale. 2 bells. Changed course SW about the same time as we ran into a travat from SE and SSE. Reduced all light sails as well as topsail and mizzen topsail. Travat and rain continued. Slaves fed as usual. Discover parted bolt rope on main topsail. Repaired ditto and later set all sails. Seamen Jens Pedersen, Antoni Olsen, Friderich Kruse and Ordinary Seaman Bendt Thomsen sick. 13 male, 3 female and 1 boy slave sick. Course SW 1/2 W Dist. 6 1/2 miles. East meridian dist. from Cook's Loaf 141 1/10 minutes."

Sunday 1 May: "Slaves given food and water. Small gale and clear air. 2 bells. Course south. Slaughtered kid, pumped bilges. Slaves washed themselves. At 11:30 Able Seaman Antoni Olsen died. At 12:00 sang a hymn and lowered the body overboard in his hammock. His belongings recorded, evaluated and auctioned for 20 Rdl. Slaves given brandy and meat in the afternoon. Of the crew Able Seamen Jens Pedersen, Friderich Kruse and Ship's Boy Bendt Thomsen sick. 15 male, 3 female and 1 boy slave sick. Course SSW. Dist. 3/4 mile. East meridian dist from Cook's Loaf 138 4/10 minutes."

Monday 2 May: "In the morning dead female slave found in the 'bodega' and thrown overboard. Ship's Surgeon Sixtus said she had internal ailments and he had given her a powder only once. Travat building up and very hot. Caught a small shark, the slaves rubbed themselves with palm oil and later were all given brandy. Smoked out the 'tween-decks and took up a barrel of coal from the hold. Tighten topmast

*The female slaves and the children were allowed to move about more or less freely on board. Five days after their departure the "female slaves entertain themselves by dancing their 'Negro dances' on the quarterdeck."*

shrouds fore and aft. 15 male and 5 female slaves sick. Among the crew Seamen Jens Pedersen, Friderich Kruse and Ship's Boy Bendt Thomsen sick. Course SSE 1/2 E. Dist. 4 3/4 miles. East meridian dist. from Cook's Loaf 156 3/10 minutes."

A few days at sea and we already have an idea of life on board a slave ship. The female slaves have danced their "Negro dances" on the quarterdeck, no doubt to the unanimous approval of the crew! However, it is doubtful whether the dance was intended as an expression of joy. Sickness is a constant worry among the crew, and the first seaman has already died. Two slaves have been in a fight. The space is cramped; perhaps two former enemies have been shackled and bolted together. According to Danish sources, it appears as if several of the ethnic groups in Guinea were constantly at war with one another and the many prisoners were captured and sold as slaves.

The weather is still variable – from calms to sudden travats – which means that the seamen constantly have to go aloft in order to reduce and set the sails. Travats and light breezes have led to a loss of 23 nautical miles, the distance run. By this time the ship's bottom is already covered in barnacles which reduce the speed. Fishing, especially for sharks, is a favourite pastime on board. They have brought along 116 fish hooks, including some larger hooks for sharks. Strangely enough, the crewmen ate the first shark that was caught after their departure. When they caught the second shark, quite understandably, there was no mention of whether it was eaten. By this time both Antoni Olsen and a female slave had been thrown overboard, and sharks that fed on human flesh were not very appetizing. There is reason to believe that a number of caustic comments were made in this respect. As a rule, the sharks followed in the wake of the slave ships. According to Clergyman H.C. Monrad, in his book *The Guinea Coast and Its Inhabitants*:

"Predatory sharks are to be found here by the thousands; it is not seldom that the Negroes are devoured by them, when their canoes capsize or they fall overboard, I myself have been witness to such a dreadful sight. The sharks continually follow in great shoals, and I have seen them tear apart in a moment bodies thrown overboard from the ship, despite their having been sewn in their hammocks as is customary, and been provided with weights of coal, cannon balls, etc., to force them to sink."

Dead slaves were unceremoniously thrown overboard. There is reason to believe that this was done on the port side. The starboard side, which was the "best side" of the ship, was probably reserved for the white man. There is no sign of emotion in the formal style of the journals, at any rate not when it concerns the death of a slave.

It was customary for the deck slaves, who had considerable contact with the crew, to be given European names. On the *Fredensborg* we find "Oliver", "Roland", "Ragge" and "Samson". They worked at no cost to the Company and did not even own themselves. As a reward they were given some of the white men's clothing and a little extra food. Without the deck slaves, who made up one-fourth of the the ship's crew, the *Fredensborg* would hardly have been able to sail with her great cargo of slaves. One day Ferentz himself was "down in the hold to have a look at the sick slaves. And then they were given water."

The Guinea Company had a smart system for officers and others who had the most important positions on board. They were supposed to receive a 5% commission on the total slave sales, and the scale was duly recorded in the captain's instructions. For this reason there was an even greater incentive to keep the slaves alive, because each dead slave represented a loss of about 10 rixdaler or more for the chosen few on board. As keeper of the records, the ship's assistant had to be informed of and, preferably, see every dead slave for himself. When the next death occurs on 4 May, Hoffmann writes that "a male slave died, which has been recorded on the basis of the Chief Officer's statement alone, since I have not seen it myself." He is annoyed on behalf of both the Company and himself, because he is also entitled to a provision. The Company's economic interests in keeping the slaves alive also find expression in the instructions:

"When any of the slaves become sick, the Captain shall see to it that they are immediately released from the irons and brought to a separate hold, to keep them apart from the healthy slaves. Thereafter, the Captain shall immediately order the Quartermaster to frequently examine these same slaves, and take great pains to restore them to health as soon as possible. For this purpose he shall also use *brambas* (limes) or lime juice, which the Captain shall allow him to have as often and in whatever quantity he needs for their treatment and cure. In addition, once or twice when the weather is good and the sun is high, the Captain shall order the slaves to be washed and rubbed with oil."

As the days go by, the routines on board begin to fall into place, but everyone seems harassed and strained. Ferentz has too few seamen, and the pressure on those who are left is all the greater. The weather is constantly changing, alternating between travats and periods of calm, while the distance covered varies from 6 to 11 3/4 miles per day. In the oppressive heat of the equator it is easy to visualize the situation below deck in the black ship.

Despite the canvas funnels, the temperature must have been unbearable. In addition, the funnels had little effect during a calm. There are examples of candles that barely burned in the slave hold because of the lack of oxygen! The smell of sweating slave bodies chafing against raw planks, along with the stench of excrement, must have been intolerable.

Friday 6 May: "Black clouds. The watch secured the light sails. A strong travat blew up from the east with wind and rain. Secured the topsails and courses, collected rainwater for the animals. 3 bells. All sails set again. Opened a barrel of pork and cabin bread, of which some was taken up. While slaves are eating, discover two sick male slaves. Cooked porridge of ground millet and Spanish pepper, which they enjoyed. The slaves ate as before. A female slave has a swollen thigh and leg. Same sickness."

The bill for 686 rixdaler for refreshments, which had come from the fort, also included several local products which were important to both the crew and the slaves:

| | |
|---|---|
| 98 "Negro hens" | 9 chests (6,340 l) of millet |
| 1 cow | 2 tortoises |
| 1/2 buffalo | 7 pigs including one with piglets |
| 7 kids | Onions |
| 2000 sticks of firewood | Vegetables |
| 2 barrels of beans | Potatoes |
| 2 sacks of same | Eggs |
| Spanish Pepper | Honey |
| 26 jars of "palm oil" | Brambas (limes) |
| Grains of Paradise | |

*Opposite page: Ration, or "Scale of Victualling", for the slaves during the Fredensborg's maiden voyage in the triangular trade in 1753 as the* Cron Prindz Christian. *Notice that the ration of brandy is crossed out for Tuesdays.*

Three "millet stones" were brought on board the *Fredensborg* shortly before departure. These were millstones hollowed out of sandstone, for grinding millet grains. When Ferentz writes that the two sick slaves were given a porridge of ground millet and Spanish pepper, it had been ground in one of these stones. Millet formed part of the slaves' fare, which had been carefully calculated and used without change by Danish ships for decades. It has been possible to find the rations for the *Fredensborg*'s maiden voyage as the *Cron Prindz Christian*. No doubt the list in Ferentz' expedition chest was very much like this one:

## RATION AND SCALE OF VICTUALLING FOR THE SLAVES
*Which accordingly shall be eaten on The Royal Chartered Danish Guinea Company's frigate called the* Cron Prindz Christian, *during the impending Voyage from Guinea to St. Thomas.*

One Slave's weekly Fare
1/2 write One Half Pound Pork
One Ottingkar (2,17 l) Beans
One Ottingkar Grits
1/3 write One Third Ottingkar Millet
1/2 write One Half Pægl (quarter pint) Brandy
1/8 write One Eighth Pound Tobacco
1 Tobacco Pipe

*Palm oil is always mixed into porridge, which can be estimated weekly at 1/4 pægl per Slave. 10 skjepper (1 skjeppe = half a bushel) grains of paradise for one hundred slaves throughout the entire Journey. One Barrel Brandy for the Remidors and the Negroes who replenish the Water Supply.*

The Daily Meals are as follows

| | | | |
|---|---|---|---|
| Sunday....... | Pork, Beans, Groats | Tobacco and Pipe | |
| Monday...... | Beans, Groats | Tobacco | Brandy |
| Tuesday...... | Beans, Groats | Tobacco | |
| Wednesday... | Beans, Groats | Tobacco | Brandy |
| Thursday..... | Beans, Groats | Tobacco | Brandy |
| Friday........ | Beans, Groats | Tobacco | |
| Saturday..... | Millet Twice | | Brandy |

This is the diet on which thousands of slaves lived while the ships were crossing the Atlantic. From a nutritional point of view it was probably acceptable, as it included vegetables. The brandy and tobacco were intended more for the psychological effect, and were included to help keep up their spirits during the wearying passage. As we can see, the brittle clay pipes were supposed to last a whole week, and were probably collected after use. The slaves were largely fed out on deck whenever this was possible. They were taken up in groups, needing fresh air and exercise as well as fresh food. The slave stove on which the porridge was cooked was out on deck. The cook had to see to it that the slave food was well-prepared and clean. It was not to be served too hot on the platters, and the slaves who did

not like palm oil in their porridge were not forced to eat it. Throughout the journey it was important that the food was good, since the slaves were to be offered on the market in the best possible condition. But, as we shall see, the diet regulations were not always followed to the letter.

It sometimes happened that slaves refused to take food on board the slave ships. In order to counteract emaciation these slaves were force-fed. For this purpose a special mouth-opener called the "speculum oris" was constructed. After the mouth had been opened, the food was poured down a funnel. No instances of this were recorded on board the *Fredensborg*, nor is a mouth-opener listed among the supplies.

Sunday 8 May: "The sailmaker improved the awning. 4 o'clock Seaman Jens Pedersen was cured of the fever – that is to say, he was dead. The deceased was sewn into the Company hammock, the flag lowered to half-mast, a hymn was sung and he was cast overboard by the starboard forechains. Butchered a pig for refreshment, weighed 4 stone 10 pounds, secured light sails. Slaves fed as usual. 1 sick female slave with a swollen thigh, and a male slave sick with stomach pains. All the other slaves had good appetites. Set all sails, handed out brandy, pipes and tobacco to all the slaves."

As usual Hoffmann is better informed about the sick on board than Ferentz, who wrote this. On the same day he notes that Seaman Friderich Kruse and Ship's Boy Bendt Thomsen are sick, along with 16 male and 6 female slaves. On the following day there was quite an uproar on board. Aye the African, who has signed on as ordinary seaman and interpreter, proves that he is an important member of the crew.

From the Captain's journal: "Have been told in confidence by a Negro woman and Aye that several male Akwambo slaves have banded together to plan a rebellion. That one day, while all the seamen were eating, the male slaves would seize their knives and murder all the Whites. At a suitable moment an Akwambo woman would give a sign to one of the boys to let them know the best time to carry out their evil intentions. Whereupon, made inquiries and learned that the Crepes were unwilling to take sides with those planning this evil. They told Aye that we should be on our guard, that there are now 3 male slaves, 2 female slaves and one boy who were behind this. They were punished with the cat-o'-nine-tails, and later all the Akwambo and a few Crepes, a total of 15 pairs, were placed in wrist irons connected to long chains, and secured."

The wrist irons were rarely used on the slaves, "except those who were so wild and dangerous that it was necessary". In this case there were no doubts about the necessity, because the disclosure of the plans to revolt was a terrifying discovery. Somehow, two of the women who were kept aft had been in contact with several of the male slaves. This suggests that the two female slaves functioned as spies who were supposed to find out the right time to strike. The use of one of the young boys as a messenger was a good idea, because they probably ran wherever they liked on the quarterdeck. The most important villages of the Akwambo, or Akwamu, were situated by the Rio Volta, a good distance from the coast, while the Crepes lived further to the east. Rivalry between the two groups must have been one of the reasons why the Crepes were unwilling to take part in the attempted revolt. Another reason could be the fact that, considering the circumstances, they found it hopeless. Aye's role is clear enough. He understood the language that was spoken in a large area, among others by the Akwambo, and he became the hero who was able to report to Captain Ferentz. Several later episodes reveal that Ferentz set great store by Aye after the disclosure.

This story reveals that on several occasions riots broke out on board the slave ships. If the slaves managed to take possession of the ship and kill the white seamen, they would still have problems in handling the large ships. Not to mention navigation and knowledge about winds and currents. Their ideas of geography were limited to the part of the coast they were familiar with, if they had come from the coastal region. If they did manage to reach land, there was a considerable risk of falling into the hands of enemies and being sold again as slaves. Another serious obstacle was the ship's cargo of alcoholic beverages, which could result in wild victory celebrations and drunken stupors. In reality, the possibility of gaining freedom and later finding the way back to the coast and one's own people was very small.

On this day Ship's Assistant Hoffmann is concerned with something entirely different from a planned slave rebellion. While Ferentz is struggling with interrogations, punishment and retaliation, Hoffmann is writing yet another critical letter to the Captain. He has been inside the cabin and seen that a number of the late Captain Kiønig's belongings are being used by his successor. This will not do! The Ship's Council, which is responsible for the effects, has left them in the care of Ferentz. And the Ship's Assistant has no confidence in him:

"…It is with no little surprise that I am informed that the trunk in which Captain Kiønig's possessions are kept has merely been locked and the key to this is in your hands. One pile of his things is lying here in the cabin, another there, and what's more, even up on the quarterdeck! I have had to be content with protesting about such an unlawful treatment of a dead man's estate. Since the auction, the gold watch which the late lamented Captain Kiønig left behind has been hanging on the wall of the Captain's bedroom. Because of the rolling of the ship, the watch is in such a state that it no longer keeps time and consequently is damaged. The Captain has admitted this in the presence of myself and others. The unvarnished truth is that the watch has lost its value, which would not have happened if the estate of the deceased had been treated in a lawful manner. You alone are duty bound to answer to the heirs or creditors for the damage done to the gold watch. As far as the other belongings are concerned, as long as we have been under sail from Fort Christiansborg, you have constantly been using Captain Kiønig's octant. It is as clear as day that the unauthorized use of something belonging to a dead man is unlawful!"

Hoffmann waits two or three days before he delivers his letter of protest to Captain Ferentz. If the relations between the two have previously been strained, they are out-and-out hostile now. Ferentz is furious. As the one who is responsible for a Company ship of tremendous value, he regards this as making a fuss over trifles. His everyday life is full of problems which have to be solved if the *Fredensborg* is to arrive safely at St. Croix at all. The reaction is not long in coming. Hoffmann: "In the afternoon I came up on the quarterdeck. Captain Ferentz had Captain Kiønig's octant, and asked whether I saw that he was using it, and whether I wished to protest again. I said no, but that I would make note of it in the journal. Whereupon he answered me in such a manner that I would not give offence to the worthy Board of Directors by repeating it. Seamen Peder Holm and Claus Larsen can bear witness to this, seeing that one was standing by the wheel and the other at his post. I have every hope that the worthy Board of Directors does not give the Captain leave to speak in an abusive and shocking manner to an Assistant who is doing nothing more than his duty."

Ferentz feels obliged to reply in writing: "I cannot cease to marvel at his incipient refractoriness." Point by point he refutes Hoffmann's accusations and insists that he must not interfere in matters concerning the command on board. "As far as the gold watch is concerned, the truth is that the watch still works; when it is wound up it runs as well as it has at all times. As far as Kiønig's octant is concerned, I confess that I have used it up to now, and that I intend to use it until we come to the West Indies, and even beyond. An octant is handier and more reliable than a quadrant, and I have therefore used it as befits a faithful officer of the Company and self-respecting man." Hoffmann is severely criticized for not being present in the morning. "By 6 o'clock in the morning he could have had a good night's sleep, and risen and been present when the slaves' food is handed out, in the morning as well as in the afternoon. To date I have yet to see him, even though he has said he will be present and supervise the serving of the food and water of the slaves, which I believe is his duty. Therefore, as his commanding officer, I ask that hereafter he carries out his duties as Assistant and stops making protests."

Life on board the ship goes on. Chief Officer Beck is so weak after his illness that he is still unable to walk about on deck, and Sixtus is completely taken up with all the sick. Two men have "durchlauf" – diarrhoea – and a third has a tumour in his head, while a female slave has "worms in one of her legs". This is probably the dreaded Guinea worm.

On 16 May, after 23 days under sail, Ferentz can take bearings of the little island of Principe, or Prindzens Eyland, ahead. He orders the flag to be hoisted. It was customary for the slave ships to take on board the final refreshments and fill up the water casks on one of the innermost islands in the Gulf of Guinea. It was at Principe Island that the slave ship Cron Prindzen exploded in 1705 with 826 slaves in the hold. The reason for the fire that reached the powder-magazine may have been a slave rebellion on board. There were only five survivors of the worst catastrophe in the history of the Danish-Norwegian slave trade.

According to the instructions, in the event of considerable delays because of bad weather or calms, the captain could put into one of the three islands of São Tomé, Annobon or Principe, "in order there to take on rice, chickens, pigs, coconuts, papayas and other delicious fruits, as well as water." When the slave ship arrived at one of the islands it was customary to rent one or two warehouses so that all the slaves could come ashore to regain some of their strength. After a suitable stay they should "with the first good wind and opportunity, with God's help, continue the journey".

No doubt the crew of the Fredensborg has been eagerly anticipating such a stopover, but because of contrary winds and strong currents they have to give up, and sail on "with sails as full as possible," and manage with the provisions they have on board. On 17 May a "very emaciated" slave dies, and Seamen Peder Holm, Jocum Bollvardt and Ship's Boy Anders Skaaning receive several lashes for falling asleep during the watch. Their punishment is light for this serious negligence, because, according to the Ship's Articles, the worst punishment they could have received was keel-hauling (being hauled under the keel of the ship). As far as Jochum Bollvardt is concerned, he did not doze off because of ordinary fatigue. This was the first sign of the dreaded fever; two days later he lies delirious in his hammock, which is to be his final resting place.

Thursday 26 May: "Hazy, travat, reefed topsail, gale. Slaves rubbed themselves with palm oil. The sailmaker repaired a funnel that was down in the after hatch for the female slaves. Three slaves complained of stomach pains, but ate all the same. 5 bells. Veered with the wind SE, immediately afterwards the fore topsail broke in the middle. Took down same in addition to the topsail that was torn to shreds. Took in lower spritsail yard and lashed this to the topsail yard again, and also bent the other old topsail. The old yard was delivered to the cook for firewood. Jochum Bollvardt, Friderich Kruse, Peder Madsen, Bendt Thomsen, Mistress Møller and Hoffmann sick. Of the slaves, ten male, five female and four boy slaves sick. Course SE. Dist. 10 miles. West departure from Eyland Prindz 240 1/10 minutes."

Sunday 29 May: "Strong topgallant breeze, overcast. Smoked out the slave holds with tar, juniper and gunpowder. Slaves fed as usual, received brandy and meat. 1 male slave dead, ship pumped dry. Found a leak in the quarterdeck in a rotten waterway seam. Caulked and finished by me. Pump ship dry. Peder Madsen recovered. Jochum Bollvardt, Friderich Kruse, Bendt Thomsen, Mistress Møller and Hoffmann sick. Eleven male, five female and four boy slaves sick. Course W to S. Dist. 19 miles. West departure from Eyland Prindz 317 6/10 minutes."

Thursday 2 June: "Strong topgallant breeze. Set lower studding sail on port. Tidied up in the cargo forward and stowed 3 hogsheads. Took up one hogshead coal to the cook. 1 male slave dead and thrown overboard. Took bearings on the setting sun, according to this observe compass error of 14 degrees NW. Near gale, dense air with rain. Took down lower studding sail, which was later set. 1 female slave dead, had tumour and worms in one leg. Run down topgallant sail, took down lower studding sail. The same are sick. Eleven male, five female and three boy slaves are sick. Course W to S. Dist. 35 3/4 miles. West departure from Eyland Prindz, 701 minutes."

The *Fredensborg* crossed the Equator on 30 May. There is no indication of a special ceremony when crossing the Line, with "King Neptune" or "the Man in the Line" as he was also called in those days. Considering the situation on board, they had more than enough to do to keep the *Fredensborg* under sail and the slaves alive. The southerly equatorial current was taking them in the right direction, even though they were driven several miles to the southeast before they were able to stabilize the course to the west. Without difficulty they came though the dreaded Doldrums, which in some instances could be a matter of life or death. Many slave ships had lain week after week with slack sails, while a blazing sun and heat increased the thirst of those on board. In several instances the captains had rid themselves of the slave cargo, to enable the whites to survive on a scanty supply of provisions and water. During the leakage in the quarterdeck, we see that Captain Ferentz took care of the repairs himself. Whether this was a captain who could turn his hand to almost anything is hard to say – this could just as well be a reflection of the fact that they had no carpenters on board. Later during the voyage Ferentz repairs the longboat along with the boatswain's mate.

Friday 3 June: "Strong topgallant breeze the whole day. Crowded all sails, scoured and swabbed the slave holds. All the slaves rubbed themselves with palm oil, and with the help of one of the deck slaves Aye barbered all the female slaves. Some of the late Kiønig's woolen stockings were aired out. Same are sick. Course W to N all day. Dist. 39 1/2 miles. West departure from Eyland Prindz 838 minutes."

Saturday 4 June: "Moderate breeze all day. Washed down the platforms in the hold for the female slaves. The cooper made two small gutters for water. Aye the African, and one deck slave barbered all the male slaves. Slaughtered a pig for refreshment and smoked out the 'tween-deck. Hoffmann recovered, along with 2 male slaves, otherwise the same are sick. Course W to N the whole day. Dist 38 1/4 miles. West departure from E.P. 1013 minutes."

The reason for all the barbering, in which Aye takes the leading part, is not given. Whether there were vermin on board is better left unsaid, but after 42 days at sea a haircut was certainly necessary. Now, day after day goes by while the routines on board are tightened. There are constant incidents which are recorded in the journals, like the one on Sunday 4 June: "All the slaves given pipes and tobacco, discovered 5 or 6 female slaves who had stolen salt and Spanish pepper. They each received 10 lashes with the cat-o'-nine-tails."

The next disciplinary matter does not concern any of the slaves, but Ordinary Seaman Erich Ancker from Christiania. He has been sick, but has been recovering. At any rate it is clear that he has fully recovered his appetite, while the rations are on the scanty side. On Wednesday 8 June the Ship's Council is summoned, and afterwards Ancker is called in to explain an episode a few nights earlier, when he is said to have knocked a candle out of the hand of a female slave and thereafter, in the dark, stolen food from the cabin. Ancker admits the theft and explains that he was hungry. He is then accused of several other thefts that have taken place on board, and after considerable pressure confesses to having stolen pork and butter from Third Mate Runge. After this confession the seaman is ushered outside, and each member of the Ship's Council is asked to present his views about a suitable punishment for Ancker.

Boatswain's Mate Peder Thorsen: "Erich Ancker has confessed to the entire Ship's Council that he has stolen food from the cabin and several other places on the ship. I think that since this is a minor offense he should receive a thrashing of half a hundred lashes, on the port side of the capstan."

Boatswain Rosenberg: "Since he has been stealing so often, it seems to me that he deserves 50 blows at the capstan."

Third Mate Runge: "Since we have been informed that the other evening Erich Ancker was down in the passage to the cabin to steal, and that he has stolen many other times, he should be punished as a thief with 50 lashes."

Officer Beck: "He deserves 70 lashes for the theft."

Captain Ferentz concludes: "Since such deeds should not remain unpunished, as an example to others and to prevent him from doing this sort of thing later, my vote, in accordance with most of the votes, is that he should be given 50 lashes with the cat-o'-nine-at the capstan."

Erich Ancker is then called in, the verdict is announced, and he is asked whether he has any objections, which he does not. Then he is tied to the port side of the capstan, and receives "the 50 lashes as counted by the boatswain and the boatswain's mate."

It may be of interest to see the prevailing victualling regulations for Company ships engaged in long-distance trade. The following list is from 1753, the year the *Fredensborg*, under the name of *Cron Prindz Christian*, set out on her first voyage in the triangular trade:

*"RATION and Scale of Victualling*
*for the food to be eaten on the Ships of the*
*Royal Chartered Danish Guinea Company*

*The Weekly Ration for One Man:*
*A half pound of Pork*
*Two pounds of Meat*
*One and a half pounds of Dried Fish*
*One pound of Butter*
*Five pounds of Groats*
*Two pounds of Peas*
*Four pounds of hardtack*
*Seven pounds of soft bread during the first 4 – 6 Weeks*
*One pint of Brandy*
*One Barrel of Beer for each man for the whole voyage*
*Two pints of Water daily when all Beer has been consumed.*

*Oil, Malt Vinegar and Prunes, which are not ordinary fare, shall be given at the discretion of the Ship's Council.*

*The Petty Officers and Assistant Barbers, Chief Boatswain, Constable, Cook, Steward and their Assistants who are transported out of the Country, and dine in the Cabin and with the Chief Steward, are given one and a half rations of Pork, Meat, Butter and Brandy, and when someone is sick, no rations are due him, but then he is given Food and Drink in compliance with the Orders and at the Discretion of the Ship's Council."*

This looks relatively good, but most often the reality was quite different. Nothing is said about the quality of the food, which could be extremely poor, especially during a long voyage after lengthy storage. The hardtack was usually full of weevils, and most seamen preferred to pound out the weevils before they ate it. The crew of the *Fredensborg* escaped scurvy and epidemics, but were hard hit by the climate fever. It is not easy to stop a hungry young boy, but fifty lashes with the cat-o'-nine-tails served to keep Erich Ancker within his allotted ration during the rest of the voyage. What the female slave was doing in the passage to the cabin with a candle in her hand may leave room for speculation. It was well-known that amorous incidents occurred on board the slave ships; if anything like this took place on board the *Fredensborg*, there is no mention of it in the ship's log or journal – one did not write about that!

# RANSON og Spise-Taxt,

## Hvor efter skal spiises paa de Kongl. Octroyerede Danske Westindiske & Guineiske Compagnies Skibe.

### Een Mands Kost Ugentlig:

Et halv pund Flesk
Toe pund Kiød
Et og Et halv pund tør Fisk
Et Pund Smør
Een og tre ottendeel Ottingkar Gryn
Et halv Ottingkar Erter
Fire Pund hart Brod
Syv Pund bledt Brod i de forste 4 a 6 Uger
Een halv potte Brændeviin
En Tonde Oll til Mands for heele Rejsen
Een pot Vand daglig naar Ollet slipper
Af Olie, Oll-Edicke, og Svidsker, som icke er nogen
ordinaire Spiise, spiises efter Skibs-Raadets got-
findende.

Under-Styr-Mændene og Under-Barbererne, Høybaads-Mand, Constabel,
Kok, Botteleer, og hvis Assistenter, som bliver transporteret udi Landet,
og spiser i Hytten og hos Botteleren, gives een og een halv Ranson, af Flesk,
Kiød, Smør og Brændeviin, og naar nogen syg er, bekommer hand ingen
Ranson, men da gives Mad og Dricke, efter Skibs-Raadets Ordre og Got-
findende.

Udi Cahytten skal spises efter Menage og Billighed, efter Opperhovedet eller
Skibs-Raadets Gotfindende.

Naar Skibet her paa Reeden, eller udi Sundet for Affejling er beliggende, ny-
der en Person til Forfriskning halvandet Pund færsk Kiød, 2de gange om U-
gen, nembl. eengang om Sondagen, og dend anden gang om Onsdagen,
en fierendeel Pund Smør, et pund blodt Brod, 2de Potter Skibs-Oll om
Dagen, ligeledes og derforuden til Cahytten, et Lam, eller Faar, og ey
videre.

Actum Kiobenhavn d/10 Octbr 115..

When the *Fredensborg* crosses the line for the second time on 11 June, they are still at some distance from St. Paul Rocks. The speed is not very great, but a distance of 20 to 30 miles a day helps considerably. On that day "the slaves were given millet to eat for the first time." According to the slaves' "Bill of Fare" they were supposed to receive millet twice every Saturday, but this does not begin until 50 days after their departure.

Captain Ferentz continues to navigate precisely with Kiønig's octant and writes conscientiously in his journal every single day. He has read his instructions and sees to it that the crew's memory of the Ship's Articles is refreshed at regular intervals.

Hoffmann has been badly shaken by Captain Ferentz' reply, which he feels is both insolent and insulting. He retaliates with a new letter to the Captain; it covers page after page in the ship's journal. With the adroitness of a lawyer he argues his case in a way that must have left Ferentz speechless and exasperated. He explains why Ferentz has not seen Hoffmann in the morning as follows: "In spite of everything, the fact that you have not seen me has its natural explanation since, while the slaves are eating, you usually drink your coffee and smoke your pipe in the cabin, where you are unable to see whether I am on the deck. Besides, the ship is quite large."

Ferentz has had enough. In his reply to Hoffmann he retracts a few points, but one thing has irritated him considerably: "As long as one or two of the other officers are on deck, I do believe that I may be allowed to go to and from my cabin, and drink my own coffee and smoke my own tobacco, as long as my duties to the worthy Company are not being neglected."

Hoffmann now decides that everything should be passed over in silence, but adds a few comments in his own defence in the journal. It is well known on board that he and Ferentz are bitter enemies, a fact which may have caused one or two to overstep the mark. Hoffmann describes what happened on 12 June: "In the morning the slaves were given meat and brandy. Because of extremely insubordinate behaviour towards me by Ordinary Seaman Aye, I boxed his ears twice on the quarterdeck. Boatswain's Mate Peder Thorsen witnessed this, since he was standing on the gangway. He heaped abuse on me and said he would punch my nose if he ever saw me strike a boy again. All this took place in the presence of the Captain and several of the others. I couldn't help taking offence at this, whereupon I asked the Captain that Peder Thorsen be reprimanded and ordered to keep within his proper limits. This was done, whereupon he came to my cabin, thanked me for my advice and more, and said that he would serve me again. In truth, a great deal may be read into these last words, the significance of which I leave in the hands of the worthy Directors."

A few days later Ferentz has noted that Cooper Weis has made a new log-chip. This is the little triangular chip of wood hanging at the end of the logline that was used for measuring the speed. Had the sharks been at work there? When they overhauled the logline they found that "it is a little too short between the knots." But in all probability the *Fredensborg* didn't sail any slower for that reason. They had entered the north-east trade wind, the most important ally of the slave ships, along with the favourable currents. The triangular trade had been blessed with favourable natural conditions; when they were not sailing, they were drifting in the right direction. Many of the *Fredensborg*'s daily runs were no longer than the drift of the current.

Opposite page:
*A Menu or "Ration and Scale of Victualling" for the crew on board the ships of the Danish West India and Guinea Company dated 1753.*

*From Captain Fer-
entz' journal during
the crossing of the
middle passage.
Deaths of the slaves
were marked by a note
in the margin.*

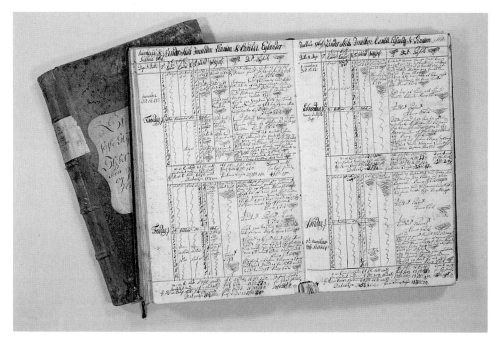

23 June. Seaman Jochum Bollvardt died. He "was then taken up and sewn into the Company's hammock. Lowered the flag to half mast, sang a hymn and he was thrown overboard. In the afternoon his belongings were recorded, evaluated and auctioned off, which brought in 11 Rdls 3 ort and 6 shillings."

Poor Jochum did not have many belongings, but he did have a little gold. In his sea chest they found some gold dust which he had obtained by barter on the Coast. It appears as if the active seaman, who had been to Quitta in the longboat, may have exchanged his shoes for gold. However, in the records only a single shoe is listed! The next one to splash overboard was a male slave. The deaths continued, despite the fact that Sixtus was doing his best with all his jars. In all probability, they did not escape smallpox. This was a sickness which the plantation owners were especially on the lookout for when buying new slaves. It must have been diffi-cult for Sixtus to make a correct diagnosis with the medical knowledge of the day. But he reported that death no. 15 was a woman who died of venereal disease.

According to the captain's instructions: "Seeing that it is difficult for the slaves, and in part may cause sickness when they are shackled together in this manner throughout the journey, the Board of Directors will leave it to the discretion of the captain from time to time, especially after he has entered the middle passage, to allow some to be unbolted. Or alternate in allowing some to be unbolted and oth-ers bolted again, to the extent that those slaves from the north called 'dunke', i.e. northern slaves, in preference to others, could be unshackled from time to time, but the meanest and most dangerous must always remain in irons. The Board reminds the captain that this is solely a means for preserving the health of the slaves, and when he sees fit to allow some to be unshackled he must set out such guards as he deems necessary, so the slaves at all times can see and hear that the crew are watchful and at their posts."

However, the prescribed airings do not appear to have had the desired effect; slaves died practically every day:

Thursday 30 June: "1 male slave died and towards evening was thrown overboard."

Saturday 2 July: "1 male slave died of a stroke."

Sunday 3 July: "2 male slaves died, including one of our first deck slaves named 'Ragge'."

The cause of death was not always given, but it is well known that mental suffering also resulted in many deaths on board the slave ships.

Our friend Hoffmann has not been well for a long time, and one day he remains in his bunk. He is so weak that he is unable to go up on deck, and has to base his entries in the journal on the reports of others.

The trade wind is steady day after day. The distance being covered is absolutely satisfactory, and elegant frigate birds are a sign that they are approaching land.

Thursday 8 July Hoffmann writes: "Early in the morning, and otherwise the whole day, we can see the islands of the West Indies on both sides. A schooner passes us, and a frigate on its way to Antigua, which is one of the islands. The slaves were shaved today. 50 pieces of firewood were taken up to the cook from the hold, and the last barrel of brandy, which showed a leakage of 5 1/2 inches. Slaughtered a pig weighing 47.6 kg. for refreshment that was shared among the cabin and the crew. Hoffmann recovered. Friderich Kruse, 14 male, 5 female and 4 boy slaves sick."

Now that they have arrived safely in the West Indies, both Captain Ferentz and the crew can finally begin to relax a bit. He is quite familiar with these waters from his time as chief officer on the *Planteren* from Copenhagen. Now he is certain that the water and provisions will last during the final leg to St. Croix. The ship is a hive of activity. While flying fish soar past the frigate, the cables are hauled out of the hold and fastened to the anchor rings. Hoffmann describes the last day at sea and the arrival at St. Croix:

*After a long voyage across the middle passage, they finally arrived in the West Indies. It looked something like this when the* Fredensborg *sailed along the north side of St. Croix before they dropped anchor. Notice all the slave huts in front of the main building. The vessel in the picture is a brig.*

*The harbour in Christiansted drawn from the seaward side. A pilot cutter, with a red stripe in its sail, is on its way in, followed by a larger vessel. Several of the ships lying at anchor have taken down their masts or are partly dismantled. This bears witness to a lengthy stay, probably laying up for the winter in order to escape sailing in northern waters. The inset shows the harbour square at Fredriksted with a fort and "water battery".*

Friday 9 July: "In the morning we fired a 7-gun salute. One male slave died. In the afternoon we sighted land which we assumed was St. Croix. At 4 o'clock in the afternoon a female slave died and was thrown overboard. At 4:30 the pilot came to us, and at 5:30 we joyfully dropped anchor at St. Croix. Praise the Lord who has aided us thus far. May He continue to have mercy on us and assist us in our venture, and may we complete our journey happy and well.

Royal longboat arrives with the commanding officer. Fired 7-gun salute with the 4-pounders in honour of the fort, which is answered by 3-gun salute, and is returned by three. Many vessels came to congratulate us on our arrival. Among our slaves there are still 5 or 6 for whom there is no hope. At 6 o'clock, the captain, Reimers and I go ashore. We meet the Company's agent, Mr. Thalbitzer who is in the best of health, and are informed by him that on the coming Tuesday the 12th, we should begin to unload with all possible speed. At 8 o'clock we were brought back to the ship in the longboat. Friderich Kruse recovered today. Peder Madsen sick. Of the slaves, 10 male, 5 female and 2 boy slaves sick."

Upon their arrival at St. Croix, Seaman Friderich Kruse had finally recovered. He had been sick throughout the voyage from Africa to the West Indies, but he had survived. Whether this was the result of Dr. Sixtus' medical knowledge, or the natural resilience of a young boy is better left unsaid. Twenty-four of the slaves had died during the 78-day voyage, and they had been joined by three members of the crew. A total of 15 members of the crew had lost their lives since the *Fredensborg* left Copenhagen.

CHAPTER 6

# *Slaves and Colonies*

T HEY HAD MADE IT! THE LONG STAY IN AFRICA, the many deaths and the middle passage, with its uncertainty and strain, were consigned to oblivion in the ephemeral wake of a ship. Now they had come to a different world, to a town with houses, regulated streets and "civilization". The *Fredensborg* lay at anchor in the roadstead close to the town of Christiansted on St. Croix, within range of the guns at Fort Christiansvern.

The streets were bustling with activity, and elegant coaches drove back and forth with their black coachmen and white passengers. The plantation owners, or "planters", as they were called, were the island's upper class, along with the governor and the King's other officials. These were prosperous times and they had plenty of black domestic slaves to wait on them. Their women were beautifully dressed and took life easy, while the social life flourished and madeira and rum flowed. The second of the two towns on St. Croix was called Fredriksted, and was situated on the west side of the island. There was also a fort, with soldiers and cannons to protect the whites. It was best this way, because in those days there were around 18,000 slaves on the largest of the colonial islands in the Danish-Norwegian kingdom. The free residents made up only 10 percent of the population.

To the crew on board the *Fredensborg*, it must have been a tremendous relief to come to St. Croix. How the slaves felt is a different matter. Some of them must have felt a degree of "relief" now that the long and unpleasant voyage was over, while others, perhaps, were even more depressed. Everyone feared the unknown, as they stared at the shore.

The danger of a slave rebellion was over for the time being – on board the ship, at any rate. Now it was a question of getting rid of the troublesome cargo of slaves. Rumours of a newly arrived ship, with prime quality slaves, always spread quickly among potential buyers. There was a constant demand for new manpower, because the slaves were worked hard and the death rate was high. Before the slaves from the *Fredensborg* were to be offered for sale, it was important that they were in the best possible condition. Now their rations could be increased. If any-

*Map of the West Indies from 1824. The Danish West Indian Islands of St. Croix, St. Thomas and St. Jan, which today comprise the U.S. Virgin Islands, are located just east of Puerto Rico.*

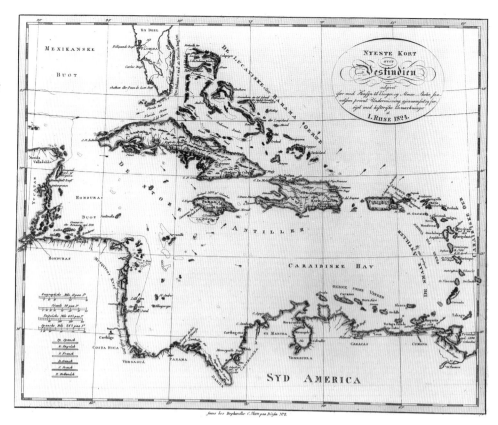

thing was lacking they received supplies from land, which was taken care of by the Company's own agent. In order to manage their business on St. Croix, the Company had hired Carl Heinrich Thalbitzer. He was to be found in the Company's own building down by the harbour. Ferentz describes the events of the next few days:

Sunday 10 July: "In the morning we immediately started lowering the longboat. Third Mate Runge went ashore to obtain provisions from the agent, and came back with 48 pounds of beef and some vegetables, in addition to a large quantity of limes and yams for the slaves. 1 male slave died. The assistant and I went ashore in order to dine with Mr. Thalbitzer. The slaves have received brandy, pipes and tobacco, and rubbed themselves with palm oil, and afterwards danced and jumped about to the accompaniment of their songs and drums."

Monday 11 July: "The slaves washed themselves and rubbed themselves with palm oil. At 9:30 the slaves were fed. Cleaned the ship above and below deck. At 8:00 I went ashore in the longboat in order to obtain clearance. At 9:30 I returned with Mr. Thalbitzer in order to inspect the slaves. At 10:00 we went ashore again. I immediately returned to the ship in the longboat. Unbent all the light sails. Obtained 5 pieces of 'salempuris' cotton from Mr. Thalbitzer for slave loincloths."

*Opposite page:*
*A map showing the location of St. Croix, St. Thomas and St. Jan.*

Tuesday 12 July: "The slaves washed and rubbed themselves with palm oil. Captain Krog set sail for Copenhagen. Sent with him all the letters I had received from Fort Christiansborg, and then I purchased a little dinghy from him. Captain Lemvig set sail for Amsterdam. Pipes and tobacco brought ashore to the slaves at the request of the agent."

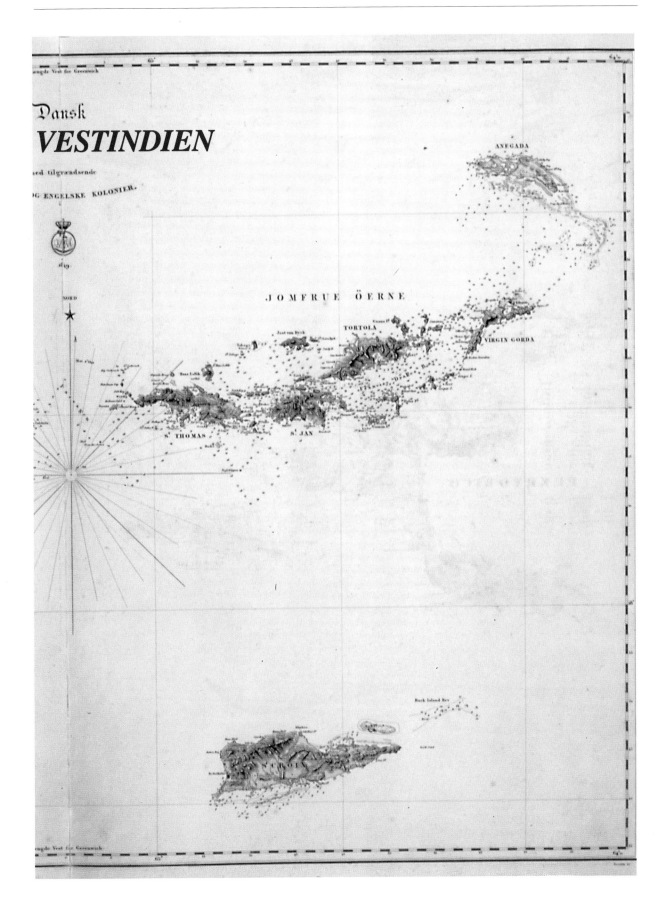

*The view from Governor-General Peter von Scholten's country house, Bülowsminde. Here we have a good impression of the topography on the north side of St. Croix, with the town of Christiansted, the harbour and the island of Protestant Kay. To the left of the balcony we can see a group of slaves who have prepared the fields for planting sugar cane. The drawing from January 1834 was made by the Governor-General's brother, Frederik von Scholten, who was a naval officer and inspector of customs in Fredriksted.*

Hoffmann, who was responsible for keeping the accounts, paid close attention on the day the slaves were unloaded in two groups. He stood and recorded every single slave that went down the gangway ladder:

|  |  |
|---|---|
|  | *Remaining on the ship for the time being:* |
|  | *5 male slaves for work on board* |
| *123 male slaves* | *7 ditto who are sick* |
| *19 boy slaves* | *8 ditto female slaves* |
| *73 female and girl slaves* | *1 ditto boy slave* |
| *4 freight slaves* | *1 freight slave* |
| *219 slaves in all* | *22 slaves in all* |

| | |
|---|---|
| *A total of 18 male slaves and 6 female slaves died* | *24 slaves* |
| *Brought ashore* | *215 slaves* |
| *and for Mr. Reimers* | *4 slaves* |
| *Remaining on board* | *22 slaves* |

*A total of 265 assorted slaves*
*which is the number we received at the Danish Fort Christiansborg.*

"One male slave died. In the afternoon the longboat left the ship with the Captain, Chief Officer Beck, Doctor Sixtus, Third Officer Runge and myself. Took ashore food for the slaves, which consisted of porridge. The Agent insisted that the food for the slaves be taken from the ship's provisions and cooked on board the ship. Held a meeting of the Council in the Agent's house. After the meeting was over, we went back on board. Peder Madsen and Erich Ancker sick. 3 male and 2 female slaves sick."

Early the next morning Captain Ferentz orders the men to start dismantling the large slave bulwarks. First the cannons are removed and then the planks and the framework are taken down and stowed away.

Cook Ørgensen has already started preparing the food for the slaves, because as early as 8 o'clock in the morning Ferentz, Sixtus and Runge go ashore with steaming cauldrons of porridge. This is repeated at 4 o'clock in the afternoon. The Assistant Pilot comes on board at the Captain's request to see to it that the ship is moored properly, and the stream anchor is cast. The dreaded hurricane season is approaching, but they can still relax.

Captain Ferentz summons a meeting of the Ship's Council in the cabin. This time it is not about punishment, but about the cabin provisions. As captain, Ferentz is entitled to a certain standard, but this has only been so-so since he took over. According to the specifications, little remained after the gluttonous Captain Kiønig. In addition, there have been many sick on board the ship; they have received special provisions, which has increased the consumption of certain foods.

Ferentz believes this is reason enough for the purchase of new supplies, and that the worthy Board of Directors would agree to this were they present. A unani-

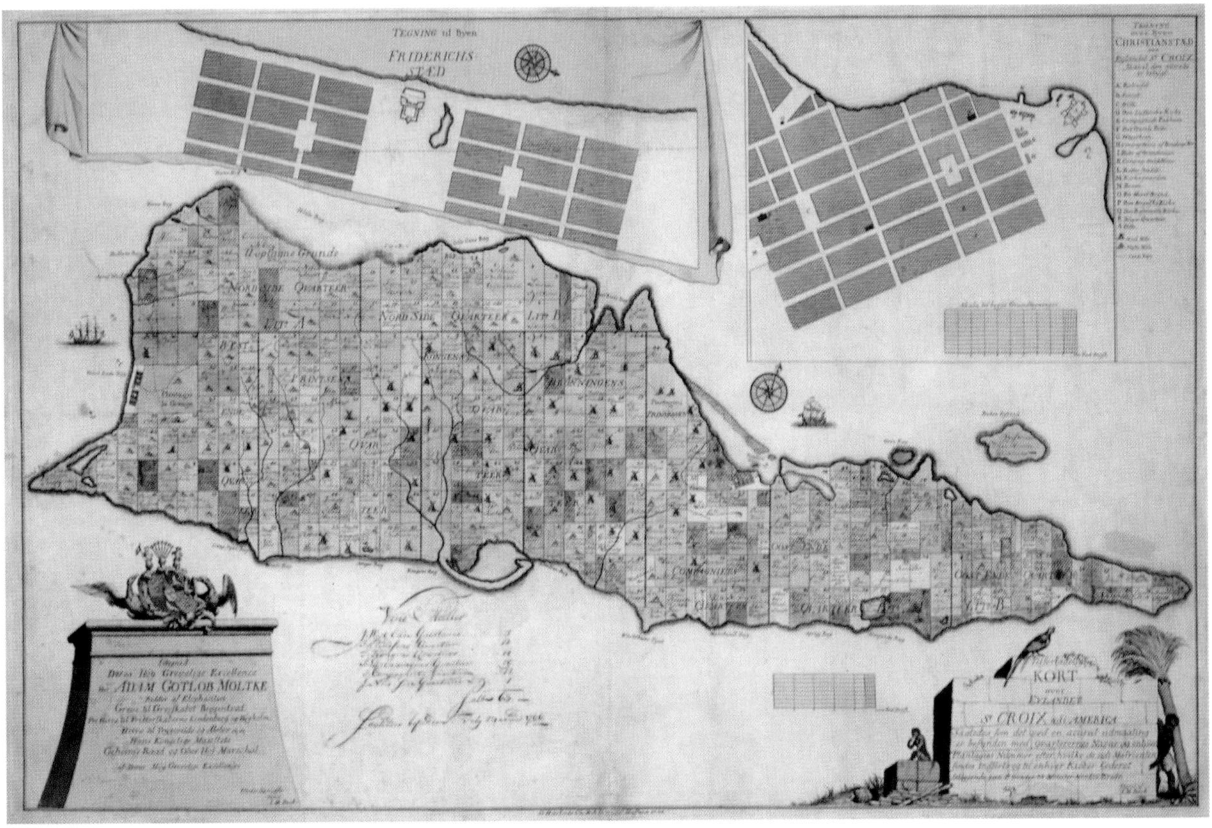


*Revised version, circa 1766, of a map of St. Croix engraved in Copenhagen in 1754 by J.M. Beck, and dedicated to Count Adam Gotlob Moltke. The map is a rough sketch, but shows the shape of the island very well. The plan of Frederiksted was not completed. The Princess Plantation, close to the town of Christiansborg, delivered barrels of sugar to the* Fredensborg. *An inset added in 1766 reveals there were 63 windmills for the production of sugar.*

mous Ship's Council agrees to the purchase of wine, prunes, currants, pepper, ginger, saffron, nutmeg, cloves, cinnamon, cardamom, molasses, green tea, Bohea tea, and herbs. An order list is made up for Thalbitzer and sent the same day. Third Mate Runge often goes ashore. He delivers food for the slaves and brings back fresh beef and vegetables for the crew. The daily rhythm on board is changed, and except for two men on watch they are able to sleep at night and work during the day. Three customs officials come on board to inspect the gold and the elephant tusks. They are shown the gold and several small tusks, but are unable to inspect the large elephant tusks, which are stowed deep in the hold and difficult to reach.

Thalbitzer reacts quickly to the request for provisions for the cabin. On the following day he sends on board Madeira and French wines as well as tea and various spices. Seven male slaves who have been purchased "at His Majesty's expense" are also brought on board. These slaves are to be kept on board temporarily, until the sale of the slaves has taken place. Ferentz takes every precaution. He secures the longboat with a solid chain alongside the ship in case anyone should try to escape.

The Ship's Council has yet another meeting with Thalbitzer, "to negotiate the sale of the slaves in the best possible manner". The Company's instructions are clear in this respect. Both the agent and the Ship's Council are bound by detailed instructions from "The Yellow Palace" in Copenhagen, but there is always room for a few finishing touches. The meeting is concluded with a glass of the finest Madeira.

The next group of slaves is taken ashore along with the the slave food. The poor wretches have hardly any appetite, because they include "3 males and 3 females who were the sickest and most emaciated slaves on board to date". They are taken up to the Company's manor, some to die on land, others to be sold as "trash slaves". Captain Ferentz is more concerned about Friderich Kruse. He no longer believes that Sixtus is able to cure the seaman: Saturday 16 July: "At 7 o'clock in the morning I went ashore and took Seaman Friderich Kruse to Dr. Herring, as I thought he might be able to cure him. To date he has not been well enough on board to serve the Company since we sailed from Fort Christiansborg."

Hoffmann has a relapse and is confined to bed on the ship. As the Company's faithful servant, he is informed about most of what takes place, and takes pains to note that, at the insistence of the agent, a barrel of beef weighing 386 pounds has been opened. Yet another male slave is dead, and Friderich Kruse has remained on land. But the flow of information does not always function equally well, because on the following day the shortest note appears in the ship assistant's journal: "I am still sick and confined to bed and was therefore unable to observe what took place today."

In the Company's courtyard the slaves receive better care. They are washed and rubbed with palm oil, and the slave food is rich and ample. Now they experience better days, and are able to relax after the rigours of the middle passage. The open sores that resulted from chafing against the slave platforms are beginning to heal, and they are given pipes and tobacco and a drop of rum to help lift their spirits. Thalbitzer knows from experience how the goods should look in order to obtain the best possible prices. A week on a special diet, in new surroundings, is good business in spite of the operating expenses.

The *Fredensborg* is anchored in poor holding ground and, foot by foot, the trade wind presses the frigate closer into the shallows. Ferentz observes that the starboard anchor has lost its hold in the coral sand, and the ship's heel is touching the bottom. After hectic activity they manage to warp the ship out into a safer position, after first hauling up the bower. The *Fredensborg* is riding higher after getting rid of the slaves and large quantities of water and provisions along the way. Every day the work continues on board, because now the *Fredensborg* is being made ready for a new cargo on the third leg of the triangular trade.

On land Thalbitzer makes the final preparations for the sale of the

*The slaves from the* Fredensborg *are brought ashore and taken up to the Company's building. Among the slaves to be sold were several children between the ages of 5 and 8.*

slaves. He has written a placard that has been posted on St. Croix and St. Thomas. It proclaims that "a cargo of slaves from the Gold Coast that I have lately imported" shall be sold on Monday next in the Company's courtyard.

Sixty-nine slaves are sold on the first day, and thus far the agent is satisfied. Good prices have been obtained from fifteen different buyers, and they have taken the slaves with them.

Captain Ferentz has a more relaxed attitude to the sale, even though he is keeping himself well-informed. If good prices are obtained, he can look forward to a commission far greater than his total wages on the entire journey. Cook Ørgensen is also keeping an eye on things. He is coming to the end of a strenuous period, preparing great quantities of porridge on the slave stove. In addition, he may also earn a few extra rixdaler on the sale of the unfortunate slaves.

The best slaves have already been sold, and on the second day of the sale Ørgensen feeds the remaining slaves 30 pounds of salt beef. They will look more presentable with full stomachs. Ferentz, Sixtus, Reimers and Hoffmann are present. With regard to sales, the second day is bad, because only four slaves are sold. Nor do things improve during the next three days; only ten slaves are sold altogether.

But if the sales are slow, Ferentz has other and more serious worries. He is left with twenty-seven men to bring the *Fredensborg* safely home to Copenhagen. He must count on autumn storms and rough seas during the Atlantic crossing and in the Skagerrak and the Kattegat. Friderich Kruse is confined to bed at Dr. Herring's, and the outcome is uncertain. Undermanned as they are, Ferentz tries as

*Danish-West Indian 12-shilling silver and 2-shilling copper coins. Minted in 1740 in Copenhagen for the West India Guinea Company, intended as local small change and wages for functionaries and soldiers.*

hard as he can to find more seamen, beginning with a letter to the captain of the royal barque which is stationed in the West Indies:

"As the journey from Copenhagen to the Gold Coast, and from there to this place, has occasioned many deaths among the crew, the frigate *Fredensborg* whereof I am master is not manned as it should be. I therefore feel obliged to request of Your Honour to let me have 3 or 4 good seamen which I am truly in need of for the continuation of my journey to Copenhagen. I pray that these not be men who are forced to do this, but those who sail with me should do this of their own free will."

But the oral reply from Captain Grundt, who commands the King's ship, is discouraging, because he too lacks men.

On board the ship a great deal remains to be done to clean up after the slaves, and remove the special arrangements necessitated by the slave transport. In addition, the *Fredensborg* shows considerable signs of wear from her long voyage, the stay at the Gold Coast and the crossing of the middle passage. Owing to sickness, death and a shortage of crew members the maintenance has been somewhat neglected.

The ship's bottom is covered with barnacles that pose a threat to the continuation of the voyage. Alongside the other West Indiamen that have sailed directly from Europe, the *Fredensborg* is far from a pretty sight. But Ferentz has made his plans. The ship is scoured and washed down and barrels containing wood tar are brought up from the hold. While the sale of slaves is in progress, they have "taken down the rest of the female slaves' privy and pigsty on the port side, and then cleaned it in order to tar it."

The nauseating smell is dispelled by the heavy odour of tar which makes life easier on board. But they haven't completely eliminated the foul stench from the holds.

Even though the slave food is still being cooked on the ship, Thalbitzer insists that a part of the slave provisions be brought ashore. 25 barrels of groats and 4 barrels of white peas are transported in the longboat, and on the following day Runge goes ashore with the rest of the horse beans. The beans are ground in the afternoon, and the Agent's clerk takes possession of 25 barrels. The remainder are brought back on board. The leftover slave food and water reveal that the *Fredensborg* was well-stocked for the passage. But a few weeks in the Doldrums could have quickly changed this. The surplus provisions and empty barrels are handed over to the agent "in order to sell and make as much money as possible".

Hoffmann is hard at work with the agent, and Reimers goes ashore every day in order to look after his interests. He has been fortunate, because all of his slaves have survived the middle passage. Since Reimers has sold his slaves privately, the total sales price is unknown. But he has at least 800 rixdaler left after the freight charge has been paid to the Company.

The harbour at Christiansted is bustling with activity, and Ferentz tells us that Captain Meyer has sailed to the Netherlands and Bergen, while Dirk Bøyesen is going to Copenhagen. Ferentz continues his persistent search for more seamen. He visits several of the other vessels anchored in the roadstead, and one day he is successful. Captain Solberg is able to spare Seamen Rasmus Mathiessen and Hans Winter, and they come on board with their sea chests and are immediately put to work. On board Captain Grundt's ship Ferentz has finally found a carpenter who is willing to sign on the *Fredensborg*. Grundt has given Ferentz a verbal promise that this is all right, but later, to Ferentz' extreme annoyance, he demands a seaman in exchange. Ferentz needs every seaman he has for the demanding voyage home.

One day, while Runge is working with the provisions in the hold, he sees "a barrel of salt beef in which the nails were broken and the brine had run out. The meat smelled, but was still good inside, whereupon it was again covered with brine." There is no mention of whether the slightly tainted meat was intended as slave food, but on the same day, at the agent's request, Runge weighs 100 pounds of meat which Ørgensen prepares for the slaves the following day.

Ferentz has approached Thalbitzer in order to find out when he can count on departing from St. Croix. He is told that if it is too late in the autumn, it is safer to lie up for the winter than to risk the ship and cargo. The answer makes Ferentz uneasy, because this implies that he cannot count on weighing anchor before the middle of September, which is rather late.

In order for the remaining slaves to look as good as possible, Thalbitzer increases the meat rations. He has sold a large consignment of 84 slaves to the nearby Spanish Colony of Puerto Rico, and he wants them to arrive as quality goods. The price is so-so for the large shipment, but since the sale had been slow the last day or so, the agent thinks it wise to offer a solid quantity discount. Now he only has the sick slaves left, in addition to those who are to be shipped to Puerto Rico. Even the sick are worth something as long as they remain alive.

Hoffmann spends most of the days in the Company's house, but receives pitifully little information about the progress of the slave sales, prices and buyers. The only figures he is allowed to concern himself with are the deaths of the slaves. He has now arrived at 29 dead slaves: 22 males and 7 females.

27 July is the final day of the sales in the Company's courtyard. Only two sick female slaves remain in a corner, awaiting their fate. John Johnsen wins the bid with a total sum of 160 rixdaler. Even if only one of the women survives and recovers, he has still picked up a reasonably good bargain!

Ferentz is delighted to learn that three of the deck slaves from the middle passage have been sold to a buyer in Copenhagen. He is able to provide free passage and food in exchange for their working during the crossing. The three, who are renamed "Oliver", "Roland" and "Samson", come on board and the *Fredensborg* is again transporting slaves during the final leg of the triangular trade, even though on a modest scale.

Even if the sale has been modest in the Company's courtyard on 27 July, it is even livelier on board the *Fredensborg*. Four days earlier the Ship's Council decided

*The Prosperity Plan-
tation on St. Croix.*

that Captain Kiønig's merchandise and several other items shall be sold at auction on board. At the same time Quartermaster Engmann's navigation instruments are also to be disposed of. The advertising of the coming auction has been of the very best. The auction has been announced in the church, in the taverns and on all the ships anchored in the roadstead, while seven placards have been posted in Danish and four in English. Everything has been arranged for a successful auction, and a longboat is waiting at the quay in order to bring the prospective buyers out to the *Fredensborg.*

People from the other ships in the roadstead come flocking, looking for a good bargain. When the auction begins around 10 o'clock, "quite a number of strangers" have come on board.

Hoffmann starts by announcing the conditions that have been endorsed by Ferentz: "Every bid is to be made in Danish currency and the sum of the auction sale is to be paid fourteen days after the auction is over. If a bid is not regarded as economically sound, then the ships' captains shall be held responsible and are guarantors for what is purchased by their men."

Now it begins, and the bidding is spirited. Kiønig's white embroidered vest goes to Reimers, while the bolts of cloth are sold to various buyers, including Dr. Herring and Master Nelly, the assistant pilot. When the red and white double silk kerchiefs come under the hammer, Hoffmann puts down his pen for a moment and procures eight for himself, while Sixtus buys the remaining nine. Third Mate Runge wins the bidding for two pieces of silk, while Ferentz becomes the owner of a piece of red checked cotton, and 3/4 alen black Manchester cloth. "Captain Eigen living in the West Indies" buys a kerchief. Then they go over to the shoes, a total of 156 pairs, which are sold 6 pairs at a time. Among those who buy shoes for their homecoming, we find Ferentz who buys 12 pairs, while Hoffmann is content with half that amount. For a brief moment Aye, the African and Ordinary Seaman, is the centre of attention when he becomes the proud owner of 6 pairs of shoes. He has hardly ever owned as many shoes before, but then this will cost him almost his entire earnings from the middle passage. The seamen from the *Fredensborg*, who secure for themselves some of the warm Icelandic woolen stockings, do not regret it later during the voyage. Boatswain Rosenberg buys 12 pairs, and so does Runge from Arendal, who is no doubt thinking about cold Norwegian winters. Then they proceed to the remainder of Kiønig's belongings.

First they hold up the chest with the lock and key. This is the one that has been standing in Ferentz' cabin and has been the object of Hoffmann's biting criticism. Now the time has come for a small triumph for Ferentz, who manages to secure this particular chest for himself. After two barrels of flintstones and a few other small objects have found their buyers, the great moment has arrived. Captain Kiønig's octant in its case is shown to the gathering. The strangers who make their bids are hardly aware of the bitter quarrel between Hoffmann and Ferentz over the octant. It is mentioned several times in the ship's journal in connection with Hoffmann's claims about the improper use of the deceased's estate. But in spite of this Ferentz has used the instrument every single day. It is no coincidence that Ferentz secures the octant for himself, because he has made up his mind to buy it regardless of the price. He has to pay 15 rixdaler, and it is not unthinkable that he has triumphantly waved the instrument under the nose of the offended Hoffmann before the auction continues. Ferentz does not stop at this; he also becomes the owner of several charts and a pair of calipers, while Runge can pack away six stoneware plates.

Not everything is sold at the auction. No one is interested in the three barrels of

*Slaves at work producing sugar in the West Indies around the end of the seventeenth century. In the mill, which is turned by oxen, the sugar cane is crushed between the rollers, and the juice runs down to the cookhouse in a leaded trough. The juice concentrates as it is ladled from kettles to kettles before it crystalizes, cools and is poured into barrels. The slave huts are on the right.*

*Working with tobacco and cassava on a plantation in the West Indies in the seventeenth century. Tobacco leaves are being dried in the building to the right, while two slaves are twirling chewing tobacco. On the left they are working with cassava root, the meal of which is dried on the roof and used to bake bread.*

"simple Negro pipes". Ferentz is responsible for the unsold items, including the gold watch and a copper chamber pot. Some of Kiønig's most personal effects will be taken home to his family in Copenhagen. The auction brings in 720 rixdaler and 13 shillings. When the quartermaster's nautical equipment is offered for sale we find Ferentz, Beck, Runge and Rosenberg among the buyers. Finally Petty Officer Engmann gets hold of an old, grey "broadcloth coat" from his brother's estate for one daler. This amounts to about one-quarter of the total amount of Engmann's estate.

On the following day the *Fredensborg* is again bustling with activity, but now there are other tasks that demand attention. Early in the morning they have already started careening the ship over to port, so that the starboard side below the waterline is accessible. Ferentz has hired five carpenters from several of the other ships in the roadstead, and soon they are busy scraping and cleaning the bottom. This work is being carried on from two barges. Down by the water's edge fires have been lighted under two big cauldrons, in which a "lubricant" is being made. After the side of the vessel has dried a little, it is caulked and finally coated with pitch and tar, which was the ship-bottom paint of the time. On the following day they repeat the process on the port side. While this is being done, a barque sails away with the 84 slaves who have been sold to Puerto Rico.

Cook Ørgensen can look ahead to better times, now that he only has 33 men and 1 woman to feed on board, including the 3 deck slaves. The slave stove and the large cauldrons have been stowed. In addition, with regular supplies of fresh fish, meat and vegetables, complaints about the food have ceased. For the time being the slave irons are lying in a heap in the 'tween-deck, while the muskets have discharged their loads of peas and have been polished and oiled.

Ferentz can also relax a little between tasks. The nerve-wracking careening is being carried out as well as possible, but there has been no question of a thorough cleaning. Most of the parasites that slow down the vessel have been removed from the bottom, but thousands of the 6-7 cm long barnacles are still stuck below the waterline and can seriously hamper the sailing in the Skagerrak in winter.

The slaves have been scattered forever to their new "homesteads", but the crew care very little about that. They have more than enough to think about with their own exhausting everyday life, and, in addition, the health of many has been impaired by sickness. The carpenters continue caulking the outside of the ship, and the port gangway is erected in its normal position again. They have taken on ballast, which is brought out by a barge from the quay.

Ferentz conscientiously reports to the Board of Directors, and in a letter he writes on 30 June in order to send it with Captain Selvogh, he is able to report to "the worthy Board" that "yesterday all the slaves have been sold privately, though it is unknown to me at what price, to whom and in what way. At the last meeting of the Council it was decided, if possible, to sell all the slaves privately, in order to receive cash payment and thus free us from risk."

So far Thalbitzer has furnished no particulars about the sales of the slaves and the economic results, but it is evident that the cargo of slaves was disposed of without an auction. Thus far, Ferentz has shown that he is a capable captain, because by the end of July the *Fredensborg* is ready to take on a new cargo. On 1 August 58 mahogany planks are loaded on board, and on the following day 20 barrels of sugar – a fact worth calling attention to:

"With the first barrel that came over, flags and jacks were hoisted and 5 four-pounder salutes were fired," writes Hoffmann.

The loading of the huge barrels of sugar, which may weigh up to 700 – 800 pounds, is a complicated process. First they have to be loaded on board the long-boat and ferried out to the *Fredensborg*, which is anchored some distance from land. From there they are hoisted onto the deck and down into the hold, where they have to be stowed properly. This operation requires many men, and Ferentz has found it necessary to hire several extra seamen. The last of the ballast is rowed ashore in the pram, while the carpenters stuff oakum into the seams between the planks. Thereafter the seams are coated with pitch, in order to keep the oakum dry and in place. It is important that the frigate is in the best possible condition before the coming voyage. The departure from the West Indies will take place during the dreaded hurricane season, and afterwards the terrible autumn and winter storms in northern waters will be a constant threat.

There is also a lot of work to be done up in the rigging. Ropes that have been exposed to wear and tear and the tropical sun have to be replaced, and coil after coil is brought up on deck. Captain Ferentz is high and low on board, and keeps himself posted on practically everything. Barrel after barrel is lowered down in the hold, planks of mahogany are piled up, and then come barrels of campeachy or dyewood. Every day Hoffmann is working with the agent on land. Runge takes charge of a large cask of rum that comes on board for the crew. One day a visitor arrives along with the barrels of sugar. "A little Negro boy was sent on board by the Agent". There is nothing in the journal that tells what he is supposed to do, but he is certainly not there just to have a look around the large frigate – a task no doubt awaits him. Nothing more about the little boy appears in the journals.

*A country road on St. Croix where a team of oxen is pulling a load of 5 barrels of sugar on the way to the harbour. The* Fredensborg*'s cargo of sugar amounted to 55 loads of this kind.*

It appears as if Ferentz' devoutness has diminished after his arrival at St. Croix. In the space of three weeks he has not recorded a single prayer in the journal. On Sunday 7 August, however, he sends the longboat to land with several members of the crew who are going to church. They return around noon, and in the afternoon the next group is sent ashore. They hardly search for a place of worship; perhaps they end up in one of the local "Punch Houses"; the rum and the women are cheap on St. Croix. By 10 p.m., however, everyone is safely back on board.

Poor Mistress Møller is facing an uncertain future, and is literally on shaky ground on board the ship. Whether she will be allowed to return home on the *Fredensborg* depends on the goodwill of the Agent. If she is left behind on St. Croix she will be facing considerable difficulties, about which she has not hesitated to inform the agent. Thalbitzer no doubt feels sorry for the impecunious lady, who is one of the few white women to have survived life on the Gold Coast for any length of time. In a letter to Ferentz he requests him to grant the housekeeper a passage on the ship back to Copenhagen, which is done.

Two days later the captain shows extra solicitude for the lady who has become a regular part of the ship's inventory. She has gone ashore to Christiansted, and Ferentz is anxious when she does not return to the ship long after nightfall. "At 9:30 the Captain goes ashore in the longboat to find Mistress Møller, who was on land." When they row back, Ferentz has an unharmed housekeeper on board.

Sickness strikes again. On 12 August the situation is really serious, with a total of 5 ailing seamen. Six barrels of sugar, 75 planks of mahogany and several barrels of dyewood are the result of the day's loading. When Hoffmann comes on board in the evening, for once he is the centre of attention in the cabin. He has calculated the commission from the sale of the slaves. It amounts to 2,054 rixdaler, which is 5 percent of the total selling price of 41,092 rixdaler. There are eleven men who will share the profit. The Captain, of course, receives the most; he is entitled to 2 percent of the selling price, or as much as 2/5 of the commission – in other words, well over 821 rixdaler. The chief officer receives 308 rixdaler, and it gradually decreases to the cook, who receives 34 rixdaler – corresponding to 1 1/2 percent of the sum from the sales.

The Company's clever system of commissions must have been a strong incentive to those who derived benefit from it. For some of them the commission represented a larger amount than they could earn during the entire voyage in the triangular trade. The amount was not paid in cash, but "in articles of value, paid in local products according to the fixed price in the country, with permission to take the goods home without paying freight rates".

There is no documentation about what happened to the commissions of the second and fourth mates and the carpenter who died, as these positions had not been filled. In accordance with the captain's instructions, the estates of the deceased should receive 1/3 of the premium since the deaths had occurred on the Gold Coast, but before the slaves had come on board. Thus, both Ferentz and Beck should have given up 1/3 of their commissions to the heirs of both Kiønig and Lundberg, if the rules were observed.

Sunday 14 August: "The men on the King's watch have been given shore leave…" Aye is with them, probably wearing brand-new shoes. But when the long-boat comes back in the evening, he is absent. Aye spends the whole night on land without permission; perhaps he is enjoying himself up in the quarter known as the "Negergottet" ("Negro Gutter"). He hardly has any money, but a pair of new shoes certainly must be satisfactory legal tender for most things! The next morning Ferentz himself goes ashore to search for him, and soon returns with the runaway. Aye is not punished for his night on land, and Ferentz merely notes: "Ordinary Seaman Aye has been ashore all night."

The next report from Ferentz to the worthy gentlemen in Copenhagen is sent with Captain Kjølsen on 17 August:

"I beg to inform you that I have written to the worthy Board of Directors by means of Captains Grundt, Krogh and Selvogh, which communications I trust your excellencies have received. Since then I have continued to repair the ship in order to sail by the middle of September, and have found 3-4 or 5 carpenters and 4-8 seamen for the necessary work, and at the present time I am still paying daily wages to 3 carpenters and 4 sea-

*Barrels of sugar and bales of cotton are being prepared for shipment, while the gentlemen in the foreground are carrying on a lively conversation. Products from the colonies were highly sought after in Europe, and the trade flourished.*

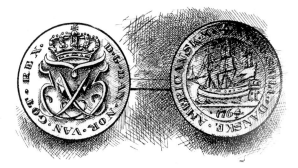

*West Indian silver 24-shilling piece from the time of Frederik V, 1764. A ship stamped on the obverse side is the coat-of-arms of the West India Guinea Company.*

men. By the same token, I have taken on a carpenter to make the journey to Copenhagen, at a monthly wage of 16 rdl. His belongings have been brought to the ship, but he has not yet come on board.

Loading is in full swing, as we have taken on 197 barrels of sugar, a considerable amount of mahogany and dyewood and 4 bales of cotton. At present the men are checking the rigging. But there is constant sickness on board; there are still five who are confined to their hammocks. In addition, there are several who probably have something wrong with them, but are neither sick nor well. It is hard to tell what it is. Consequently, I am forced to sign on several seamen, if it is possible to find any. Today the royal packet boat has arrived. I remain your faithful…"

Hoffmann, who enters a copy of the letter in the journal, concludes the day's entry as follows: "The carpenter who was hired by the captain came on board today and inspected the magnificence but then left the ship."

Not everything was equally "magnificent" on board, because shortly after the visit they discover that the mizzen topsail-yard had rotted all through and had to be discarded.

The next things to come on board are 150 rolls of good Puerto Rican tobacco leaves, followed by 48 barrels of sugar, including 30 from the Princess Plantation, brought in the plantation's own pram. They only have a short distance to row because the plantation is favourably situated not far from the harbour. The Princess is one of two plantations owned by Schimmelmann on St. Croix, and they owe the Company money for the purchase of eighteen slaves from the *Fredensborg*. This is probably the first installment, which is now being paid in sugar. That same evening a violent storm with thunder and lightning reminds them that they must soon set sail if they are to get home by the end of the year. Ferentz finds it best to repair and clean the longboat, which is tarred both "inboard and outboard, and then caulked on top of the tar." In case of an emergency the boat may mean the salvation of the crew, who otherwise have no life-saving equipment on board. This was not common in the eighteenth century.

On Sunday 21 August the men on the Queen's watch are given shore leave, while Ferentz takes Mistress Møller ashore later in the day. It appears as if everyone comes safely on board again, while poor Hoffmann encounters greater difficulties on the following day:

"When it was dark I was at the customs house, but for want of a boat I was unable to come on board before 8 o'clock. When I arrived, supper was already over in the cabin so that as usual, and also this evening, I had to go without my supper. I had to be content to go to the crew owing to the lack of order on board, as several had gone ashore without breakfast."

All sorts of things are going on that Hoffmann is not supposed to know about, but which he discovers all the same. Runge keeps himself posted, and his observations usually find their way into Hoffmann's journal. One day a "Negro" comes to the ship in a dinghy. When he leaves, he takes with him a keg of gunpowder from "the hand of Chief Officer Beck. It had been thrust into a canvas sack and taken from the gunner's storeroom. It is my duty to inquire about the reason for this, as it is apparent to me and everyone else that this is unlawful. But since, with God's help, we shall soon be coming home where the worthy Board of Directors will be able to call everyone to account, I most humbly hope it will not be misconstrued when, at this time, I merely make note of the same. Additional questioning will not help in the least, but only lead to further insults and the bad treatment from which I suffer at this time here on board."

The ship's live provisions are of great importance. Well ahead of the departure, the surviving ship's pigs have been joined by two little pigs on board. In addition they have acquired 2 sheep, 17 chickens, 3 geese and 2 ducks for the homeward voyage, and the necessary ship's provisions have been ordered from the Agent.

Captain Ferentz has used part of his slave commission for the purchase of five barrels of sugar. He is counting on a good profit from the sale of the sugar back home in Copenhagen, and has had the barrels delivered to the customs house. To his dismay he sees that one of the barrels has been broken and the sugar is pouring out. He quickly gets hold of Cooper Weis and Cook Ørgensen, who come running with tools and balers. Along with Ferentz they manage to tighten the barrel, but some of his investment has literally run into the sand. In the end the unfortunate investor is left with four large and one small barrel which, in fact, is only half full. The barrels are brought on board with great care under the supervision of the owner, and stowed in the hold.

Ferentz is extremely annoyed, because more than 200 barrels have safely arrived on board without a single mishap. The fact that it was his barrel that was destroyed is more than he can stand, and he presumes to "borrow" a little sugar from the Company. When Ferentz' small barrel is filled up, his two helpers are told to keep this to themselves. But as usual the officious Hoffmann discovers what is going on. Why Hoffmann's usually neatly recorded journal is suddenly messed up for one entry, with huge splotches of ink where this has been described, may only be left to speculation.

Reimers, the passenger and slave trader, has been taken ill. He is in such a bad state that he believes he is dying, and sends for Hoffmann in order to set up the provisions concerning "the disposition of my effects after, God willing, my demise." He decides that his money, clothing and other belongings are to be sent to his dear mother, Sara Fridschers, or other legitimate heirs in the event that she is dead. His papers are to be delivered to the worthy Board of Directors of the Company, "from which it will be apparent that I have served the Company as an honest functionary. My conscience is clear that I have behaved as an honourable and self-respecting servant of the Company should. I therefore leave it up to the fair judgement of the worthy Board of Directors, since I was denied the right to present my case fairly by the existing Government at the Guinea Coast."

To his amazement, and certainly to his delight, he survives the crisis this time. His anxiety about his homecoming will last a few months longer. Otherwise, during the homeward journey, he shall also enjoy the company of several new passengers from St. Croix, namely Mistress Wimmeløv, Søren Kipnasse, Jacob Grim and a seaman.

Sunday 4 September. For the first time during the voyage money is paid to several of the crew members. It is Sunday, the Queen's watch has been given shore leave, and the money is certainly burning a hole in the pockets of those who go on land. Of the 104.5 rixdaler that have been paid out, Aye and Erich Ancker have received a monthly wage of 2 1/2 rdl. apiece. With hard cash in their pockets the group wander through the streets of Christiansted. There is no mention of how much of the money ends up in the Church collection box. The taverns certainly receive their share, and no doubt one or two women are richly rewarded for their entertainment. Like most seamen, they are probably generous and in a spending mood as long as the money lasts. Then they return to the ship to sleep for a few hours in a swaying hammock.

It is obvious that Hoffmann and Runge cooperate very well on board. As steward and ship's assistant they are both legally bound to keep accounting records, and their positions require them to pay strict attention. While Hoffmann is working with the agent on land, Runge is the one who observes all the irregularities. If something unusual occurs, Hoffmann is informed as soon as he comes on board in the evening, in order that the episode be included in the day's report. The two keep their observations to themselves, thereby avoiding confrontations with the guilty parties.

"Today, I have been informed by Third Mate Runge that yet another keg of gunpowder has been taken ashore by a Negro. By the same token, one of the rum casks of bread has been weighed and sold to Captain Bildhugger. The worthy Board of Directors will be able to judge the disloyalty of Captain Ferentz from this."

There is hardly any doubt that a little private trading has been going on with the Company's resources. On the other hand, no fault can be found with Hoffmann's own commercial undertakings. With his slave commision he has purchased 50 rolls of tobacco. Chief officer Beck has sent ashore 3 barrels of stoneware which, according to Hoffmann, are his own property. The stoneware is sold which, along with the slave commission, is enough for two barrels of sugar. Among other things, this will guarantee the chief officer a well-earned holiday when he comes home. Reimers has regained some of his vigour and staking on an anker (38.64 litre) of Madeira wine. For his part Ferentz invests in 2 ankers of madeira. In addition, he jumps at an offer of 2 more barrels of sugar and a consignment of beverages. This consists of 3 vats, 6 tønner (1 tønne = 139.39 l) and 1 anker of rum, most of which are stored in the powder chamber. Some of the money from Kiønig's auction is used for the purchase of a couple of barrels of sugar, thereby safeguarding the interests of the heirs. 150 private rolls of tobacco are also stowed away in a dry and safe place on board.

Just before their departure Ferentz finds it best to send a final report directly back to "the Yellow Palace" with Captain Giønge. This is probably the same Giønge who was the chief officer during the *Fredensborg*'s first dramatic voyage in the trianglar trade, at the time the frigate was called the *Cron Prindz Christian*.

Ferentz is able to report that the ship is in a good navigable condition, and that they have brought on board 277 barrels of sugar, 1,313 rolls of Puerto Rico tobacco, 4 bales of cotton, 9 barrels of cinnamon bark and a considerable amount of mahogany and dyewood. Owing to a shortage of goods and high prices from the producers, he fears they will have to be content with this.

Ferentz is quite pleased with the fully loaded and refurbished *Fredensborg*. They have managed to paint the stern as well as the gallery and the figure-head, while masts and yards have been covered with pitch. They have removed the last unwelcome barnacles, and tarred and caulked the ship along the waterline. The water from Copenhagen, which has been standing on the quay, has been carried back on board along with water from the island. The local water, which is undoubtedly of a more dubious quality, is quite simply called "puddle water".

Wednesday 14 September: The *Fredensborg* weighs anchor in the inner harbour. The ship is warped out to the opening in the reef, and at sunrise they hoist the blue flag and fire a salute. When passenger Søren Kipnasse has come on board, they take up the longboat and the dinghy. The rest of the day is spent cleaning up on board and preparing to sail in the morning, which is described by Ferentz:

"At 3:30 in the morning, turned out and cleaned the ship. At 5:15 fired a salute with a 4-pounder to summon the boat to help warp us out. Thereafter I went ashore to fetch all the letters and documents from Mr. Thalbitzer. At the same time the assistant pilot came on board. Inspected the ship's draught and found the draught aft is 14 1/2 feet and forward is 13 3/4 feet. The boats of Captains Kierkegaard, Smidt, Solberg, Pettersen, Kaas and Bildhugger came alongside, and we weighed anchor. Calm, loosened forward topsail and fired sail shot at 7 o'clock. At the same time we had the anchor in the crane. All the ships were ahead of us and towed us out through the reefs. After I had attended to my business I came on board with our passengers, Mistress Wimmeløv and Mr. Jacob Grim. When we were out by the sandy reef there was a strong breeze and we loosened both topsails. Around 9

*Here we have a good impression of the crowd and activity in Christiansted harbour on St. Croix. "Foreign varieties of wood" are lying down by the water's edge, ready to be shipped out, and an ox-drawn wagon arrives with heavy barrels of sugar.*

143

*The goods the Fredensborg was to take back to Copenhagen were marked with the Company initials, which varied according to the respective products. KOGC means "Kongelige Oktrojerede Guinesiske Compagni" (The Royal Chartered Guinea Company).*

o'clock we fired a 9-gun salute which was returned with a 3-gun salute from the royal barque. Thereafter I cleared the boats and we braced aback in order to wait for Mr. Thalbitzer who arrived in Capt. Solberg's dinghy. Upon his departure a 7-gun salute was fired and he was given three cheers. Took up our dinghy and, in the name of Jesus, set all sails. Headed NNW."

They departed on the date that had been suggested by the agent, after a stay of 67 days on St. Croix. Thus far, 44 slaves and crew members had lost their lives, but the final stage of the triangular trade was yet to come.

CHAPTER 7

# *Homeward Bound and Shipwrecked*

By nightfall, after their first day at sea, they have sighted the west side of St. Thomas, another of the Danish-Norwegian colonial islands. The crew now numbers 30 men, and, in addition, there are the 3 deck slaves who are on their way to an unknown buyer in Copenhagen. The passengers include Mistress Møller and Mistress Wimmeløv, and the Messrs. Reimers, Grim and Knipnasse. The price for a passage from St. Croix to Copenhagen varies from 70 to 100 rixdaler. In addition, a seaman has come on board who has entered into a special agreement whereby he will pay 30 rixdaler and carry out "some sailor's duties" during the voyage. Ferentz is short of seamen on board, so why hasn't the newcomers signed on as a regular crew member in order to earn money during the crossing instead of paying for the journey? There is reason to believe that he has been suffering from an illness and is therefore unable to work full-time.

The *Fredensborg* is fully loaded with good colonial products. The final inventory of the cargo is as follows:

|  |  |
|---|---|
| 277  *barrels of sugar* | 4  *bales of cotton* |
| 1,044  *rolls of tobacco* | 106,630  *pounds of dyewood* |
| 4  *barrels of cinnamon bark* | 300  *planks of mahogany* |

In addition they have 150 rolls of tobacco for "Tobacco Director General" Bargum.

Now that they are again under sail there is a new rhythm on board, and the Queen's watch is set as the first watch. The cable is removed from the starboard anchor and payed down into the hold, and the final preparations are made for a rough crossing of the Atlantic Ocean while there is still fair weather. While sailing steadily on a starboard tack in the trade wind, they seize the opportunity to paint the coloured strakes on the port side. Ferentz wants the ship to look her best when they arrive in Copenhagen. He entertains the hope of being allowed to continue

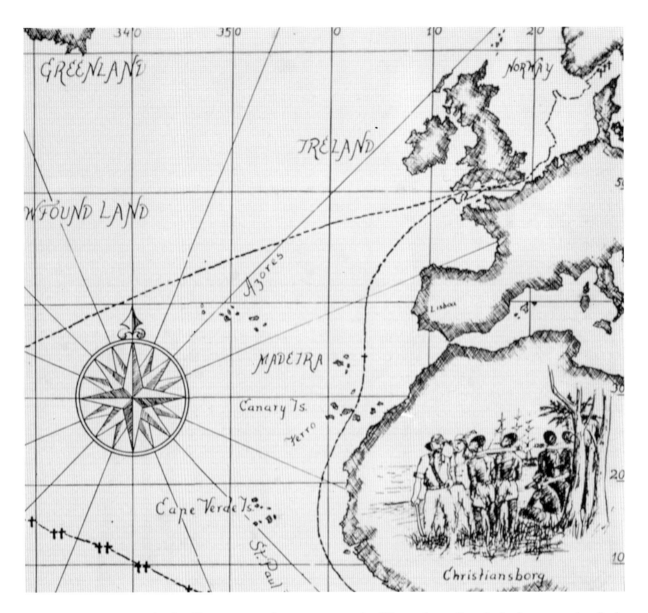

*The* Fredensborg *sailed through The Channel both on the voyage out and on the way home. Normally a "course north of England" was preferred as this was regarded as safer.*

in the Company, perhaps as a captain. Three days after their departure he finds the time is ripe for a little spiritual rearmament, and again holds a service on the quarterdeck.

The old vane on the fore masthead has been torn to shreds by the wind and must be replaced. When Sailmaker John Andersen has the vane ready, a nimble and fearless ship's boy climbs all the way up to the top with it. The new vane is white, to enable them to observe the direction of the wind against a dark, Nordic autumn sky. The next thing to break is one of the crosstrees on the main topmast. An oaken beam, lashed and wedged in as tightly as possible, is a makeshift reparation. Like all other ships at this time the *Fredensborg* consists of organic materials that are continually exposed to moisture and changes in temperature. For this reason, there was always decay despite continuous maintenance. Even though extensive repairs were carried out by Master Shipwright Ole Gad before their departure from Copenhagen, something always goes wrong, especially when the ship is heav-

146

ily loaded. With her 15 years the *Fredensborg* is not an especially old ship, but old enough for a great deal to happen on board.

Our friend Hoffmann writes that he was very sick during the departure, but he is recovering and will soon be able to make entries in his journal, thereby giving us a picture of life on board. It is obvious that wastage is a problem:

Saturday 24 September: "Took up a cask of fish-oil from the cargo. Third Mate Runge insisted that it be inspected, as the contents had decreased considerably even though I was unable to find a leak. Upon closer inspection it was apparent that the level had gone down by at least a foot, and the Captain allowed Runge to write off 50 *potter* to cover the loss. The following attestation has been prepared: Today we the undersigned, at the request of Third Mate Runge, have examined a cask of fish oil and discovered that more than a foot was lacking, to which we bear witness to the truth of this." The attest is signed by C. Beck and A.H. Hoffmann.

On the whole it is important that everything be recorded – and everything that appears in writing tallies with the facts. A few days later there is a meeting of the Ship's Council. The captain presents his receipts for provisions, expenses and refreshments during their stay in the West Indies. Hoffmann writes:

"In the afternoon a meeting of the Ship's Council was held and presented with the bills for the provisions, expenses and refreshments from the stay in the West Indies, that were to be signed. Third Mate Runge and Boatswain Rosenberg refused to sign, and made known their reasons. Third Mate Runge was willing to attest to the accounts that he had kept himself. It was impossible for Boatswain Rosenberg to know what had been brought abroad, or what it might have cost, so he too was unable to verify the invoices. Whereupon the Captain, First Officer Beck and Carpenter Lund signed the bills that were delivered to me."

This time as well, Hoffmann's sharp eyes have made certain observations, and he writes that Ferentz has listed 50 pounds of beef as lamb. What happened to the difference of more than 3 rixdaler in the prices, he does not say, but concludes: "Most of the data has been entered incorrectly, which will be shown by the ledger and the journal." It is obvious that Runge and Rosenberg had also discovered some of the irregularities in connection with the provisions and the prices, but whether Ferentz did this for his own profit, it is difficult to say.

Passengers on board the ship have also given Ferentz additional problems to contend with. The male passengers have brought along quite a bit to drink, which leads to boozing and brawling. Søren Kipnasse is especially hard to get along with. Hoffmann: Monday 26 September: "Early in the morning, came down to the cabin for my tea and found Captain Ferentz and S. Kipnasse in a furious argument. The former told the latter that if he continued with his brawling and insults, he would be forced to forbid him to dine in the cabin. He would have to eat his meals in the cabin assigned to him. The captain asked me to record this in the protocol, and that, in addition, S. Kipnasse had come down to the cabin today and had immediately started an argument for no reason at all."

A few days later Ferentz received a letter from Søren Kipnasse:

"Worthy Captain Ferentz.
As I daily, and especially yesterday and today, have been subjected to abuse by the Ship's Surgeon and the Quartermaster, I am in fear of losing my life. I therefore feel the necessity of a consultation with all the members of the Ship's Council, concerning the reprimand such officers must deserve."

As a result of this letter containing such serious accusations, a meeting of the Ship's Council is held in the cabin. The two officers, Sixtus and Engmann, are summoned, and Reimers is assigned to conduct their case. It soon turns out that there has been considerable drinking and brawling on board, and in this connection two things have come to light. "The drunken officers have vowed and confirmed that, with the help of the medicine chest entrusted to their care, they would forcibly and violently poison every man on board the ship." Since all the members of the Ship's Council agree that it would be best for the contending parties to become reconciled, Ferentz concludes: "I am not at all averse to this being done, and that complete agreement and full harmony can be maintained on board the ship. But to date, Heaven help us, drunkenness has caused considerable inconvenience to one and all. Whereas I am not learned in the law, a reconciliation between them has pleased me very much."

Shortly afterwards there is a knock at the cabin door, and Reimers enters with a "letter". He has obviously been mediating persistently among the parties, and now that the intoxication has worn off, they have come to their senses. In the letter it says:

"Worthy Mr. Captain Ferentz.
The disputes that have prevailed among the undersigned have now been settled among ourselves. To date none of us can find fault with the other, but we are good friends. Whatever has been written and said, by both sides, to the Ship's Council shall be declared null and void, for which reason this case is withdrawn. We did not wish to neglect to notify Mr. Captain of this. We remain, Worthy Mr. Captain Ferentz, your humble servants.
Carl Friderich Engmann Kipnasse Sixtus."

But the passengers are not the only ones to give Ferentz grey hair. Like most captains, Ferentz can also be abusive when giving orders on deck. Boatswain Rosenberg is tired of this, and after Ferentz has received several clear signals of Rosenberg's resentment, he finds it best to summon the Ship's Council again.

Ferentz says he has seen Boatswain Rosenberg take offence several times, "after I have been free with my commands, when in my judgement I have felt it was for the good of the Company. In order to maintain peace and harmony I have chosen to let everything the Boatswain has to say about this pass without comment." In answer to direct questions, the other members of the Ship's Council say they have no objections to Ferentz, and they cannot see that he has done anything that was not for the good of the Company.

Rosenberg, who is disqualified, is not allowed to be present at the meeting of the Ship's Council when this matter is being discussed, but he later receives a report of what has been entered in the protocol. A superior will sometimes swear, especially in a stressful situation. Hoffmann has let us know that Ferentz can be arrogant when he is provoked, but it appears as if he is not too bad. To what extent Beck and Runge have told the whole truth during the meeting of the Council is another matter. But Runge, in particular, previously showed that he has a mind of his own when he refused to sign the bill for the refreshments. Some captains could be out-and-out tyrants and abuse their position of power, but there is no indication that Ferentz fits into this category.

Nor were they spared sickness and death on the homeward voyage. Thursday 11 October Hoffmann writes: "Samson, the sick Negro, died and was thrown overboard. I looked over his things, which consisted of one white and one blue shirt, a vest, a linen greatcoat, one pair long and one pair white canvas pants, a pair of shoes, a pair of Icelandic stockings and a Turkish rug. On orders from the Captain these were distributed to the two other Negroes, who were called "Roland" and "Oliver". Passenger Kipnasse, Jens Jansen and Cooper Weis sick."

Here we can see what a deck slave possessed. Strangely enough Ferentz passes over Samson's death in silence. As far as the accounts were concerned Samson no longer belonged to the Company. Nonetheless, it would have been appropriate to mention it. Including Samson, a total of 30 had died among the *Fredensborg*'s cargo of slaves. On the other hand, Jens Jansen is a new name that appears. This must have been the seaman who was supposed to do a little work for his passage. After they had been under sail for little more than a month, Hoffmann can tell us that the storms had struck in earnest:

Tuesday 18 October: At 9:30 P.M. a severe storm arose from the south and south-southwest, which increased in such intensity that at 12 o'clock we had to shorten sail and scud under bare poles. When it was no longer possible to steer the ship, we had to heave to during the night."

Wednesday 19 October: "Same wind force in the morning, and in addition the

*Most deaths at sea were caused by falls from the rigging or by drowning, and in a storm the risks were even greater. Chief Officer Lundberg was the unlucky one on board the* Fredensborg.

wind veered round to the northwest. By 9 a.m. the storm had subsided. Half of our mizzen has blown away out there, mizzen topmast, staysail torn to shreds and the new topsail that was bent a few days ago has a damaged bolt rope."

The bad weather continues with gales, rain and thunder and lightning. There are "monstrously high seas", and the sailmaker has more than enough to do repairing tattered sails. Ferentz is particular about the spread of canvas, and for periods he uses only the fore course and a try sail.

23 October: "8 bells. Heavy hailstorm and at the same time the studding sail yard broke on the portside as well as the mizzen sheet."

When it has subsided a bit, they are able to slaughter a pig which is served in the cabin and to the crew, and later they open a barrel of ship's bread. One afternoon the gale blows up again at full strength, and throughout the night they have to ride out the storm under bare poles. Ferentz constantly has men at the pumps, but they do not take in much water, as they have done a good job caulking at St. Croix.

Since their departure from St. Croix they have been sailing in a northerly direction until they were clear of the trade winds and have entered the zone of prevailing westerlies. There they are greatly assisted by the Gulf Stream. Centuries of sailing across the Atlantic have taught captains and navigators to utilize the elements as well as possible during the homeward voyage. For the *Fredensborg* this is the contribution of the forces of nature to the final leg of the triangular trade. As they approach England, they begin to observe ships every day. And one day they finally take a sounding of the bottom at 70 fathoms.

3 November: they have entered The Channel, and are paid a visit: "An English guard-vessel came alongside and asked where we came from and where we were bound." After six days of sailing with a moderate breeze they sight Jutland, and later "took a bearing of the high ground at Skagen, S 1/4 E." One severe autumn gale follows the other as they are fighting a turbulent Skagerrak, as Ferentz calls

the North Sea. They observe another sailing ship which signals its position by lighting a fire, and Ferentz finds it wise to do the same in order to avoid collisions in storms and the dark of night.

After struggling with bad weather and constant damage to sails and rigging, both the ship and the crew are beginning to show signs of wear and tear. This is precisely what Ferentz feared with this late departure from St. Croix, and for this reason he pays extra-close attention:

Friday 11 November: "A three-masted ship sailed astern of us to the windward. Continued lighting fire throughout the watch for the aforementioned ship. 6 bells. Sighted the coast of Norway." Hoffmann continues: "The Ship's Council is meeting to discuss whether it is in the best interests of the worthy Company to remain at sea or put into port in Norway, which was in sight."

Carpenter Laxell believes that with the prevailing winds everyone would seek the first and best harbour. Boatswain Rosenberg claims that since the weather is changeable and the men are sick and in poor condition, these circumstances necessitate seeking a harbour. Third Mate Runge maintains that it is most advisable to put in at the first and best harbour, far more advisable than remaining at sea in the storms. Chief Officer Beck feels it is most advisable to put into port. Captain Ferentz agrees with the other members of the Ship's Council. Because of changeable winds, and considerable wear and tear on standing and running rigging, he finds it to be in the best interests of the Company to locate a suitable harbour. In addition, few of the crew members have the health or strength to continue struggling day after day in the bad weather.

Ferentz suits action to words, and is able to make a note in his journal: "5 bells. Hove to at Stavern in order to take on a pilot, but none came. Bore away to an easterly course. Fired a four-pounder and a pilot from Kierringhavn came aboard, and steered us in to Sandefjord harbour east of Laurvig. We anchored at 7 p.m. and furled the sails. Mr. Kipnasse very sick and 4 seamen sick. The pilot disembarked at 8:30."

Saturday morning the pilot comes back on board, and they put over warp to East Valen where she is moored. During the day they are able to wash down and clean the decks and clear away the mess on board. It is bitterly cold when Ferentz, Reimers, Hoffmann and the two ladies row ashore, where among other things they secure a supply of fresh bread and milk. On Sunday Ferentz and Hoffmann go to Laurvig while some of the men are given shore leave. Ferentz is quick to write a letter to the Board of Directors; which is to be sent by "the early morning mail":

"By means of this I humbly take the liberty of notifying Your Worships that on the 11th, after 57 days of sailing, I have safely arrived in the harbour of Sandefiord in Norway. Since 18 Oct. we have almost daily had extremely bad weather so that at times we had to scud under bare poles, at times sail under the foresail and at times under the double reefed topsail. The rigours connected with such weather have left the men so exhausted that upon our arrival four men were sick and almost everyone else was weak. These circumstances, along with a southerly wind at all times and the narrows in the North Sea, finally necessitated, though unwillingly, my putting into port in Norway. For the ship's provisions I have run up an account for 200 daler with Shopkeeper Bugge in Laurvig and because of that issued a

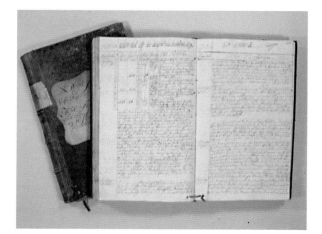

*From the Captain's Journal 1 December 1768. This is the final entry before the shipwreck at Tromøy and the days that followed.*

promissory note to Messrs. Krüger and Rahling in Elsinore. And with God's help, upon my successful return home, I shall submit the accounts. Otherwise the ship, God be praised, is in good condition, but the crew is weak. At the present time the wind is southerly, and the sea is already such that if one is to go ashore one must break through the ice with a Norwegian boat built for such conditions. As soon as the wind and weather become favourable I shall not fail to continue the journey.

Ferentz."

As usual Captain Ferentz is particular about provisions from land. He brings lamb and beef on board as well as vegetables, but this does not help Søren Kipnasse very much. He is now so sick that "any hope of recovery has more or less been abandoned". A high wind is rising again from the southeast, and the ship is swung around with such force that the tree to which the warp was fastened is uprooted. This time they fasten the mooring to an iron ring at West Valen, while "Mr. Kipnasse was worse and the sickness had gained the upper hand."

On the following day Kipnasse draws his last breath. The body is dressed in a clean dress-shirt, a pair of lisle stockings, a white cotton cap and a white kerchief, while the carpenter goes ashore to order a coffin. Jens Jansen, who has undertaken the task of attending to the body, is allowed to keep the clothes Kipnasse was wearing when he died. On the same day some tar is brought on board, as well as 388 servings of ship's bread and beer for the men. The pram that brings out the goods takes back two cabin windows in order to repair the glass.

Kipnasse is buried two days later. He is accompanied to his final resting place by Reimers and Beck, while Boatswain Rosenberg is confined to bed on land. On the following days three boatloads of wood, some vegetables and a calf are brought on board. Hoffmann is again vexed and suspicious because the captain has given orders not to weigh the calf. Nor does he find out what is in three sacks that are brought on board by the captain himself.

On 28 November the *Fredensborg* slips out of Sandefjord after a stay of 16 days. The departure has posed problems; the anchor was stuck so fast that the handspikes broke before it came loose. In addition, a man fell overboard: "As we were about to hoist the dinghy onto the ship, Andreas Fredriksen fell overboard. Immediately put about and was happy to rescue him in the dinghy".

When the pilot leaves the ship early in the afternoon, a new storm is brewing. Ferentz is in a hurry, and "claps on all the canvas she can carry". With a favourable wind it is only a 2 to 3 days' run to Copenhagen after a voyage that has lasted a total of 17 months. In the evening they sight Færder Lighthouse five miles away, and the ship's boys go aloft in the darkness in order to reef the topsails. On the 29th they catch a glimpse of Skagen before they tack north into an increasing southeasterly wind with the air heavy with rain. On the following day the gales increase, and the heavily loaded ship is forced out of the Skagerrak. The visibility is poor: "a sailing ship passed with a light, whereupon we also lit the lantern in the stern."

Thursday 1 December 1786: Hoffmann notes: "Around 12:45 p.m. the Ship's Council was summoned by the captain and asked to pass judgement on the following. At the present time the wind was from the southeast, and rising with heavy rain. If they remained at sea, and the wind blew up for a storm, they were in danger of being driven all the way back into the North Sea. In addition, three men were sick and the others were weak, and most of them could not be expected to withstand the cold. Under these circumstances it was best to put into a port. Then changed the course for land."

Captain Ferentz: "3 bells. Sighted land ahead. The Ship's Council was again summoned and asked if they stood by the decision to seek a port. The unanimous answer was that they thought it would be best for the Company as well as for the men themselves. Shortly afterwards the ship hove to and 3 shots were fired for the pilot. At 2:30 the pilot came on board from a place called Sandøen. Following the pilot's orders we veered off and sailed along the coast until we were at the approach to Narestø, where we observed a rock ahead to the leeward. The captain reminded the pilot to beware of that, whereupon he answered that he could certainly take care of the ship. Shortly afterwards he shouted, "BEAR OFF"! But too late. We did get past the rocks, but immediately afterwards the forepart of the ship struck a cliff on an island, whereupon the vessel immediately swung towards land with her port side, and ran aground. This was at 4 o'clock. Efforts were immediately made to get a hawser ashore. The wind was easterly, the air heavy with rain. Everyone immediately tried to save their lives. The expedition's chest, the Company's letters and the ship's documents were forthwith salvaged. With the help of two spars and a plumb line we tried to haul each other ashore. By 4:30 everyone was on land." Hoffmann adds: "Praised be the name of the Lord."

The brief comments in the journal reveal little of the drama that was taking place on board. There was not a moment to lose to get everyone safely up on deck, before they were swept away by the enormous waves that washed over the deck. The shipwreck has occurred so abruptly that they have to save their lives in the clothes they are wearing, even though the temperature is close to zero. Numb with cold they must scramble ashore on the swaying spars that are used in the rigging. First come the Mistresses Møller and Wimmeløv, followed by the remaining passengers, the crew and the two deck slaves from the Gold Coast. As luck would have it, they end up in a spot where the frigate is being driven in towards land by the wind and sea. Finally, all 37 on board are huddled together on the top of the high cliff. Now it is almost completely dark, and the rain is turning into snow as they start walking in search of people. Pilot Svend Jensen from Sandøya leads the way with swollen lips and a bloody nose. He has received most of his injuries during the dramatic shipwreck. However, they are not the result of an impact with the local granite, but with Chief Officer Beck's fist. Beck was so furious after the shipwreck, which he believed had been caused by the pilot, that he struck him without warning.

"The Captain went to the Pilot Master in order to arrange for someone to keep watch by the ship, which has been taken care of. The men looked after themselves, one here, the other there. The Captain, the mates and I went in a body to John Nielsen at Hastensund. Stormy weather with snow all night," notes Hoffmann.

*With the help of a few spars and a plumb line every life is saved when the* Fredensborg *is wrecked. The ship's journals and the important expedition chest are also removed to safety.*

There is no mention in the journal about what happened to the three in the open pilot boat. The pilot boat was being towed by the *Fredensborg,* and the pilot's apprentices, Gunder Nielsen, Svend Sørensen and Andreas Engelbretsen from Sandøy, found themselves in a very dangerous situation. They must have come loose in a hurry when they saw the ship was about to be wrecked. Then followed a struggle against waves and currents before they were safely back on land.

The unfortunate pilot from Sandøy, who received the blame for the shipwreck, had a difficult time ahead of him. The same was true of Captain Ferentz, who had lost his first command. The triumphant return home to Copenhagen, which Ferentz had dreamed of, had ended in a humiliating shipwreck. His personal investments, which had been purchased with the hard-earned slave commission, were in danger of being destroyed. The same was true of the valuable cargo of colonial products which were to reinvigorate the Guinea Company, and bring pleasure to the King's city. Ferentz was a beaten and unhappy man. The Captain's Instructions explained what he was supposed to do: "If it should happen – may the Almighty God help him prevent this! – that the ship is stranded or wrecked, then the Captain, if he is alive, or whoever is in command in his place, shall salvage everything that is possible to salvage."

That night, Captain Ferentz is probably unable to fall asleep in John Nielsen's house, and is thinking about his next letter to the Board of Directors in "the Yellow Palace".

# CHAPTER 8

# After the Wreck

"To the Board of Directors.

I am exceedingly distressed to be the bearer of the sad tidings to the worthy Board of Directors that the frigate *Fredensborg,* under my command, has run aground and been wrecked at Jethmar Tangen, in the eastern approach to Tromøy. I will describe the circumstances as briefly as possible. On the 28th, with quite a few ships, we left Sandefjord harbour with a N.E. wind. It was around 3 o'clock when we reached open sea, but it was scarcely 5 when a high wind blew up from SE, with heavy rain.  However we stayed at sea until the 1st, when we held a meeting of the Ship's Council at 12:45 p.m., and unanimously decided to put into port in Norway. Whereupon we headed for land, which we sighted around 1:30 in the afternoon. Then hoisted the flag, and fired three signals from time to time. Finally, at 2:30 the pilot came on board, and took over the command. The weather was heavy and we were sailing for one jib and double reefed main topsail. We observed a large rock just ahead of the ship. I warned the pilot to beware of this and bear off in good time, but received the answer that he would certainly take care of that. Shortly afterwards he gave the command "BEAR OFF!" But too late. The ship struck the rocks at an incredible speed. It was around 3:30 when this happened, and everyone had to think of saving his life, and God be praised, we succeeded. Everyone on board was saved with difficulty, although in what they were wearing, as there was only enough time to throw a few clothes onto the rocks, of which most have been lost. The ship is lying with its starboard side in the water. Throughout the night when the ship was stranded, as well as the following time, the sea has been high and rough, so we have been unable to salvage anything except for a few insignificant things that have washed ashore. However we dropped anchors and fastened a cable on land. We hope the wreck will remain steady and not be driven away, in order that we may salvage whatever we can when the weather improves.

Thomas Pedersen from Arendal was with us and assisted us in word and deed. I intend to obtain the necessary money for the sustenance of the men from him. I have placed the pilot, who is undeniably to blame for the shipwreck, under arrest for the time being. I await orders as to how I am to proceed in this matter. By the same token I await orders as to the way the salvaging is to be carried out, if we should be fortunate enough to salvage anything. The Pilot Master has arranged for the necessary guard to be mounted around the ship day and night. However, as we are are lacking in everything, I humbly pray that I may be allowed to raise as much money as is necessary in order to provide for myself and my men. Owing to the long journey they are in poor health and weak, and need clothing and food in the bitter winter cold so that in their misery they do not perish. I herewith await the merciful orders of your worships. Tomorrow I intend to hold a maritime court of inquiry which I shall send by the next post. The ship's gold has been saved, as well as copies of the agent's main ledger and journal, the ship's log, records of provisions and wages, logs and several of the ship's documents. In addition to 21 letters which it is my duty to forward. (…)

May it please the worthy Board of Directors to show us mercy and I will endeavour to remain

Ferentz"

*Even though Captain Ferentz was a defeated man after the shipwreck, he was in full activity. Here he supervises the salvaging along with Chief Officer Beck.*

When Captain Ferentz signed the letter to the Board of Directors on the evening of 2 December, he had a long and exhausting day behind him. He was a defeated man, and the former and elegant flourishes under his signature have now almost vanished. In the letter it appears as if he was unaware of the fact that the "rock" they had struck was Tromøy itself.

When they came out to Gitmertangen early in the morning they were met by a distressing sight. The *Fredensborg* was lying on her starboard side with her masts in the water and the "terrible sea and breakers prevented us from coming to the ship with any vessel". The only things they had managed to salvage were one of the compasses and a single package of water-soaked tobacco. And to make things worse, the package of tobacco was duly marked with the captain's initials J.F. – as a reminder that his path to anticipated riches had gone down along with the ship!

They had succeeded in finding quarters for most of the crew in Narestø on the other side of Tromøysund; some also stayed with the pilot master in Kjørvika. In Narestø there were several seamen's widows who could use an extra shilling by renting rooms to the shipwrecked seamen. Hoffmann had finally managed to distance himself from Ferentz as well as the others he disliked; he had found lodgings in Hastensund with John Nielsen, who was highly esteemed as both a skipper and shipowner. The unfortunate ship's

*This section of Admiralty Chart Director Jens Sørensen's general map from c. 1715 shows the skerries at Arendal. The* Fredensborg *went down at the spot marked "Giedmersøe" all the way to the east on Tromøy, while Narestø is situated by the bay north of "Skindfeld Tange". Outside of Arendal we can see "Merdøe" where the* Fredensborg *lay at anchor on the voyage to Africa.*

assistant was very glad to have escaped from the shipwreck with his life, but his joy was soon overshadowed by his personal loss of valuable rolls of tobacco.

Christian Runge from Arendal had received a homecoming he would rather have done without, at any rate during the first days. Later he realized that the dramatic shipwreck had been an Act of Providence. He had sailed from Arendal to Africa, sweated through months on the Gold Coast, and shared the burdens during the middle passage. In addition, he had taken part in the sale of slaves, the loading of the cargo and a stormy voyage across the Atlantic, only to be shipwrecked close by his hometown. This was a long and arduous detour only to find a sweetheart in Narestø, a few miles from his homestead! Christian Runge was probably lodged in Thomas Svendsen's house in Narestø, all the way down by the shore. Here lived Widow Svendsen, who had lost her husband in an accident at sea, and she had a pretty daughter named Gunhild. Young Christian had a lot to tell about, and during the long winter evenings Gunhild no doubt heard about life on board, and about exotic places, enslaved Africans and voracious sharks.

As a rule a shipwreck had legal consequences. Two days after the shipwreck Counsellor and District Judge Brøndsdorph had arrived in Hastenstund by boat from the official residence in Kolbjørnsvik. The maritime court of inquiry into the loss of the ship was held in John Nielsen's house, and a number of witnesses were summoned. The court was in session and the first lines of the records of the court proceedings read as follows:

"Peter Buch Brønsdorph His Royal Majesty's duly appointed Counsellor, District Judge, as well as Notarius Publicus in Nedenes Fief in the diocese of Christiansand, hereby makes it known that, in the year 1768 on 3 December, a Maritime Court of Inquiry, upon the requisition of Captain Johan Frantzen Ferentz, is con-

vened in John Nielsen's house in Hastensund, in Tromøy parish under the jurisdiction of Nedenes Fief, in order, then and there, to receive the final testimony
from his ship's crew about the shipwreck."

After a description of the course of the journey, and what happened during the
shipwreck, the witnesses were called in to testify one by one. A total of sixteen
members of the crew had to take the oath, "so help them God and His Holy word".
They all gave the same explanation and when asked about the cause of the shipwreck, they all said that neither the captain nor the crew had done anything
wrong. They were all of the opinion that if the pilot had turned the ship before
they came so close to land, the shipwreck would never have taken place, "and the
ship brought to her salvation".

The pilot, who was present without being summoned as a witness, said he had
exercised all the caution and seamanship he was accustomed to using. He produced good testimonials to his capability signed by Captains Friis and Schieldrup,
whom he had piloted into Kjørviga. Ferentz immediately challenged the pilot's
defense strategy, and presented a claim for compensation for the ship, cargo,
inventory and equipment. Ferentz was fighting for his own future. He knew the
Company would show no mercy if the blame for the shipwreck were to be placed
on him or anyone else on board.

In a letter from the pilot, which was delivered a few days later, we are given a
more detailed explanation of what took place during the approach and the shipwreck: "...with the jib, main topsail and mizzen we were carrying, I gave the command to head for the approach to Tromøysund in order to come into Kiørvigen
harbour. Since it was impossible to harden in the sheets, because of the tremendous gales and heavy seas, we had to proceed on the same course. When I noticed
the ship was taken by the current and wind, I asked the captain whether the ship
would tack in order to bear away from land. He said no, and for this reason we had
to veer round or bear away, which would also have succeeded if the mizzen had
been standing bare. The ship had already begun to change course when I discovered that the topsail brace broke. In addition the mizzen could not be reduced.
The wind took hold and the ship headed in to land. Shortly after the ship had
struck, without the slightest reason or previous warning, I was attacked by Chief
Officer Beck while I was standing on the deck. He struck me in the face with his fist
so the blood flowed from my nose and mouth."

While the preparations for the maritime court of inquiry were being made,
there was hectic activity out by the wreck. In a short time twenty-four local men
had been hired, and when the weather had improved a bit everyone was busy salvaging sails and spars. A powerful cable that had been lent by John Nielsen was fastened to the main mast, and together with another borrowed cable and some of
the ship's own rigging they managed to bring the ship on an even keel four days
after the wreck. Now the salvaging was easier, and six of the cannons and some of
the equipment were brought on land. A hole was chopped in the deck of the cabin
above the sail locker and the sails were taken up, and many soaked rolls of tobacco
were fished up through the after hatch. Even though the ship was "lying with half
the cannon wheels under water and in addition largely down by the head", the
hull appeared to have stood up very well, in view of the collision and the storm.

*These are dangerous waters where the* Fredensborg *went down. Just beyond is Tromøysund with safe anchorage in Kjørvigen to the left and Narestø to the right.*

They clearly hoped to salvage the ship with the help of two large barges and 36 empty wine barrels that came out from Arendal. Then they could tow the wreck in to a safe place for repairs. But the December days were short, and they were struggling against time and feared new storms.

Hoffmann had borrowed a boat and gone to Risør with two of the seamen as rowers. There were said to be vessels there from Jutland that could take some of the seamen to Copenhagen, to avoid "draining the Company's funds". Hoffmann was able to place fourteen men on six different ships, where they could work their passage home for the fare. On the way back he dropped in at Lyngør and arranged for transport for Mistress Wimmeløv. With well qualified local salvaging assistance, there was no reason to use the exhausted crew from the *Fredensborg*, but some stayed behind to help all the same. Thomas Pedersen, who had been hired as commissioner by Ferentz, did everything he could to obtain the necessary equipment for the salvaging and cash for current expenses.

In the days up to the middle of December, weather permitting, there was a bustle of activity out by the wreck. It was cold and Tromøysund froze over, but not enough to prevent Brønsdorph from coming to Hastensund and taking a statement from a witness in the case against the pilot. The general opinion after an inspection by various experts, including Master Shipbuilder Christen Hansen Riiber, was that it would be best to move the *Fredensborg*, even though the risk was great. The ship was lying in such a way that the possibility of salvaging anything more was very small. The men who had been staying with the master pilot in Kjørvika were moved to Narestø, so that, with the exception of Hoffmann, Ferentz had gathered the rest in one place. Weather permitting, they salvaged ship's equipment and a little of the cargo, largely tobacco. Everything was brought into Hastensund and Narestø, and the rolls of tobacco were cut open in order to dry.

The storm struck with full intensity on 14 December, and the *Fredensborg* was again exposed to a heavy strain in the mighty waves. Again and again the hull was hurled against the cliffs, but it still remained intact. This attracted considerable

*159*

attention among the salvage crew, and in a new report to the Board of Directors Ferentz wrote: "However, one cannot cease to wonder about the incredible strength of the ship. The Norwegians unanimously agree that there is nothing like her in all of Norway. As soon as the weather permits I will try to move her."

On Christmas Eve there was hectic activity out by the wreck, which was now a pitiful sight. The masts and bow sprit had been chopped away, and the wreck had been hauled to a better position further into the bay. There is no mention of the way Christmas was celebrated, but eight men had been posted in to keep watch every night during Christmas. The close collaboration with Thomas Pedersen as the commissioning agent came to an abrupt end when Ferentz received the first letter from the Board of Directors on 27 December:

"Captain Ferentz
We have been distressed to examine your letter of 2 December owing to the sorry state of the ship. We see from the same letter that the pilot who commanded the ship has been arrested, but after receiving a letter by the last mail from Mr. R. Lassen in Arendal, who informs us that the pilot has been set free, we do not know what to think. If it is true, as you have written, that the pilot has been arrested, then he must not be released before the case has been lawfully heard. By today's post we have written to Mr. Lassen in Arendal and asked him to assist you with both money and good advice, and informed him how to deal with the pilot. Otherwise you must pluck up your courage, and do the best for the Company by salvaging as much as possible, in expectation that nothing be neglected. Thomas Pedersen has written to us, but as he is a master pilot we do not think it best to hire him as commissioner. You must refer to Mr. R. Lassen who will assist you with money. By today's post Lassen has received orders to pay Thomas Pedersen the money he has advanced. We remain obligingly

Bargum    Engmann    With"

The year 1768 ended with strong, southeast gales and heavy seas. It became more and more apparent that the ship could not be saved, and Ferentz was in no doubt that the keel had been heavily damaged when he saw the rest of the fore mast rise two feet above the deck after the last storm. Lassen, who had assumed complete responsibility, aimed at salvaging as much of the cargo as possible with the help of special salvaging instruments which he had ordered from a blacksmith. Among other things, there were hooks and claws on long poles that could take hold of things under water. These special "wreck tongs" later proved to be very useful. With the help of these they managed to bring up several elephant tusks and other objects from the ship. Lassen fired all the local salvage workers, as he felt their wages were too high, and asked that the members of the crew take over as much of the work as possible in order to reduce the expenses.

On 11 January Erich Ancker said goodbye to his shipmates in order to go home to Christiania. He was paid 4 rixdaler for travelling funds. The journals do not tell whether he had saved any of his personal belongings after the shipwreck.

The work at the exposed site of the wreck was a terrible strain on the crew from the *Fredensborg*. The transition from tropical waters to snowstorms and freezing temperatures was considerable, and they were poorly equipped for this highly dangerous work. In a letter to Customs Officer Lassen, Ferentz and Hoffmann write, among other things: "We are using the seamen wherever we can, but they must be treated as human beings. It would be unchristian to make them work by the wreck, and in the cold of winter have them stand up to their knees in water, wearing shoes and stockings. All the more, as most of them have only one pair, and accordingly must let them dry on their feet. It would be best for them if they could go home."

On 20 January new storms set in, and now the strong ship's construction had to submit to the elements. On the following day the weather had improved a bit, and Ferentz writes:

"Early in the morning, with considerable difficulty in the snow and wind, the mates and I, along with the crew and several of the salvagers made our way across the fjord and out to the wreck, which had broken into a number of pieces. Then salvaged around 60 mahogany planks, some red wood and a number of beech planks and beams. But around 3:30 the heavy sea and storm were so bad that everyone left the wreck and went home since they were soaking wet, except for the guards who remained in order to salvage whatever they could. The mates and I, along with the boatswain, went by land to Hastensund, as the boat was unable to carry any more over the fjord to Narestøe."

When the hull collapsed, the cargo was released. Now it was a question of salvaging as much as possible before it drifted away, and people from Kjørvika and Hastensund came to help. The mahogany planks floated along with splintered ship's timber, while the heavy dyewood sank. But it turned out even worse with the barrels of sugar. The result of months of toiling by the slaves was destroyed by a few heavy waves that took hold of the barrels and crushed them against land. All the elephant tusks, which had been stowed in the bottom of the hold, settled nicely in a pile on the seabed. Two of the 4-pounders that had not been salvaged also sank heavily to the bottom. The salvage crew struggled and saved whatever they could, but some of the wreckage drifted along Tromøy to Alvekilen a little further to the west. It was inevitable that some of the men became sick from working in the winter cold. One of them was Aye.

One evening, when Ferentz came home wet and cold after working for many hours in a near gale, a new problem awaited him: "Aye, the Negro, had been caught red-handed stealing and deserved to be punished, but was treated leniently in that he was allowed to change lodgings and move in with the boatswain, which happened in the evening when the boatswain came to fetch him. Whereupon I noticed that the Negro was only

*In order to salvage as much as possible of the ship's equipment and cargo, Customs Officer Lassen ordered special "salvaging instruments" from a local blacksmith. Here we see a suitable selection which reveals that there was no lack of inventiveness in those days.*

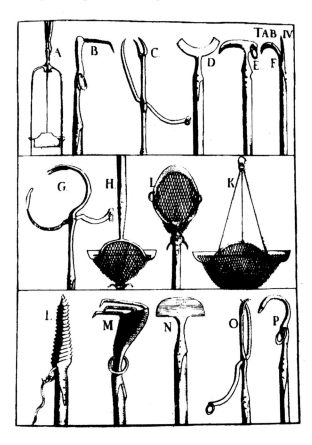

*This is the way Arendal looked at the time the* Fredensborg *was wrecked. In the middle of the picture is the church on Tyholmen where slave trader Reimers was buried.*

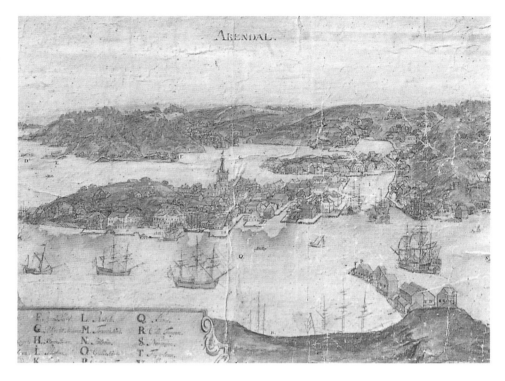

ARENDAL.

pretending to be sick, when he scampered about as fit as a fiddle when he discovered that he would not receive additional punishment." Ferentz had not forgotten that Aye had revealed the plans for the rebellion among the Akwamus, and allowed him to escape punishment once again.

Slave Trader Reimers had found lodgings in Arendal. He was in poor health and he was worried about meeting the Board of Directors to defend his actions on the Gold Coast. However, on 27 January he quietly passed away. The slave trader found his final resting place in the churchyard at Tyholmen in Arendal. While Hoffmann accompanied the slave trader to the grave, Rosenberg was very ill and delirious with fever. Two men had to keep an eye on him, as he was very restless and at times furious. The boatswain, who had gone in the longboat to Keta with supplies, ended his passage through life in a loft in Narestø. Even after such a long time, malaria claimed its victims. The ship's carpenter and a local carpenter produced a coffin, and a bellringer and a grave were ordered at Flosta graveyard. On 3 February a silent body of shipmates carried the unpainted coffin up to the church. On the top of the hill they were met by a biting northeasterly wind, and the snow was beating into their faces as the coffin was lowered into the frozen ground. Rosenberg was buried at the expense of the Company, as his scanty belongings were not enough to cover the expenses.

It is obvious that Ferentz was an honest man who wished to settle accounts. He had considerable problems when Lassen periodically lacked cash and was unable to provide the most necessary support. The local salvagers, who had not received their final payment, exerted considerable pressure on Ferentz, and a demand for payment also arrived from Narestø: "I had to borrow 6 rdl from Skipper Tiøstolvsen in order to pay some of the people who had taken in members of the crew as lodgers, as they would otherwise, owing to a lack of money, be forced to give them notice

*162*

and send them away on a winter's day with hard times everywhere. The lack of the necessary payment from Mr. Lassen on behalf of the worthy Company is causing me considerable inconvenience, which increases the cruel fate of a shipwrecked man."

Lassen worked hard to obtain passage to Denmark for the remaining seamen. They demanded 10 rixdaler for travelling funds, but Lassen offered 5. After vehement discussions they agreed on 6 rixdaler. Their departures were delayed even longer when their landlords in Narestø took action once again. They took their lodgers' clothing, which they had washed and kept in order, as security for the lack of payment, and Ferentz had to endure considerable abuse even though he was quite innocent this time. It ended with his having to pay out 26 rixdaler against receipts for a later settlement of accounts in Copenhagen.

Finally, the shipwrecked seamen left Narestø. When they came to Risør, however, Cooper Weiss had to be put ashore because of fever. The others went to Strømstad, in Sweden, with Bargeman Anders Jyde as had been agreed. We do not know whether they continued by land, or obtained a passage along the west coast of Sweden. No doubt Ferentz was relieved after dispatching so many of the men, and on 9 March he sent even more. Lassen had arranged with Skipper Simonsen, whose ship was anchored at Sandvigen outside of Arendal, to take Aye and the two slaves to Copenhagen along with seamen Fredriksen and Diedrichsen.

After they had gone, Ferentz and Hoffmann were able to concentrate on the preparations for auctioning off the "salvaged goods" which the Board of Directors wished to sell there. The auction lasted for three days in Narestø and Hastensund, and both Lassen and Hoffmann kept records of the sale which brought in 2,108 rixdaler and 16 shillings. This amount barely covered the expenses that had been incurred during the difficult salvage operations and for other necessary expenses. A couple of days after the auction, which ended on 15 March, Third Mate Runge was discharged after serving the Guinea Company for 621 days. He received 4 rixdaler for travelling funds home to Arendal, the same amount Erich Ancker had to make do with all the way to Christiania.

Spring arrived, but the air was still cold. Ferentz had arranged for the transport of the remaining equipment and salvaged cargo to Copenhagen. John Nielsen in Hastensund undertook the task at a price of 150 rixdaler. The loading began. The equipment taken on board included "1 arms chest with 23 small arms, 9 pistols, 10 swords, 4 blunderbusses, 6 iron cannons, 2 swivel guns, 1 ship's bell, 260 slave irons and 1 slave stove." Of the original cargo from the West Indies and the Gold Coast, 17 elephant tusks, 193 pieces of dyewood, 153 planks of mahogany and 2,005 rolls of tobacco were taken on board. The losses had been considerable and the *Fredensborg's* final journey, which was intended to boost the Company's economy, burdened it with a loss instead.

In a loft in Narestø Boatswain Rosenberg's few belongings were hanging to dry. When they packed his ship's chest Hoffmann discovered that an old silk kerchief and 2 pairs of woolen stockings were missing. The stockings, which Rosenberg had bought during the auction of Kiønig's merchandise, no doubt continued to wander in Narestø and certainly came in handy.

After a stay of more than 4 1/2 months in Norway the last five were ready to depart. Hoffmann, Beck, Sixtus and Mistress Møller went on board the snow *Quind*

*Here is a good view of the skerries where most of the events took place. Top right we can see Gitmertangen on Tromøy, with the outport of Narestø just inside. Boatswain Rosenberg was laid to rest in the slope below Flosta Church. Målen, where Rømer's ship went down, may be glimpsed top left.*

*Anne,* which, after an uneventful voyage, cast anchor in the Copenhagen roadstead ten days later. Their arrival was not one of the golden moments of the triangular trade, but the survivors were all the more wiser.

Whatever became of the seamen and the slaves who sailed with the *Fredensborg* on her very last voyage? Most of them quietly faded into the mists of history, but we can still follow two of our acquaintances for a while. In spite of a shipwreck and petty transactions, Captain Johan Frantzen Ferentz revealed that he was ready for similar assignments. When he and Hoffmann made their way with trepidation to "The Yellow Palace" on 30 April 1769 they took with them more than a kilo of gold and the expedition chest with all the important documents and journals from the voyage. Future generations can only guess what was said during the meeting between the unfortunate captain and the Board of Directors. Bargum, Engmann and Reindorph were most concerned with the economic consequences of the shipwreck. No doubt Captain and Director Jesper With was also interested in receiving a first-hand report about the hardships of the journey and not least the shipwreck. As a seaman he was in a far better position to evaluate the sequence of events than the other members of the board, and no doubt had a sympathetic understanding of the accident. The pilot had received the blame for the shipwreck, and at that time the criminal proceedings which had been instituted by the Company had not yet been decided. Upon a closer perusal of Hoffmann's journal, in which the pilot's testimony had also been recorded, Jesper With had no doubt drawn his own conclusions about the accident. He was quite familiar with the Arendal area and knew how difficult the waters could be in a southeasterly storm.

Ferentz reappeared in 1770–1773 as the captain of the sloop *Quitta,* and sailed along the Guinea Coast as an ivory trader. In 1774 he was given the command of the frigate *Christiansborg,* and set out on a new voyage in the triangular trade. The Company's financial difficulties gradually went from bad to worse, and in 1774

Director Bargum declared himself insolvent and left Denmark. The following year the Company's financial status was so poor that that they had to terminate the concessions to forts and trading stations along the Gold Coast. As the State was unwilling to come to their assistance it was decided to liquidate the Company and sell the properties. The sugar refinery was sold in 1776, and in the same year they ceased their activities on the Gold Coast. The Guinea Company carried out a total of 21 voyages in the triangular trade from 1767 to 1776. During these years a total of 4,799 slaves were exported from the Gold Coast, while 1,768 of these were transported on leased French ships in a total of 7 voyages.

Captain Ferentz, who by now had considerable experience from the triangular trade and the Gold Coast, did not remain unemployed. A new trading company, the Baltic Guinea Company, was established and took over all the concessions. One of the shareholders, who later became director, was Minister of Finance Ernst Schimmelmann. When the newly constructed *Fredensborg II* set out for Guinea, a proud Captain Ferentz was in command. Ferentz was equal to the task and carried out three voyages with the *Fredensborg* in the triangular trade. During his five voyages as a slave captain Ferentz probably transported more slaves than any of the other Danish-Norwegian slave captains:

| | | | |
|---|---|---|---|
| FREDENSBORG I | 1768, | *265 slaves of whom* | *30 died.* |
| CHRISTIANSBORG | 1774, | *336 slaves of whom* | *82 died.* |
| FREDENSBORG II | 1778, | *421 slaves of whom* | *145 died.* |
| FREDENSBORG II | 1781, | *540 slaves of whom* | *30 died.* |
| FREDENSBORG II | 1785, | *290 slaves of whom* | *61 died.* |

Captein Ferentz loaded a total of 1,852 slaves on board the ships at the Gold Coast; 348 of them died along the way. This amounts to a death-rate of nearly 20 percent but as we can see the number of deaths during the voyages varied greatly. The worst journey was in 1778 when more than every third slave died.

Third Mate Christian Runge from Arendal had made his plans for the future. At the auctions on board he had purchased charts and navigation aids, at the same time as he probably had a piece of silk or two for a girl in Narestø. Christian Runge and Gunhild Thomasdatter had found each other, and were married in Flosta church and went to live in Narestø. Before a year had passed after the shipwreck, they had a little daughter who was christened Marie Elisabeth. Later they had four more children. Christian Runge continued his career as a seaman, and in 1781 we find him as the skipper of the brig *Elisabeth Catrina*. It was probably the highlight of his career when he was given the command of the frigate *Anna Elisabeth*. Runge later encountered misfortune when this ship ran aground while entering the harbour of Dublin.

There were disputes between Runge and the female shipowner about salvaging the vessel, and Runge was summoned to court. He died in December 1789 up to his ears in debt.

Pilot Svend Jensen from Sandøy had a difficult winter after the shipwreck. First he was knocked down by First Officer Beck, and immediately afterwards he was arrested. After he was released, he bravely struggled to free himself from the serious

*It is highly possible that Christian Runge was provided with lodging here in this red-painted house in Narestø after the ship-wreck. This was the childhood home of Gunhild Thomasdatter, and this is where she and Christian lived during the first years of their marriage. Later they bought another house in the vicinity. Several of the old houses from the time of the* Fredensborg *are still preserved in the old outport.*

charges. At the same time he had to continue working as a pilot in order to support his family. In connection with the case, all of his possessions in the little home on Sandøy were recorded and evaluated. The case was not tried before 7 August 1769. Both Rasmus Lassen, who represented the Company, and the accused pilot Jensen were present when the judgement was pronounced. The court decided that the pilot had not made any mistakes and that he had to be acquitted: "The shipwreck was a chance happening, which could be nothing more nor less than a misfortune." In all probability a happy pilot sailed home to Sandøy, while Customs Officer Lassen had to inform the Company that they had lost the case. Kay Larsen, a Danish author, has written about the final voyage of the *Fredensborg* in his book *Krøniker fra Guinea (Guinean Chronicles)*, published in 1927. Here he says:

"The unfortunate Pilot, based on Captain Ferentz' claim to that effect, was arrested, but to no avail. What was his worth compared to the red gold, the precious ivory, the mellow rum – the sugar – and the elegant frigate which had been crushed by the barren cliff. Man is created in a fleeting moment, at times by chance, but a ship is built up by dint of wisdom and work – and it takes time and money to scrape together a cargo. Up to now, man is the cheapest and simplest and most transitory of all."

If we look at the crew list after the *Fredensborg*'s final voyage we can see that the "transitoriness" had been considerable. Of the original crew of forty men who had signed on in Copenhagen, fifteen were dead, which represents 37.5 per cent. In addition Carpenter Hæglund died 21 days after he signed on in Guinea. There is no doubt that a voyage in the triangular trade was one of the most hazardous journeys a seaman could embark on. The dangers of shipwrecks or accidents on board were undoubtedly greater in northern waters like the Skagerrak and the Kattegat, but it was first and foremost the stay along the Gold Coast, and its after-effects, that resulted in the greatest loss. The encounter with the tropical diseases, not least malaria, was the most common cause of death.

The death-rate among the crews of the slaveships that sailed in the triangular

*Opposite page:*
*The final voyage of the* Fredensborg *cost many seamen their lives. Here we see the crew list where all the deaths have been marked by the author.*

# Equipage Rulle

ved det Kongl. octroijerende Guineiske Compagnie Skib Fregatten
Fredensborg undtagne og med Skibet indvarende Mandskab, nemlig

| Charge. | No. | Navne | Maanedlig | Charge | No. | Navne | Maanedlig |
|---|---|---|---|---|---|---|---|
| Capitain | 1 | Espen Kiönig | 💀 | Matros | 24 | Jens Pedersen | 💀 |
| Ober Styrm | 2 | Peder Christian Lundborg | 💀 | | 25 | Claus Larsen | 5 |
| Assistent | 3 | Christ. Andr. Hinr. Hofmann | 10 | | 26 | Jens Lebertsen | 5 |
| Ober Mester | 4 | Joch. Christopher Sixtus | 10 | | 27 | Niels Matth. Fredberg | 💀 |
| 2d Styrm: | 5 | Johan Frantzen Serentz | 10 | | 28 | Peter Holm | 5 |
| inder Mester | 6 | Carl Friderich Engmann | 7 | | 29 | Pet. Dider: Grønberg | 5 |
| 3d Styrm: og Constabel | 7 | Christ. Hansen Beck | 9 | | 30 | Jochum Bollvard | 💀 |
| 4d Styrm: og Bousseman | 8 | Andr. Sivertsen Gadt | 💀 | | 31 | Frid. Jens: Kruse | 5 |
| Baadsmand | 9 | Christoph. Christens. Rosenberg | 💀 | Lods og Matr | 32 | Abraham Christopher | 4 |
| Ober Canon | 10 | Jacob Jacobs. Beck | 💀 | Oploopere | 33 | Hans Anders. Stolmage | 3½ |
| Kock | 11 | Nicolay Jørgensen | 8 | | 34 | Peder Mad: Skou | 4 |
| Quart.Mester | 12 | Abraham Engmann | 💀 | | 35 | Wogn Olsen | 3 |
| under Canon | 13 | Johan Jacob Kock | 💀 | | 36 | Andreas Skaaning | 3½ |
| Bödker | 14 | Ivert Jacobsen | 💀 | | 37 | Aye | 2½ |
| Prigler og Matr | 15 | John Andersen | 6 | Drenge | 38 | Erich Anker | 2½ |
| Baadsm. Math | 16 | Peder Thoersen Nordberg | 6½ | | 39 | Ole Erichsen | 2 |
| Matroser | 17 | Thomas Greisen | 5½ | | 40 | Bendt Thomsen | 2 |
| | 18 | Andr. Friderich Schlacke | 5½ | | | | |
| | 19 | Hans Iverstsen | 💀 | | | u Maanedlig | 272 |
| | 20 | Ragnal Nielsen | 5½ | | | og for Maaneder | 3 |
| | 21 | Ole Nicolaysen | 💀 | | | | |
| | 22 | Anthonie Olsen | 💀 | | | Summa | 816 |
| | 23 | Peder Johnsen | 💀 | | | | |
| | | Lat. | 105 | | | | |

*A West Indian store-house at Søndre Toll-bod in Copenhagen was built in 1780, a few years after Captain Ferentz returned from his involuntary stay in Norway. Later he delivered several shiploads of barrels of sugar and other good colonial products at this quay.*

trade during the period 1777–1789 has been investigated by Svend Erik Green-Pedersen. He has come to the conclusion that the death-rate for the seamen was 33 per cent, when taking all the voyages into account. During the same period the death-rate among the slaves, who were on board during the middle passage from Africa to the West Indies, was around 15 per cent. By way of comparison it may be mentioned that Erik Gøbel, Senior Archivist at the Danish National Archives in Copenhagen, has studied the death rate on board 58 East Indiamen from the Asiatic Company. During 4 periods between 1732 and 1833 that have been investigated, the average death-rate is 8.25 per cent. A comparison of the two great navigation routes, the China trade and the triangular trade, clearly reveals that the voyages with slave ships were especially dangerous.

It is striking that the ten who were at the bottom of the crew list of the *Fredensborg*, and who were undoubtedly the youngest, managed the best. We know that several of them contracted the fever, but survived. Those who had previously been on long voyages had been exposed the most to sickness and death. Above all, their constitutions had been weakened by the unhealthy and monotonous diet, the tremendous change of climate and previous attacks of illness in the tropics and the East. In addition there was the physical wear and tear which taxed their strength. The immunity which some developed against certain diseases was dearly bought and prevented neither dysentery nor typhoid. Most often the capabilities of the ship's doctors were greatly limited by the means available during that period, and both Sixtus and Engmann contracted diseases themselves. Thus it is not surprising when Gøbel points out that although some ship's doctors died while on the way to China, this did not result in an increase in the death rate.

Even though extensive Norwegian participation in the slave trade cannot be established, Norway did take part. Many of the seamen who sailed on the slavers were Norwegian, like Christian Runge, Erich Ancker, Ole Nicolaysen – and Peter Wessel Tordenskiold. In 1706, at the age of 16, he signed on as a seaman and the youngest on the slave ship *Cristianus Quintus.* Knowledge about the slave trade must have been widespread in the outports and coastal towns. At any rate they were not unfamiliar with black people. Aye and the two deck slaves remained in Narestø for several months after the shipwreck. A few years later Hans Herlofsen, a shipowner and merchant in Arendal, purchased a black child. The slave, who was born on St. Croix in 1769, was named Adam and was thirteen years old when he came to Arendal. The price of the boy was said to have been 300 rixdaler, which was quite a large sum. Another African had formerly ended up as postmaster in Kragerø. He was later murdered, but that is another story. The *Fredensborg's* final voyage in the triangular trade cost forty-eight seamen, slaves and passengers their lives. Kay Larsen:

"The journey was over. It had cost many good men their lives. Their bones were scattered around the globe, along the route of the ship, and the saga of the frigate *Fredensborg* had come to an end. The Earth devours and destroys the living. The Archives conceal the dead, who sometimes come alive again, in their fashion, through the diligence of the scholar."

*The map reveals the route followed by the* Fredensborg *during her final voyage in the triangular trade. The crosses mark the deaths among the slaves and the crew.*

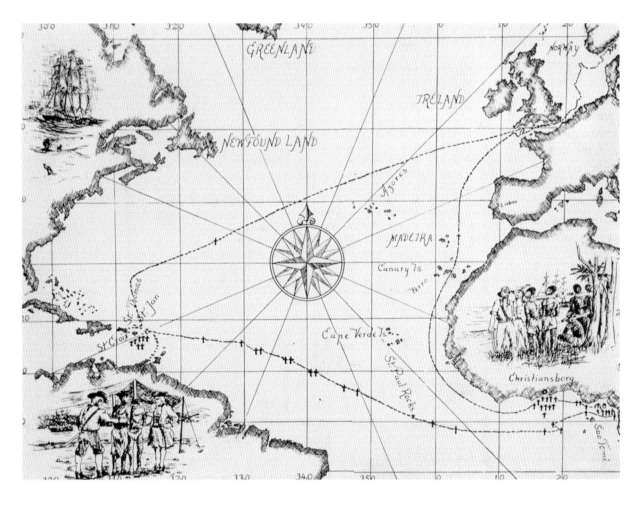

# *To the Bottom of the History*

# PART II

*It is difficult to imagine that the pieces of wreckage at the bottom of the sea were once a beautiful frigate like this. Here we see a reconstruction of the* Fredensborg *made ready to receive a cargo of slaves. The model was based on descriptions of the construction, water colours, inventories and drawings of ships from the middle of the eighteenth century. The original drawing has not been found.*

CHAPTER 9

# Objects from the Deep

T HE WRECK OF THE *FREDENSBORG* rested in peace for 206 years before being found on 15 September 1974, after careful studies of documents from the court of inquiry. Without the protocols and the journals in archives the remains of the *Fredensborg* would probably never have been discovered. After the wreck was located at Tromøy it was decided that the Norwegian Maritime Museum would undertake a marine archeological dig. The wreck was found within the coastal area for which the Norwegian Maritime Museum has responsibility, an area that stretches from the Swedish border to Rogaland. The Ministry of the Environment would provide funding, but since the wreck was found in the autumn, it was deemed most practical to start work the following summer.

On 2 July 1975 the *M/S Abelona,* hired to be a base ship, was in place over the wreck at the eastern shore of Tromøy. In addition to staff from the Norwegian Maritime Museum, under the leadership of Svein Molaug, there were many interested sports divers from various parts of the country. Some of them were already experienced in marine archeological field work; others were participating for the first time. After the necessary bearings were taken, a coordinate system oriented on the north-south line was set out on the bottom. Each square, measuring two by two metres, was marked with letters and a numbers code. It was natural that the area where the ivory was found be included in the coordinate system. As feared, digging was difficult, and much of the time was spent removing stones that lay among the remains of the wreck. In some places the ground is hard, while in other places the sediment is looser. Since it is so shallow at the wreck site, much has been destroyed. I have been there myself during storms and seen how violently the waves break over the wreck site. Then the ground mass is set in motion, which is hard on porcelain, glass, earthenware, ceramic ware and other brittle objects. During the years that have passed since the ship was wrecked, there have been hundreds of storms and even hurricanes which have torn into and broken the remains.

*The recovery work on the* Fredensborg *is in progress with the divers' boat* Capri *as a base ship. On that weatherbeaten site it is necessary to have a solid mooring to maintain the correct position.*

In the course of the first dig, which lasted until 15 June, a number of finds were made, especially of elephant and hippopotamus tusks. But there were also other interesting objects brought up from the wreck, among them an African stone mortar or rubbing stone. Such finds yield important insights into the life on a slave ship.

After the first dig is finished we evaluate what has been accomplished. The ground conditions have been very difficult, and expectations were greater than the results. However, there are several places on the bottom which have not yet been investigated because of lack of time, and we have hopes of finding more at the wreck site.

A new preliminary examination looks promising. With Molaug's permission we take some samples of the ground next to the first area of the dig. Our examinations reveal that there are great possibilities for more finds, and indeed we see a few objects, which are covered for the time being. We have obtained a copy of the Maritime Museum's seabed chart with the coordinate system drawn in, and we have left two markers on the bottom. This gives us a good basis for further marking of an extended coordinate system.

Our application for a dig in cooperation with Aust-Agder Museum is approved. The Museum will provide a low-pressure compressor and fuel, while we provide the divers' boat *Capri*, to serve as a fully equipped base ship. It is essential to increase the size of the crew, and we wind up with a team which, in addition to those of us who found the wreck, is made up of Curator Ruth Hamran, chemical engineer Ib Kjølsen and photographer Karsten Bundgaard.

In the beginning of July 1977 we are ready to act. *Capri* is anchored over the wreck, a new coordinate system has been set out, and the final preparations have been made. The dig starts the next day, and a short time afterwards the first finds are being registered on deck.

The air-lift is an important piece of equipment during a dig. We have rigged up a

110 mm hose which ends in a short steel pipe fitted with a handle. The hose goes from the wreck site on the bottom up to a grate which is hanging on the outside of the hand rail on the *Capri*. At a little distance from the bottom air from the low-pressure compressor is blown into the large hose. When the air rushes towards the surface, it expands as the pressure decreases, creating a sucking effect. Sand, mud and small stones are thus effectively transported up into the grate in a mixture of air and water. There we can check that small objects do not "sneak away" from the site.

Again we are going to experience exciting days at Gitmertangen, where we are at work from early morning until late in the evening. Our goal is clear: to find out as much as possible about the ship, the cargo, the equipment and the individuals who were on board. A slave ship which was wrecked after having nearly completed the triangle route is unique in marine archeological annals. A museum exhibition of objects from the *Fredensborg* will therefore be an important contribution to the information about the grim history of the slave trade. The objects have interest not only for a small local community close to the find site; they concern millions of people whose forefathers were victims of the transatlantic slave voyages.

Two powerful wheels of wood come to light in the sand. They were part of a gun carriage, a low wagon on which the cannons were mounted. Soon one of the *Fredensborg*'s 4-pound cannons shows up; thus we have found both the cannons which were not salvaged after the wreck. Every day we record 10 or 11 hours of effective work on the bottom, and up on deck it is also busy. All the objects must be measured, marked and registered. After that they are placed in large basins of fresh water to prevent their drying out and to wash out the salt. Several of the objects require very careful handling. Brittle objects such as leather and textiles must be sealed in plastic bags on the bottom before they are taken up. On deck Ruth, Ib and Hartvig are ready for the further treatment they require, which is done in a responsible manner.

*After great amounts of sand and stone were removed, the rest of the slave ship came to light. The wreck was an underseas time capsule whose every object was from 1768 or earlier.*

It is unavoidable that interest in the dig is great. We receive many visitors daily, among them several guest divers, and the press also wants to be part of it. Every evening we go to the outport of Narestø, just as Captain Ferentz and his crew did when they were working on the wreck. There we meet many people who want to hear the latest news and see the finds of the day.

The small fish living on the bottom where the dig is going on have palmy days in the areas where we turn the sand for them, and occasionally an inquisitive gold sinny disappears into the air-lift. Most of them survive the airy trip and are thrown back. A cuckoo wrasse that is observing the dig at close quarters steadily finds, exactly as we do, some tidbits in the sand. Even though we work on the wreck up to 12 hours every single

day, they are good days. Thanks to the favourable depth where the artefacts lie, we have few limits on our time on the bottom. We divers alternate working shifts and spend five to six hours on the seabed every single day. Since we are all so familiar with the *Fredensborg*'s history, a number of comments are heard in reference to the objects we find. A small lady's shoe probably belonged to Mistress Møller or Mistress Wimmeløv; the inkwell to the fussy ship's clerk Hoffmann who wrote so eagerly. A jug of brandy that we find presents no threat to the further work – it contains only salt water. Those who were hoping for a mouthful of "very special old brandy" were sadly disappointed!

The few metres below the surface and down to the wreck bring us 200 years back in time. Underwater we are entirely alone with the past, and our thoughts can wander freely. Because we keep working ourselves ever deeper, below the normal ground level, we cause small sand slides constantly. This can result in objects which we have sighted being buried again. Then we must simply be patient until the sand is again removed. Even after a long dive it is difficult to tear oneself away; but with an empty air tank we have no choice. During the entire process we keep a careful check on the areas we are working in. Keilon and I do most of the diving work, well-aided by Karsten and Tore. The coordinate system on the bottom is being steadily extended and registered on the underwater chart.

*During the work with the wreck we were entirely alone with the past. Since we were familiar with the ship's grim history, the experience underwater was very special.*

The low-pressure compressor is placed on the foredeck, while the high-pressure compressor for air for the divers is on the afterdeck with the air intake in clean air. Both compressors are kept running practically all day so it is not exactly peaceful. There we divers have the advantage, because down on the bottom we hear only a little rumbling from the air lift.

Much of the hull of the *Fredensborg* was crushed when she was wrecked, a fact

which we noted during the dig. A scant half metre under the normal bottom the airlift sucks up pieces of broken ship's oak, clogging the entire system. The same thing happens in a layer farther down. In other places, fortunately, there are larger structures, but we do not find a continuous bottom section of the ship.

Visibility in the water is something that concerns all divers. Sometimes the current drives the mud from our digging right into the area of the dig. Just as in the first dig, we have to remove much stone. But unbelievable as it is, between sand, stone, and pieces of oak there always lie objects which we can bring up for registration. When the dig is finished, we have the basis for an exhibit at the

Aust-Agder Museum. Preservation of the finds is left to Ib Kjølsen, who performs small wonders with these very difficult objects which lay so long in salt water.

The objects that we found during the two digs can be divided into several groups, such as ship and equipment, cargo and personal belongings.

The *Fredensborg* was fifteen years old when she was wrecked. The hull was built of oak fastened together with oak pins. Even though Master Shipswright Ole Gad had produced a solid piece of work, it was to no avail against the storm and the southern Norwegian bedrock. In the picture we can see that a solid piece of oak timber has been cracked into pieces. There were certainly several factors which caused

*Ship's oak timber, iron fittings and tropical barnacles.*

the wreck. The bottom of the ship was covered with large tropical barnacles, popularly called "long necks". This had reduced the speed and led to somewhat sluggish handling when approaching land. Some of the larger wrought iron fittings have withstood the long stay in salt water fairly well, for then, as now, there were differences in the quality of iron.

The *Fredensborg* was armed with ten 4-pound and four 1/2-pound cast iron cannons. All the cannons except two were recovered soon after the ship was wrecked. As a result of the long stay in shallow water they were heavily corroded. The cannons had been fired when the directors of the Company were on board for dinner before departure, they were fired at a death, and again, threateningly, when slaves were being loaded on board. And the pilot from Sandøya was summoned by a cannon shot. However, battles with enemy ships did not occur on the final journey. One of the two cannons was later raised by the Norwegian Maritime Museum. The tampion in the muzzle is still in place. On one of the trunnions the letters OEC have been engraved. This was the trademark of Olov Ehrencreutz, who we know was the owner of the Swedish ironworks in 1743. The Swedish "finbankere" were standard goods in a number of countries in Northern Europe. So the Danish slave ship which was wrecked in Norway had Swedish cannons! The conservation process of the cannons was carried out by the Norwegian Maritime Museum in Oslo.

The blunderbusses, guns and pistols had flintlocks for the ignition of the primer when they were fired. The flintstones that were found in the wreck were shaped or chipped. The ship carried lead and bullet-moulds so shot could be cast as needed. The powder magazine on board was protected against fire by bricks. The cannons were mounted on a carriage having three wheels, and two of these were found together with the cannon balls.

*One of the* Fredensborg's *iron cannons in the process of conservation at the Norwegian Maritime Museum.*

A ship like the *Fredensborg* had both standing and running rig and therefore great quantities of rope, cable and tackles were needed on board. Maintenance of the sails and replacement of worn gear had to be carried on while underway. The blocks had to be extra solid in order to stand the strain, so they used sheaves of *Lingum vitae*, a tropical hardwood of great strength. Some of the single blocks were found close to one of the cannons. It is possible that they had been used to train it. The rope spliced to the blocks is not original.

*Wheels and shot for the cannons, flintstones, lead, musket balls and bricks for the powder magazine.*

The triangular piece of wood is the "log chip". In order to determine their speed they used a device made of a "log chip", a log line and an hourglass to measure time. On the line there were knots spaced at specific intervals, from which we derive the term "knot" for speed at sea. On 17 June 1768, on the way to St. Croix, Captain Ferentz ordered Cooper Mads Georg Weis to make new log chips.

Food and drink were important on board. After the fourth mate and steward Andreas Sivertsen Gadt died at sea, it was Christian Runge from Arendal who was given the responsibility for provisions, beverages and firewood. The firewood that was found was beech, and must have been on board during the entire triangular journey. Wood had been purchased on several occasions while underway, so the beech wood was probably at the bottom of the heap. The weights were used by Runge to weigh the provisions which Cook Nicolay Ørgensen had ordered for both the slaves and the crew. The largest weight had Christian V's monogram, *C5* under a crown, in relief. He had introduced a standard system of weights and measures into Denmark-Norway. It is odd that several of the weights were made of lead, which could be shaved easily so one could cheat on the weight. This implies that the weights were used on board to weigh provisions, and not in trade. Like the powder magazine, the stove was enclosed in bricks. The danger of fire on board was a constant threat on a sailing ship.

*Blocks, sheaves, cables and log chip.*

Chief Curator Pirjo Lahtiperä at the Zoological Museum in Bergen has analysed the bones found in the wreck. Provisions on the ship included salted meat in barrels, and the analysis shows that they had beef and veal on board. In other barrels there was mutton from animals aged 10 to 18 months. Pork was also there, although it appears that the chops were cut away on one side before being salted. The best cuts were most often not used for the ship's provisions. The pigs were between one and two years old when slaughtered.

While the officers refreshed themselves with fine quality drinks at meals, the rest of the crew had to be satisfied with brandy of a cheaper quality. Brandy was also used as medicine. The large brandy casks probably belonged in the cabin. Many

*Bones from the ship's provisions, weights, barrel staves, firewood and bricks for the oven.*

broken bottles were found in the wreckage, both ordinary round bottles and square "canteen" bottles with short necks. The latter were usually kept in a "flaskefor", a portable case with dividers for square bottles, so they could stand steady. The round bottles had probably contained rum from the West Indies. Many of the bottles had been full at the time of the wreck because the corks were still in place in the necks. Remains of drinking glasses and a punch bowl were also found.

The dinner service was light grey English stoneware from Staffordshire, with a relief pattern. They had both

flat and deep plates and a few bowls on board. Also found were parts of a teapot of "Egyptian style", from Whieldon-Wedgewood c. 1755–1758. The German beer stein is made of grey stoneware with blue and red decor. The officers used coffee cups and saucers and platter of Chinese export. The blue pattern depicts chrysanthemums, birds, a decorative band, etc. A complete china platter was brought up. It is unsigned and has a simple blue decorative border whose style dates it to 1730–1740. It has not been possible to determine whether it is from the factory in Store Kongensgade in Copenhagen, or from another factory.

*Brandy jug, plates, bottles, a beer stein, chinaware, a glass and a teapot, a knife handle and a spoon. Leather binding for a prayer-book and a psalter, an inkwell, a slate and medicine bottles.*

There was not room for a ship's chaplain on board the *Fredensborg*, but as we have seen, the captain, according to instructions, was to hold a prayer service morning and evening for the crew. Before departure the Board of Directors sent on board twelve extra prayer books "for the purpose of spiritual healing". The bindings of a prayer book and a psalter were found in the wreck, but the written words have been swallowed by the sea. The small brass clasps of the psalter have a design in relief of angels – so-called cherubs – blowing on horns. Ship's Assistant Hoffmann conscientiously wrote down everything that happened on board. Had

he dipped his quill into this inkwell? Writing on the slate, which was broken into several pieces, was done by a slate pencil. The quills shown in the picture are of a later date.

Tools were important on board, and were guarded carefully. A whetstone was necessary to keep the tools sharp. In order to open the strands in splicing rope a fid was used. As we have seen, things were very difficult for the ship's carpenter when Kock, Beck and Hæglund died on the Gold Coast. This little planer has undoubtedly passed from hand to hand before it sank into the depths. Cleanliness was also important. During the voyage from Africa to the West Indies the slave hold had to be constantly scraped and cleaned out.

Then it was good to have brooms on board. Oakum was used to caulk the seams, which were later payed with pitch.

Ivory was a common article in the hold of the slave ships. Both elephant and hippopotamus tusks were found. Most of them were in surprisingly good condition, but some had been broken. When the ivory was loaded on board on the Gold Coast, Captain Ferentz wrote "42 Elephant tusks and 43 creveller" in his journal. The total weight was 1,855.5 pounds, or 927.75 kg. Crevelle is the term used to indicate small tusks weighing 6 to 7 kg or less. Ivory was used for many things, such as combs, knife handles, intarsia

*Plane, whetstone, diverse handles, broom, oakum and a wedge.*

work, sewing articles, and keys for the spinet, cembalo and clavichord. Doctor Sixtus on the *Fredensborg* had a small ivory syringe with him. Ivory was also popular for the carving of decorative objects. Hippopotamus tusks, which are extremely hard, were used, among other things, for false teeth. Immediately after the wreck occurred, 17 elephant tusks were salvaged. A total of 51 small and large elephant tusks and 13 hippopotamus tusks were found in the wreck. The find, together with broken tusks, totals close to the complete cargo.

Among the articles in the cargo from St. Croix, besides sugar, tobacco, cotton

*Elephant and hippopotamus tusks from the Gold Coast.*

*Mahogany and dye-wood from St. Croix.*

*Shoes, parts of shoes, textiles and tropical shells.*

and cinnamon, there were great quantities of dyewood and 300 mahogany planks. During the dig we found much dyewood and one plank of mahogany. This was of the rare sort known as Cuba mahogany, which was used for fine cabinet work in the eighteenth century. The mahogany was well-suited to the elegant and slender forms used in rococo styles. The dyewood, *Haematoxylon campecheanum*, had withstood the long stay in salt water surprisingly well. As we saw from a trial extraction of colour from the dyewood, it was still effective after 209 years underwater. There was no noticeable difference in a comparison made with fresh dyewood. During the dig the deck of the *Capri* became coloured by the dyewood as it was brought up. The old sailor's method of using lemon juice to bleach colour worked satisfactorily.

The three most important plant colour materials are indigo, alizarin and haematoxylin, which is extracted from dyewood. This particular, and important, variety of wood is known by many names, among them logwood, blue wood, Campeche-wood, and Brazil-wood. In the days of Marco Polo, Brazil-wood from the East was known in Europe. In 1500, when Cabral discovered the east coast of South America with its great forests of that special tree, he called the new land "Terra de Brazil". Dyewood also grows in other places around the Gulf of Mexico, among others on the Campeche coast of the Yucatan peninsula. Dyewood was also imported to the North. At the beginning of the seventeenth century Christian IV established a gaol in Farvergade in Copenhagen. This institution was popularly called "Raspehuset" (Grating House). The reason for this was that early in the eighteenth century special cells were designated where physically strong criminals were put to work grating dyewood – a difficult and unhealthy occupation. The grated wood was allowed to ferment in large, damp rooms before use. Dyewood was also used for furniture, but never became popular among the cabinet makers because of its hardness which made it difficult to work. This variety of wood was also used to make ink, and for various other purposes.

*A whistle, a spur, buttons, brushes, buckles, a lid for a tobacco box, a thimble, etc.*

There were shoes, parts of shoes, and textiles. A kerchief, which had been blue-checked white, may have come from the supply of Captain Kiønig's "trade goods", or from a sea chest. There were also the remains of homespun and raw silk. The smallest shoes were lady's shoes. They must have belonged to one of the female passengers. The largest man's shoe is well-preserved and has a finely worked pewter buckle. Could Captain Ferentz have "walked out of his shoes" during the wreck?

Even though some of the sea chests were saved during the wreck, there were those on board who lost everything they owned. Captain Kiønig played the violin and another crew member played the flute. Incredibly, part of that thin wooden flute was found. The officers usually wore knee pants with buckles, but the rest of the crew wore long trousers. We found many buttons. Light-coloured buttons were used for underwear and work clothes, while buttons of shell and metal were for finer clothing. Many of the buttons were simply for decoration, following the fashion of the day. The brass lid for a tobacco box is from the Netherlands and is marked with a log table for determining speed. A spinning top was undoubtedly used to pass the time when the men were free. Among the many small things there were a spur, a brush, cuff links, a key and a thimble. A lid for a needle case, or something similar, is marked with the initials P M K. – this might have belonged to Able Seaman Peder Madsen, København (Copenhagen).

The find of an oval box made of wood shavings was interesting. The measurements of the box were 19.3 x 9.6 x 6.7 cm. Everyone watched excitedly while the lid was removed. What could be hidden in this box? It proved to be buttons, buckles, cuff links, a pencil divided into two, writing chalk, a slate pencil, sewing thread, wax for the thread, a musket ball, a piece of flintstone for a gun, a few coins and an even

*Box containing coins,*
*buttons, cuff links,*
*flint, lead ball,*
*thread, wax, seals*
*and sealing wax, etc.*

smaller box. The coins, 18 in all, were very corroded and some of them were difficult to identify. They were identified by Chief Curator Bjørn R. Rønning at the University Coin Cabinet in Oslo. They proved to be from Spain and Ireland. The Spanish coins had been minted during the reigns of Philp IV, Philip V and Carlos II. The
Irish coins were minted during the reigns of George II and George III. The
youngest of the coins were from 1766, just two years before the *Fredensborg* was
wrecked.

In the smaller box there were two pieces of red sealing wax and two signets.
One was of brass and octagonal. Within a border of a pearl-like decoration the initials TBM were engraved in a mirror-image monogram under a marquis crown. A
signet is a very personal belonging and usually bears the initials of the owner.

The other signet is beautifully formed in rococo style with a handle of gilded
brass. It is fastened to a stone engraved with a dove holding an olive branch in its
beak. The text which is written on the seal is extraordinarily interesting for a find
from the wreck of a slave ship: PEACE & LOVE!

The use of a signet is very old. It served a mark of authencity and meant that one
guarded one's signet very carefully. The signet was often destroyed upon the death
of its owner, or placed with him in the grave. In the *Fredensborg*'s time the signet was
used principally to seal letters, and accompanied the owner's signature on formal
documents. As we recall, the gold which Ferentz brought with him from Africa was
sealed. The signet followed the owner, as a ring or on a ribbon around his neck.
Both signets from the *Fredensborg* have a hole in the top for such a ribbon, but they

lay in a box during the wreck. Who could have owned such signets? The initials do not fit any of those we have come to know who were on board. Could the box have belonged to a passenger, or been freight?

Karsten Bundgaard, who participated in the last of the digs, has put in a great deal of work in trying to discover the owner. Thomas Bordeaux Malleville, who was commander on St. Thomas in 1773, and later became governor, has been suggested as a possible owner, since the initials fit. Because the signet with the dove has an English text, Bundgaard continued his search in England. The Jessop and Hodson families both had a dove with an olive branch on their family shields, but they used the motto in Latin, *Pax & Amor*. The Hodson family was an Irish branch of the Jessop family, and the several coins which were from Ireland point in their direction. There were many plantation owners from Ireland in the West Indies.

In the wreck were found two special bones. They had no connection with the ship's provisions, as did the others which had been brought up. These bones, too, were analysed at the University in Bergen. One of them is from a water chevrotain, the other from a peacock.

*These beautiful signets withstood the long stay in sea water surprisingly well.*

The water chevrotain, *Hyemoschus aquaticus*, an animal the size of a cat, lives near water in the rain forest in an area stretching from Sierra Leone to Uganda. It is the smallest of the antelopes, very shy and difficult to catch sight of. It is a good swimmer, and can swim underwater. The peacock, *Pavo cristatus*, was not common on the Gold Coast, but there are descriptions of it in books about West Africa. Peacocks were found in the West Indies. Both of these bones are leg bones.

Since only one of each kind was found, and in the same area of the wreck, one might speculate about why they were there. The *Fredensborg* was a slave ship, and it is not beyond the bounds of reason to think that one, or both, bones come from an amulet or "fetish". The zoologist Dr. Chris Gordon, from the University at Legon in Ghana, informs us that the water chevrotain is common in that country, among other places at River Volta. He does not rule out the possibility of such an animal having been taken to Europe as a curiosity. Professor Nkrumah at the National Museum in Ghana, however, was of the opinion that the bones could have belonged to a talisman or amulet. The Adomehene Apea Kwasi III, in the Akwamu area of Ghana, told me that bones were commonly in use in amulets. They were tied together and hung around the neck, the upper arm, or in a belt.

In the traditional religions in Africa amulets were in use right up to our day. They were meant to protect the bearer from danger and evil spirits, to bring good fortune, or have other effects. The slaves were not permitted to bring amulets on board the slave ships, and they were usually torn off the bearer and thrown away. It

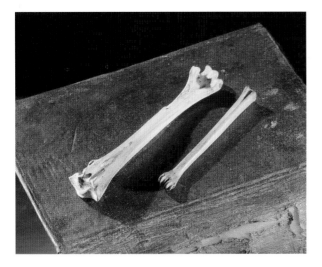

*Bones from water chevrotain and peacock.*

is not inconceivable, however, that such an object could have been smuggled aboard the *Fredensborg*, and hidden.

One of the most interesting finds from the wreck is an African stone mortar, or rubbing stone, made of sandstone. The measurements are 40 x 25 x 23 cm. The mortar is well-used and has a faint golden-brown colour. A round stone was used for grinding. Researchers in St. Croix, in the U.S.A. and in Ghana have shown great interest in the find of that stone and its use on board. Captain Ferentz himself provided the answer to the use of the mortar when he described them as "millie stones". The grain variety "millie" – possibly millet – was part of the slave diet. Two of the three stones that were taken on board were salvaged from the wreck.

The clay pipes, or so-called Negro pipes, which were given to the slaves were stored in barrels on board. They were of a cheap quality, and certainly inexpensive to purchase. Some of the heads of the clay pipes that were found in great quantities are marked "J.B." They are of Norwegian production and were produced by Jacob Boy in Drammen. Boy's factory was the only Norwegian clay pipe factory in operation from 1752–1770. According to the regulations, slaves were given one pipe per week. They were given tobacco every day except Saturday, which was "smoke-free".

Because of extreme corrosion many of the iron objects have been destroyed by rust. But some imprints in the corrosion lumps bear witness to their silent history. This applies to the slaves' foot irons – the prime tool of deprivation of freedom.

*Imprint of the slaves' foot irons, slave pipes and African stone mortar or rubbing stone.*

CHAPTER 10

# *From Tromøy to St. Croix*

I N THE REMAINS OF THE ONCE PROUD FRIGATE we had discovered objects that represented not only the unique society on board but also the gravity of the entire triangular trade. Thanks to these – and the journals of the captain and the ship's
assistant – we gained good insight into the conditions on board a slave ship. The
unmistakable outlines of the slaves' foot irons created an even stronger impression.
They were powerful reminders that, despite all the objects we had excavated from
the depths, the slave trade was first and foremost a question of human beings – of
the seamen who sailed to earn their living, and even more so of the African men,
women and children who were the victims of slavery. I soon realized that my work
with the *Fredensborg* had not ended with the final excavations. From the wreck, the
ephemeral wake of a ship could be traced back to distant waters. We had found and
examined the *Fredensborg,* but what remained of historical relics in the other places
where the ship had called during its final voyage? A plan was beginning to take
shape. I wanted to retrace the route of the *Fredensborg,* in a "reverse triangular trade."

It is very time consuming to penetrate into the past. I did not feel like stopping
with the sale of the slaves that took place in the Company's courtyard in the summer
of 1768. Would it be possible to continue following some of the slaves to specific
plantations? As luck would have it, in the Danish National Archives in Copenhagen
a very important ledger has been preserved in which the agent of the Guinea Company, Carl H. Thalbitzer, had duly recorded the sales of the slaves from the *Fredensborg.* The names of the buyers were listed along with the number and price, but one
important bit of information was lacking: Thalbitzer knew the buyers so well that he
did not find it necessary to write down the names or addresses of the plantations.

Again the Archives came to my rescue: here was to be found a census, a so-
called land register. It had been taken on St. Croix in 1768–69, in other words, at
exactly the right time for me. As coincidence would have it, Ferdinand August
Charisius, one of the two men responsible for taking the census, had later moved
to Arendal where he became a customs inspector. His exotic daughter Anna
Sophie, who was called "the Creole", married one of Arendal's richest merchants

*Christiansted with Fort Christiansvern to the left. After it was taken over by the government, the city entered a period of expansion during which a number of new buildings were erected.*

and shipowners, Anders Sørensen Dedekam. They built the magnificent house Sophienlund on Tromøy, the same island where the *Fredensborg* went down.

Charisius' census became the key document that enabled me to proceed. In those days St. Croix was divided into nine zones, or so-called quarters, with different names like the King's Quarter, the Queen's Quarter, the Company's Quarter, etc. To my good fortune, the quarters, in turn, were divided into smaller plots that were numbered. Now it was easy, and my detailed map of St. Croix received small spots of colour on the correct places. The plantations where the slaves from the *Fredensborg* ended up after the sale were found on the map, but was there anything left of them on our former colonial islands in the West Indies?

With a piece of dyewood, a copy of Oxholm's old map of St. Croix, and a well-documented history in my luggage, I set out in 1982 with my brother Tore on the first stage in the wake of the *Fredensborg*. It is an exciting moment as we approach St. Croix in a tiny seaplane at a height that must correspond to the top of the *Fredensborg*'s main mast. And now we are standing there, gazing over the roadstead where the slave ships unloaded their live cargo. The view of the harbour appears familiar from the old drawings that I have examined so thoroughly. There is the yellow Fort Christiansvern with its many cannons, and the old weighing house is still standing. Protestant Cay, just outside the harbour, still shelters the inner basin where the slave cargo was exchanged for good colonial products.

We walk towards the old customs house, the residence of Inspector of Customs Porthe, whom I know so well from Thalbitzer's journal. He was quite a speculator. Further up the street I can see the steeple of the old Lutheran church, pointing at a blazing sun. We go up to the church, on the same path taken by the seamen from the *Fredensborg* when they went to hear the Word of God instead of the moaning of the slaves. The church, now called the "Steeple Building", was built by the West

India Guinea Company at the same time as the *Fredensborg*. Both the ship and the church were put into use in the year of our Lord 1753.

St. Croix is not a large island. However, with a length of 168 km and a width of about 8 km, it is still the largest of our three old islands in the West Indies. St. Thomas is about 70 km farther to the north, along with St. Jan which is now called St. John. Our former West Indian colonies cover a total area of about 504 square km, and are situated at about 18 degrees north latitude. They have a tropical climate.

St. Croix has a variable landscape. On the west side of the island there are mountains and valleys, and a luxuriant rain forest that levels off to the south in flat, fertile fields. The highest mountains, Blue Mountain and Mount Eagle, are not quite 400 m high. On the east side, where the fields are less productive, St. Croix ends almost in a tip that points towards Africa. Christiansted, the capital, is situated on the coast on the north side of the island, while Frederiksted, the other town, is all the way over on the west end.

Columbus encountered St. Croix and all the other islands in these waters during his second voyage in 1493. He named them "The Virgin Islands" after the Blessed St. Ursula and her "11,000 virgins". Columbus was not given a favourable reception when his men went ashore at Salt River and were attacked by Carib Indian inhabitants. But in spite of this, the island received the name "Santa Cruz" which means "The Holy Cross". In the course of its history this beautiful island was owned by a succession of nations – Spain, the Netherlands, England and France. Indeed, even the famous Knights of Malta were its owners for a time. In 1733 St. Croix was purchased from France by the Royal Chartered Danish Guinea Company in Copenhagen, and later, in 1755, the island became a Crown Colony along with St. Thomas and St. Jan.

Christiansted is a charming little town which contains many buildings of historical and architectural interest. Most of them are situated adjacent to the old harbour area. The street plan bears witness to a regulated development, and here are Kongens Gade (King's Street), Dronningens Gade (Queen's Street), Prindzens Gade (Prince's Street), Strand Gaden (Strand Street), Torve Gaden (Market Street), Kirke Gaden (Church Street), Fisker Gaden (Fisherman's Street). Only the name "Neger-Gottet" (Negro Gutter) stands apart on Charisius' list, a reminder that we are far from home waters.

A wooden colonial-style building, with shuttered windows, is the goal of our first walk through the streets. A sign informs us that we have come to "The Division for Archaeology and Historic Preservation". We introduce ourselves and ask hesitantly whether anyone is familiar with the old plantations on the island.

Not long afterwards we are seated around a table on a terrace in Hill Street, with Barbara Hagan-Smith and William Chapman. She is an archivist, working on the history of the island and matters of preservation, while he is a specialist in historical architecture. The two have extensive knowledge about the old buildings and plantations, and listen attentively while we tell our story about the *Fredensborg*. When we spread out Oxholm's map on the large marble table, and tell them what we know about the sale of the slaves and the plantations where the slaves ended up, they become very excited. "This is the first time we are able to establish a direct connection between a known Company ship and the plantations here on the

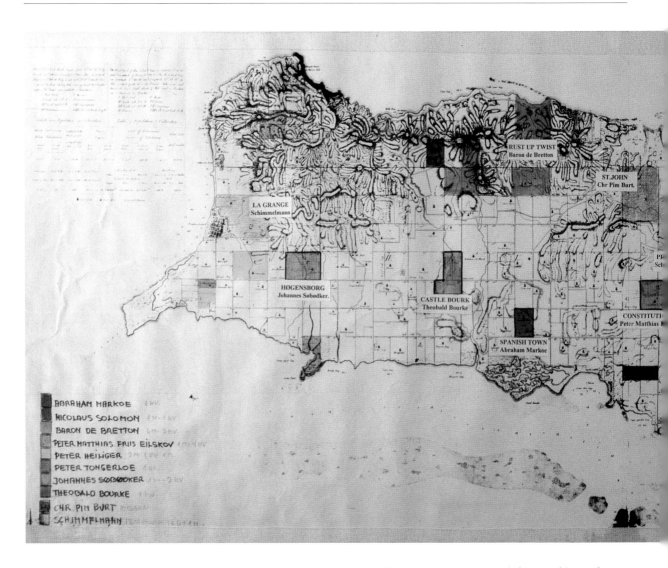

island," says Barbara. We are promised all the assistance we might need in order to find the places we would like to visit.

It is a short walk down to the Company's yellow-painted building where Thalbitzer lived. In front of the facade facing the harbour, there is a courtyard surrounded by high walls. We stop inside the walls, and I look down at the dry sand. How many thousands of black feet stood here, while the bids came thick and fast during the auctions? How many little children's feet left their mark on sand wet with tears, as merciless buyers wrenched them out of their mothers' hands? How many buyers selected a suitable victim in order to satisfy their physical needs? I am relieved that I will never learn the answer.

So this is where the slaves from the *Fredensborg* filed in through the gate. They all wore loincloths of blue cotton and glistened with palm oil. The "goods" had been made ready for sale; they had eaten their fill and had been given brandy and tobacco. Inside the building Captain Ferentz sat with Hoffmann, Sixtus, Beck and Runge, discussing the sale with Thalbitzer. Actually, there was not much to discuss because, again, the Company's instructions, written in Copenhagen, explained what was to be done: "Whereas the manner of selling the slaves cannot be accu-

*The slaves from the Fredensborg ended up in many places on St. Croix. Some of the buyers had slaves scattered on several plantations, others had them collected in one place. Here we can see Abraham Markoe's "Spanish Town", Johannes Søbødker's "Høgensborg", Theobald Bourke's "Castle Bourk", Peter Matthias Friis Eilskov's "Constitution Hill", Christian Pim Burt's "St. John" and Peter Tongerlo's plantation.*

rately determined here, because it depends on the time and the circumstances, the Captain must leave it entirely in the hands of the Company's Commissioners to sell the slaves in the best possible manner. (…) In order to turn this to the best account for the Company, we regard it to be the most favourable method that the entire cargo of slaves, as many as are healthy, whether male, female, boys or girls, is sold to a single buyer, one who is generally known to be well-established and satisfactory, or also that they be sold to several honest and well-established buyers." It is obvious that the worthy gentlemen in Copenhagen preferred a private sale to an auction, regarding the sale of both slaves and other kinds of goods: "…in general, none of the Company's goods there on the island shall be sold at public auction unless the circumstances make this imperative."

Four days before the official sale began, seven prime-quality male slaves were sold to His Majesty for 225 rixdaler apiece. In all probability these men were to work for the authorities, and were called "His Majesty's Negroes". The high price indicates that these were first-class goods, but then, his Majesty's representative was allowed to choose first. On the same day Governor General Clausen secured for himself four male slaves at 200 rixdaler apiece, and one girl slave at 120 rixdaler.

Thalbitzer had written a placard with the following text that had been put up in several suitable places:

"SIR:

I take the liberty of informing you that on Monday next at nine o'clock I shall begin to dispose of, by private sale, the cargo of Gold Coast slaves I have lately imported, under the following conditions:

Those who purchase fewer than ten slaves are to pay the whole in six weeks, & those who purchase ten or above, are to pay half in six weeks, & the remainder on or before 10 April next year.

The further particulars to be in agreement with the obligations in the already printed standard contract which are in force with each purchase. If payment is not immediately forthcoming the buyer shall provide a written guarantee. Sugar shall be acceptable as security.

C. Thalbitzer"

The great day arrived and people came flocking, some in horse-drawn wagons, some on foot, others in boats from St. Thomas. At 9 o'clock in the morning the gate was opened. Since this was not an auction there must have been a flurry of activity when the buyers inspected the slaves. First, the best-looking slaves were chosen, and thereafter followed a "health check". Their age and strength were judged, they had to skip and jump, their teeth were examined and many a blue loincloth was removed. They had to stand there naked, and were inspected before the decision was made and the price decided on.

There must have been a brisk trade in the Company's courtyard on that day. Everyone wanted to secure the best slaves for himself, and with many eager buyers present good prices were easy to obtain. Thalbitzer dipped his quill in ink and wrote prices and conditions in his ledger as the slaves were sold:

| | | |
|---|---|---|
| 18/7 1768 | 16 m 2 b | à 230 rdl. to Ludv. H. Schimmelman |
| | 9 m 5 f | à 230 rdl. to John Jacob de Wint |
| | 2 g | à 230 rdl. to Gregory Hoeg Nielsen |
| | 2 b 1 g | à 227.5 rdl. to Jacob Linberg |
| | 2 m 1 f 1b | à 230 rdl. to Peter Heyliger |
| | 5 m | à 220 rdl. to Nicolaus Solomon |
| | 10 m | à 230 rdl. to Geurt Spre de Wint |
| | 1 m | à 230 rdl. to Alexander Mark |
| | 1 m 4 f | à 215 rdl. to Friis Eilskov |
| | 1 m 1 g | à 220 rdl. to John Latoyionen |
| | 1 g | à 220 rdl. to Michael Hamrah |
| | 1 m | à 230 rdl. to Samuel Newton |
| | 1 f | à 220 rdl. to August Darius |
| | 1 f | à 215 rdl. to Peter Tongerlo |
| | 1 f | à 220 rdl. to Maria Elizabeth |

(m=male, b=boy,  f=female, g=girl)

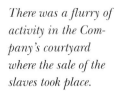

*There was a flurry of activity in the Company's courtyard where the sale of the slaves took place.*

First in line was Heinrich Ludvig von Schimmelmann. He had just arrived in the West Indies to manage the plantations of his uncle, Minister of Finance Count Heinrich Carl Schimmelmann. On St. Croix he was responsible for the two plantations: "La Grange" at Frederiksted and "The Princess" at Christiansted. There was a constant need for new labourers on the two large plantations, and this must have been his first purchase of slaves. Apart from this he did very well for himself, and by the very next year he became a member of the Privy Council on St. Croix. Throughout his career he held many positions of trust, and ended as Governor-General with the rank of Major General in 1785. He was known to treat the black population quite humanely, which was certainly an advantage to the 18 slaves he purchased from the *Fredensborg*.

When the day was over, Thalbitzer quickly summed up the results. The auction had lived up to his expectations; the sale of the slaves had amounted to 15,672.5 rixdaler. The interest in good prices was not limited to the Company alone. The Captain and certain other members of the crew eagerly kept themselves posted, since they were entitled to a percentage of the selling price. The slaves' food, which was prepared on board the *Fredensborg*, was brought ashore twice a day. As the slaves were sold and there were fewer who had to be fed, things gradually became easier for Nicolay Ørgensen, the cook, and Christian Runge who were responsible for the provisions.

Among the buyers on the first day was Captain Peter Tongerloe, a "free Negro" who owned a little plantation on a hillside overlooking Christiansted. Tongerloe had done well; he had nine slaves and was also the owner of a fine house in the town. As we can see, he purchased a female slave who had been sold by an African

on the Gold Coast, and now she had been bought by a black man on St. Croix. Maria Elizabeth, who was a free Mulatto and lived alone in a house on Kongens Tvergade, also bought a female.

On the following days the sale was slower, and the buyers had more time to inspect the goods before they agreed on the price. The quill scratched against the paper, and constantly new names and figures were entered in the ledger:

| 19/7 1768 | 1 m 2 f | à 650 rdl to Johannes Søbødker |
| | 1 f | à 200 rdl to Theobald Bourke |
| | 1 f | à 215 rdl to Abraham Markoe |
| | 1 f | à 225 rdl to John Sullivan |
| 20/7 1768 | 4 m 1 b 2 g | à 215 rdl to James Kennedy |
| 21/7 1768 | 1 m | à 220 rdl to Edwad Beach |
| 22/7 1768 | 5 m 1 f | à 220 rdl to Nicolaus Solomon |

After another five days it was all over. The final entries in Thalbitzer's ledger read as follows:

*Heinrich Ludwig Ernst Schimmelmann was 25 years old when he purchased 18 slaves from the Fredensborg for his plantations "La Grange" and "The Princess" on St. Croix. He later became Governor-General and a Major General before he died in 1793, at the age of 50.*
*From a painting at the Museum of National History at Fredriksborg.*

| 23/7 1768 | 10 children age 5 -8 | à 120 rdl to Ch. Pim Burt |
| | 1 m | à 200 rdl to Hegidius Henning |
| 24/7 1768 | 6 m 2 f | à 200 rdl to Baron de Bretton |
| 25/7 1768 | 35 m 36 f 6 g 7 b | à 160 rdl to Puerto Rico |
| 25/7 1768 | 14 m 1 b 7 f sick | à 55 rdl to Cust. Insp. Porthe |
| 27/7 1768 | 2 f  sick | à 80 rdl to John Johnsen |
| | 3 m | à 230 rdl to Lt. Thrønn |

I can see before me Charles Pim Burt as he evaluates the remaining children of the *Fredensborg* slaves, and goes around with a critical eye before he makes his choice. Was his wife Petronella with him? Was an economic motive the sole consideration behind the purchase of the ten between the ages of 5 and 8, or could he have had nobler intentions of giving the little ones a good childhood and adolescence? He had to pay 1 200 riksdaler, a considerable amount. When fully grown they might be worth twice as much, and they could work all the time as they were growing up. It must have been quite a sight as he went out of the gate with the flock of children at his heels.

Charles Pim Burt was the owner of the St. John's Plantation not far from Christiansted; the children had a short walk to their new "home". On the way they passed the Princess Plantation where some of their "fellow passengers" from the *Fredensborg* had already arrived. All of the little children had been separated from their parents but perhaps some of their parents might have ended up at the neighbouring plantation. A closer scrutiny of "Massa Burt" reveals a clearer motive: He wanted to secure manpower for himself. Burt was one of the largest landowners in the Queen's quarter, where he had a plantation comprising four tracts of land. He himself lived in Christiansted, which was customary for the plantation owners. This made life more agreeable. Not a single "Blank" or white person was listed as a resident of the plantation. But Burt had slaves, many slaves. All told they amounted to

217, almost an entire shipload! There were 164 able-bodied adults; he had 20 adolescents, and then there were all the children. St. John's was swarming with children! Charisius' census, dated 10 January, the year following the slave sale, lists a total of 33 children under the age of 12. In addition there might be 10 youngsters from the *Fredensborg*, if they were all still alive. Children and adolescents made up around one-fourth of Burt's "stock" of slaves.

It must be added that Burt was in good company, because there were also large numbers of children on the neighbouring plantations. A little long-term planning was necessary in order to guarantee a continuous availability of labour, because the life expectancy was short among the slaves on the Danish-Norwegian islands in the West Indies.

The largest buyer was Don Riera who owned plantations on Puerto Rico, another of the Caribbean Islands. A total of 84 slaves were sent there by boat. The good Puerto Rican tobacco which the *Fredensborg* carried on the return voyage was probably a part of the payment. Three of the deck slaves had been sold to a buyer in Copenhagen. The sale had been arranged by a lieutenant on the royal barque. The three, who had been given the names "Samson", "Oliver" and "Roland", were sent on the *Fredensborg*. Finally, there were all the sick slaves, usually called "trash slaves", who according to the instructions were supposed to be sold: "Of the dregs that must be found among this cargo of slaves, including the sick, the blind or the infirm, it is to be understood that they must not be sold before the healthy slaves have been sold and fetched." Customs Inspector Porthe took a chance when he purchased fourteen sick male slaves, one sick boy and seven sick females. Transportation over to the Customs House was short, as he was the neighbour of the Company's manor. He was probably hoping that as many as possible would survive their illness.

Chamberlain Johannes Søbødker secured for himself one male and two females

*Thalbitzer, the Company's agent who was German, kept an accurate record of the sale of the slaves. Here we see that Abraham Markoe was given the choice of paying 215 rixdaler cash or good sugar for a female slave.*

for his plantation, Høgensborg. In addition to his position as Chamberlain he also made a great deal of money running the plantation. On the plantation, not very far from Frederiksted, there were four whites, 87 male slaves, seventeen female slaves, three adolescents and 26 children under the age of twelve. The slave owners had to pay an annual tax to the authorities for each slave. However, the newly arrived slaves, who were called "bosal" slaves, were exempt from tax the first year. Chamberlain Søbødker now had eighteen bosal slaves on his plantation.

We visit Søbødker's plantation and clear a path through bushes and underbrush, which become thicker and thicker. Barbara goes first, stopping frequently to orient herself. There is a special atmosphere under the heavy leaf canopy, and I feel a grim past very near-at-hand.

The ruins of a stone building emerge in the underbrush. Barbara points and whispers that this is all that remains of Søbødker's mansion. She wants to show us a beautiful name plate which is supposed to hang over one of the doors, but it turns out that it has been broken off and stolen. It has probably been sold for a few dollars.

The tropical forest is taking over Søbødker's plantation, which has fallen into a state of considerable disrepair. Some of the details in the mansion are easily recognizable from a watercolour by Frederik von Scholten. There is no mistaking the characteristic stairways and the arched windows on the facade. I look through one of the windows and give a sudden start. Do I hear the laughter of festively dressed guests enjoying good food and drink, waited on by humble servants? No, I have arrived at

*The town of Frederiksted, with the vessels in the roadstead, seen from the north. On the fields below the artist the slaves are busy harvesting. The La Grange Plantation in the middle of the picture belonged to the Schimmelmann entailed estate. It is possible that some slaves from the* Fredensborg *ended up here.*

*Unlike the slaves, the Søbødker family lived according to their station. This drawing, from Frederik von Scholten's sketchbook, is from June 1838, 70 years after 1 male and 2 female slaves from the* Fredensborg *ended their long and involuntary journey on this plantation.*

the party more than 200 years too late – it was a bird cackling in the underbrush where the ballroom used to be.

We continue walking, and further on we can see a circle of black in the green underbrush. It turns out to be Søbødker's overturned sugar cauldron. The huge iron cauldron could probably contain thousands of litres. How many hours of work did it take to fill up the cauldron with cane juice, again and again, year after year? It was a long process before the cane juice ran down into the cauldron. One of Søbødker's predecessors, Chamberlain Reimert Haagensen, has given us some idea of conditions on a sugar plantation:

"Every morning around 3 or 4 a.m. on all the plantations, a shell is blown. It is shaped like a snail shell, but is exceedingly large and produces a sound like someone blowing a horn, which the Blacks must obey, whereupon they must get up at once and go out in the fields, even though it is still dark.

First the slaves cut a load of grass each, which they carry back to the house on their heads as fodder for the animals. Then each one makes his way out in the field to his work. The 'Bomba' (or overseer) follows them with his long whip in his hand, and when they do not work hard enough he gives them 10-12 hard lashes."

The field slaves had the hardest work, as they stood side by side digging holes in the ground for the cuttings. The holes had to be fertilized and the cuttings planted. A working day of 10 to 12 hours in the blazing sun took its toll. Judging from the number of slaves, they probably had at least two Bombas at Høgensborg. As a rule these were big, husky blacks who were given better clothes and other advantages for swinging the whip and taking care of the interests of the plantation

*The slave houses were well concealed in the dense vegetation at Høgensborg. Barbara Hagan-Smith believed they were from the 18th century, very likely from the Fredensborg's time. The roof reveals that the huts have been in use more recently.*

*A special iron collar, with projecting rods and hooks, was fastened around the neck of a slave who repeatedly tried to run away. This made it difficult to move through the fields of sugar cane and the underbrush.*

owner. After a period of growth of 14 to 15 months the sugar plant turns yellow and is ready to be harvested. The sugar cane is cut with a knife called a "kapmesser", and driven to the windmill.

The harvesting period was extra hard for the slaves. The trade winds drove the wind sails around, and the three large iron rollers pressed the juice out of the sugar cane. The slave who stood in front of the mill had a considerable advantage, because then the cane was stiff and easy to handle. After being crushed between the rollers it was limp, and difficult for the slave at the back of the mill to get hold of, and send back in order to press out the final drops of juice. Sometimes an exhausted slave would catch his hand between the rollers. For this reason a broad-bladed knife and a sharp-edged axe were hanging in the mill, which were used to quickly cut off the unfortunate slave's arm.

How many times had the juice that ran down into Søbødker's great cauldron in the cook-house been a little redder than it should have been? That made no difference. The sugar was boiled and evaporated before it ended up in big, heavy barrels that filled up the holds of the ships. Syrup and rum were other products connected with the production of sugar. The strong, newly-distilled rum was aptly named "kill devil".

Barbara leads the way through the thick forest and underbrush. Up in the trees we can see black termite nests and hanging lianas. The huge sugar factory chimney is visible amid the foliage. Suddenly I catch sight of a row of slave huts ahead of me. They are dilapidated, but are still standing with their black doorways. I quietly go inside and look around. The walls are made of coral stone. There are no windows. Were these wretched huts standing here when 1 male and 2 female slaves from the *Fredensborg* came to their new "home" at Høgensborg? Now the earthen floor is covered with leaves. In those days there were probably straw mats here. Children were born here, and others died. According to Chamberlain Haagensen: "A slave's life is one of servitude. (…) When he dies, that same evening, without the slightest ceremony, he is thrown into a hole in the ground, without a coffin and without further ado."

Many slaves were unable to cope with the transition to a life of toil. Some committed suicide; others ran away. This was called "running maroon". Maroon Mountain, out by the coast to the north of Høgensborg, was an inaccessible area. This was where the runaway slaves fled, and they defended their paths, among other things, with sharp pointed staves of poisonous wood. In 1770 the newspaper *The Royal Danish American Gazette* appeared. "RUN AWAY" announcements were customary in the newspaper's columns, which might also provide a logogram depicting a running slave.

Severe punishment was meted out to the runaways who were caught. The whip was frequently used, and those who repeatedly tried to run away were usually equipped with a special iron collar with projecting rods that ended in hooks. This made it difficult to escape through the fields of cane and underbrush. Charisius' census reveals that in 1768 there were 18,002 slaves and 1,837 whites and "free Negroes" on St. Croix. Thus it was not strange that the fear of a dangerous uprising prevailed. A planned rebellion that was exposed in 1759 led to several executions after extensive torture. The bailiff in Christiansted who pronounced judgement was Engelbret Hesselberg, a Norwegian. On St. Jan, the Akwamu slave known as "King June" went even further with his "evil intentions". He and his people killed large numbers of the population on the island in 1733. To the whites this was a brutal slave revolt, to the enslaved Africans a desperate struggle for freedom.

It is not far from Høgensborg to the tropical forest. We are searching for dyewood. Is there anything left of this special wood that was such an important part of the *Fredensborg*'s cargo? When it comes to size and appearance, the contrast between our Northern varieties of wood and tropical species is considerable. After searching for a time the unmistakable dyewood trunks appear before us. The trunk has a grooved surface just like the many logs we found in the wreck. A sample

*The punishment of slaves for running away, or other offences, could be inhumane. Governor Philip Gardelin's regulations for punishment from September 1733 prescribed severe punishments which included whipping, being broken on the wheel, pinching with glowing tongs, cutting off ears, removing limbs or hanging.*

*The newspaper the Royal Danish American Gazette which was published on St. Croix, often contained advertisements for both sales and "Run Away".*

*It is obvious that some slaves took a chance and ran away, even though severe punishment awaited those who were captured. Here, among other things, we see that plantation owner Bourke, whom we know from Thalbitzer's ledger, is looking for a runaway slave called Tuam.*

*Opposite page:*
*Frontpage of the Royal Danish American Gazette with an announcement for new shiploads of slaves delivered on St. Croix.*

Jan. 26, 1771.

Abfented for 9 weeks paft from the Subfcriber,

A NEGROE GIRL, named ANCILLA, about 15 years of age, of a low ftature, flender, and fmooth faced. Whoever apprehends faid Negroe Girl, and will bring her home to her miftrefs, fhall have Ten Pieces of Eight Reward paid them. And as it is apprehended that fhe may be carried off the ifland by one or other mafter of a veffel, who has been ignorant of her being the property of the Subfcriber, if fuch mafter of veffel will give intelligence where faid Negroe Girl may be found, and the manner of her being carried away, he fhall be entitled to the above reward, without any profecution from FRANCES COOPER.

Chriftianftæd, Jan. 26, 1771.

Juft imported from the Windward Coaft of AFRICA, and to be fold on Monday next, by

### Meffrs. Kortright & Cruger,

At faid CRUGER's Yard,

### Three Hundred Prime
# S L A V E S.

\*\*\* The terms will be made known at the place of fale.
Jan. 23, 1771.

---

# R U N  A W A Y,

From the eftate of THEOBELL BOURKE, Efq;

A NEGROE MAN, called TUAM; a ftout well made fellow, 6 feet high, coal black, about 26 years of age, fpeaks ftrong and rough, a houfe carpenter by trade, Whoever takes him up, and puts him in the Fort at Chriftianftæd or Frederickftæd, or brings him to the manager on the above eftate, Mr. LUCK STRITCH, or to EDMOND KELLY at Chriftianftæd, fhall have Ten Pieces of Eight reward. All perfons are forbid harbouring faid Negroe; and as he has an inclination to get off the ifland, all captains are forbid harbouring or carrying him off, under the fevereft penalty the law directs.

Nov. 7, 1770.

---

TO BE LET,
# Three Excellent CELLARS,
ONE of them capable of holding 100

from a fallen tree confirms that this is dyewood. Jeannie Pitts, the Director of the Whim Plantation Museum, took part in this "discovery". With recipes from Norway an arts and crafts group at the Museum was later able to use this "forgotten" natural source of colour in their work.

Another name on the list of those who purchased slaves from the *Fredensborg* is Abraham Markoe. He owned the plantation Spanish Town in the King's Quarter and secured for himself a female slave for 215 rixdaler. Today there is little evidence of Markoe's activity on St. Croix, even though the ruins of a once beautiful, two-storeyed stately home lie there against a background of an enormous silver-coloured oil refinery. On the other hand, Markoe has secured a place for himself in the history of North America.

A few years later Markoe handed over the management of the plantation to a member of the family and went to Philadelphia in Pennsylvania, one of the thirteen British colonies in North America. Here he formed a cavalry troop which he called "the Philadelphia Light Horse Troop". He had with him 28 "highly esteemed and prominent gentlemen".

Like other military units Markoe's troop had its own banner. This was later called "The Markoe Ensign" and was the first to show thirteen horizontal stripes – one for each of the thirteen colonies.

At this time, among the colonists in America – on whom higher duties and tariffs were constantly being levied – there was growing discon-

# THE
# ROYAL DANISH
# AMERICAN GAZETTE.

VOL. I.  WEDNESDAY, December 26, 1770.  No. 50.

Just imported in the schooner *Elizabeth*, GEORGE WELLS master, from *Boston*, and to be sold by

## JOHN NEALL,

COD-FISH in hogsheads,
White pine boards and plank,
Red oak staves, and hiccory hoops,
Lamp oil, spermaceti candles,
And, fire bricks.

St. Croix, Dec. 26, 1770.

On Friday the 28th Dec. next will be sold by PAUL PRIHN, at his house,

## The Cargo of Gold Coast NEGROES;

Which arrived here from the coast of Guinea the 19th December instant, by the snow Eleonora, commanded by Capt. Tadsen.

St. Croix, Dec. 26, 1770.

## TO BE SOLD BY
## Capt. JOHN WILLIAMS,

At Mr. MALLEY's stables,

## Five choice Northward HORSES,

Very reasonable for cash or short credit.
⁂ Said WILLIAMS intends settling here. Any Gentlemen pleasing to employ him in the Seafaring-way, as master of a drogger or coaster, he being very well acquainted among the islands, and the bays round this, may depend upon his doing their business with the utmost dispatch and care.

Dec. 26, 1770.

ALL those who have had any papers recorded in the Jurisdiction of Fredericksted, during the time I have administered the office of Judge and Recorder, and not called for the same, are desired to take them out and pay for them before the expiration of next month, otherwise they may expect that the papers remaining by me, after such time, will be destroyed, as I would willingly acquit myself of all unnecessary incumbrances.

W. SCHAFFER.

St. Croix, Dec. 22, 1770.

The Subscriber also begs leave to remind the Publick of his former advertisement, which has hitherto proved fruitless.

WHEREAS Augustine Malley intends to leave this island in two or three days, he desires all Gentlemen who have any demands against him to bring in their accounts that they may be settled.

St. Croix, Dec. 22, 1770.

THE Subscriber intending to leave the island immediately, he gives this publick notice to all persons who have any demands against the said Subscriber to send in their accounts that they may be discharged; and those who are indebted to him are requested to make payment.

SAMUEL DARBY.

Frederickstad, Dec. 19, 1770.

## TO BE SOLD BY
## JAMES OGILVIE,

At his House,

A Few firkins of good Butter,
Cyder and ale by the dozen,
Mens thread stockings, and umbrellas.

Dec. 22, 1770.

Just imported in the brigantine *Morning Star*, THOMAS CALLENDER master, from *Philadelphia*, and to be sold by

## JOHN NEALL,

SUPERFINE and common Flour,
Ship bread in tierces,
Kegs of white ditto,
Indian meal in rum hogsheads and barrels,
Oats in rum hogsheads,
Albany peas in tierces,
Rice in ditto,
Ship stuff in barrels,
White oak staves and heading,
Red oak ditto,
Cedar shingles,  and
Fire bricks.

Dec. 19, 1770.

## TO BE SOLD BY
## CHARLES MAGENIS,

In the Rum-shop adjoining FRIIS EILSCHOW,
New best and middle sort Flour.

WHEREAS the Subscriber intends leaving this island in a short time, she desires all those to whom she may be any ways indebted, to bring in their accounts that they may be settled and paid off.

JANE TAYLOR.

Dec. 19, 1770.

Just imported, in the ship LOUISA, from Copenhagen, and to be sold by

## LAURENS EBBESEN,

ENAMELL'D coffee pots,
Do. tea pots,
Do. milk pots,
Punch bowls, five in a set,
Small bowls,
Enamell'd tureens,
Table services complete,
Single soup and flat plates,
Butter cups,
Superfine black, white, & carmoisin cloth,
Sail duck,
Mens and ladies white gloves,
Silk lining, and flowered tabby, different sorts,
Iron in bars,
Silk ribbond, different colours,
An assortment of white tin utensils for the kitchin,
Rose water, mint ditto,
Iceland tobacco in bottles,
Barley, pearl do.
Corks.

WHEREAS the Subscriber intends leaving this island in a short time, he desires all those to whom he may be any ways indebted to bring in their accounts that they may be settled and paid off: he likewise prays the favour of them who are indebted to him to pay immediately, otherwise he will be under the disagreeable necessity of compelling them by law.

JOHN KIRWAN.

To be sold at the PRINTING-OFFICE, and by Mr. TUCKER at Frederickstæd,
[ Price, Three Bits, CASH, ]

# THE
# ST. CHRISTOPHER ALMANACK,

For the Year 1771; being the 3d after Bissextile or Leap Year; Calculated to serve all the other Charibbee Islands.

❋❋❋❋❋❋❋❋❋❋❋❋

*Frontiers of Italy, Aug. 24, 1770.*

ADmiral Elphinstone, who, after the defeat of the Ottoman squadron, failed to block up the Dardanelles, has taken twelve Ragusan, and two French vessels laden with provisions and ammunition for the Captain Pacha. As a squadron of Russian ships is also cruising between the Isles of Candy and Cerigo, the Russians are masters of all the Archipelago.

*Leghorn, Sept. 7.* The Russian squadron, which is cruizing off Tenedos, has taken 40 vessels for Constantinople, many with provisions, and others with most valuable Asiatick and African effects. The Commanders of these vessels knew not of the defeat of the Turkish fleet.

PETERSBURGH, *September 7.*

The following is an extract of a private letter from Count Tottleben, dated from Cotatis the 27th of July: "After I had overcome the most unthought of plots and treacheries, and had brought the body of men intrusted to my care by the Empress, even by force, together, out of the mountains of Caucasus and from Teflis to Russia, I had the good fortune not only to take all Georgia and its fortresses, Annaleri, Tuchet, Iimpole, Goresuram, and Alexis, from the deceiver Heraclius, and lodged imperial troops in Teflis, but have also plundered the Turkish fortresses of Scheripa, Bagdad, and Cotatis, all of which were well provided with artillery; and have made the three commanding Bashaws, with as many Agas and garrisons, prisoners of war. The Czar Saloman Imoslen, the Patriarch, and all the inhabitants of this extensive dominion, as also Georgia, have taken the oath of fidelity and subjection to her Imperial Majesty. I have now but three short days journey to go to proclaim the glorious name of my illustrious sovereign in the Black Sea."

*Warsaw, Sept. 19.* All we learn from the Russian army is, that it is posted along the Danube, and that the Turks are only seen in small bodies. We know nothing of the fate of Bender. It is said Count Tottleben is not far from Constantinople, and waits the issue of the Russian fleet passing the Dardanelles.

*Hague, Oct. 6.* We hear from Barcelona, that the king of Spain has laid an embargo on all the Dutch ships in that port that are not laden; which these letters say his Catholick Majesty proposes to employ in sending troops and military stores to the Spanish West-Indies; that these ships were intended to sail as soon as the troops and stores could be got on board; and that they were actually employed in embarking them. The proprietors of the ships are very largely paid for this service. This step of the court of Spain occasions great speculation; and it is even said the English Ambassador presented a memorial yesterday upon this subject to the States General.

*Paris, October 5.* The Count de Noailles, appointed minister plenipotentiary to the States General of the United Provinces, has received orders to depart immediately for London, to negociate some affairs of importance with that

*Abraham Markoe purchased a female slave from the* Fredensborg. *He later became famous as a cavalry captain and freedom fighter in the USA.*

tent against Great Britain, and in 1775 the War of Independence began. Here, Markoe and his men played an important role. They were the ones who escorted the newly appointed Commander-in-Chief of the army, George Washington, when he rode from Philadelphia to Kingsbridge, and Markoe's banner waved in many important battles against the English.

This had come to the ears of the Danish king. He had entered into a treaty of neutrality with England and regarded Markoe's fighting spirit with alarm. Markoe received word that unless he withdrew, his estates in the Danish-Norwegian colonies would be confiscated. For a while, Markoe appeared as an "honorary member" of his troop. But in the battle of Brandywine he fully participated.

Abraham Markoe's banner was to make a lasting impression. It is obvious that the idea of the thirteen stripes caught on. And it is perhaps no coincidence that "Markoe's stripes" in the Stars and Stripes are the same colour as that of the Danish flag that waved on St. Croix.

I am standing by the old weighing house in the harbour of Christiansted. It is noon; the sun is high in the sky and it is hot. The trade wind is refreshing to a Scandinavian as it blows steadily into the harbour. The mountain top to the east is called "Mount Welcome". Here welcome salutes were fired when a new ship glided into the harbour and dropped anchor. The cannon is still standing on its old site, but it is silent now. It has been a long time since the slave ships and West Indiamen dropped anchor with their assorted wares. Some of the "goods" unloaded themselves. They walked up to the Company's courtyard on their own two feet in order to be sold.

While Africa was the main supplier of manpower, the Europeans took care of the transport and the other supplies which the colonial society required. This could include building materials like yellow Danish bricks, equipment for the production of sugar, bullets and gunpowder for the forts, or a Western Norwegian horse. The needs were many and varied, and they were filled. Years with a good sugar cane harvest resulted in extra prosperity among the planters, who readily enjoyed a good Madeira at their table.

The need for transport was considerable, and most of it was taken care of by the direct traffic to the West Indies. This also took advantage of the trade winds, and the ships often stopped at Madeira in order to fetch wine for thirsty planters and government officials. The return freight included colonial products because it was impossible for the slavers to take charge of the entire production of the islands. The *Fredensborg*, or *Cron Prindz Christian*, as the ship was called then, had made five direct voyages to the West Indies. This traffic was far greater than the triangular trade, and could be carried out by private shipowners on certain conditions.

Charlotte Amalie is situated on St. Thomas. It was once the nextlargest town in the Danish-Norwegian kingdom, and a busy port in connection with the slave trade. With the old street names from the Danish-Norwegian period, and buildings in a typical colonial style, there are many charming places to see. The red Fort

*The Constitution Hill Plantation was owned by Peter Matthias Friis Eilskov who invested in 4 female and 1 male slave from the* Fredensborg. *The slave huts are standing on the hill behind the windmill which has been dismantled.*

Opposite page:
*The great house on the Spanish Town Plantation was once Abraham Markoe's beautiful home on St. Croix.*

*203*

*Old map of St. Thomas.*

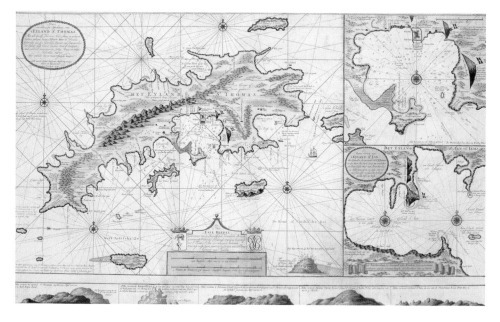

*The approach to the harbour of Charlotte Amalie on St. Thomas. The harbour is good and sheltered, but during the terrifying hurricanes there has been considerable damage to ships and buildings. After the sale, ten of the slaves from the* Fredensborg *came to the Wintberg Plantation, which is situated on the north side, behind the hills to the right of the town.*

Christian is still standing down by the harbour. North of the fort lies Emancipation Garden, the great slave market that was given its name after the slaves were set free.

In the harbour of Charlotte Amalie there are still ships that are engaged in the transport of human beings on a large scale. The Norwegian flag is waving briskly in the cooling trade wind, and I can see happy tourists pouring out of the cruise ships. The "Scale of Victualling" on board looks quite different from that on the

*Fredensborg.* Horse beans are probably not on the menu. Brandy and tobacco, on the other hand, are common to them all, even though the quality is somewhat different.

We are looking for the Wintberg Plantation, where ten slaves from the *Fredensborg* ended up. My old map is not the most reliable to steer by, but an elderly, white-haired gentleman shows me the way. With a black, crooked finger he points up a hill, and soon I can see the characteristic chimney of the boiling-house. A circular plateau has been constructed just beyond the chimney. These are the remains of the horse-drawn mill, because they had no windmill at Wintberg. Here the draught animals walked around in a circle, pulling the rollers that crushed the sugar cane. This was a much safer method for the slaves who operated the mill, because the draught animals could be stopped quickly in case of an accident. One might believe that a place like Wintberg, which means "wind hill", would have a windmill, but the name comes from the Dutch family name "de Wint".

We continue along a path that leads up to a grass-covered hill. Then I catch sight of a piece of rusty iron sticking out of the ground. It is an old mattock like the ones the slaves used in the fields of sugar cane. Here they toiled side by side. Geurt Spree de Wint was one of the first to purchase slaves from the *Fredensborg.* He had to produce 2,300 rixdaler for ten first-class male slaves from the Guinea Coast. Quietly and anonymously they wandered through the Company's protocols, and on to their buyer. No mention was made of their origin in Africa. All that mattered was whether or not they could work. In Africa the women were engaged in the farming; now the men had to adapt to new conditions and do the women's work. "Encouraged" by the Bomba's whip, the readjustment no doubt went off "without a hitch" – also at Wintberg!

*The chimney of the factory on the Wintberg Plantation is still standing.*

*The de Wint family lies buried in a dense thicket on the Wintberg Plantation.*

In a dense thicket we catch sight of an old burial ground that nature has done its best to conceal. We have to clear away leaves and rotten branches before we can see that the graves were made of yellow Danish bricks. Eagerly I bend over a tombstone that is broken into several pieces. The jigsaw puzzle is easy, and soon I can read the name "Geurt Spree de Wint". The purchaser of the ten slaves from the *Fredensborg* is lying a few feet beneath me. I can come no closer to any of those who purchased.

Not only de Wint, but also Markoe, Søbødker, Burt and all the

Forordning

om

Neger-Handelen.

Christiansborg Slot den 16de Martii 1792.

Kiøbenhavn,

trykt hos Directeur P. M. Hopffner, Hans Kongelige Majestæts

og Universitetets første Bogtrykker.

*Denmark-Norway was the first to pass a "Resolution about the Slave Trade" that would put an end to the slave transports. This led to hectic activity in order to guarantee enough manpower before the prohibition took effect at the end of 1802.*

others who purchased slaves had a few quiet years in which to manage their plantations. But they were undoubtedly aware of the growing opposition to the slave trade that was beginning to make itself felt in Europe around the end of the eighteenth century. Especially in England the opposition was on the increase, led by Thomas Clarkson and William Wilberforce, who played a central role. Dr. Paul Erdmann Isert paved the way in Denmark. When it was expected that a resolution to end the slave trade would be passed in England, a Danish "Commission for a Better Organization of the Slave Trade" was established.

Count Ernst Schimmelmann, the Minister of Finance at the time, was the originator of the Commission, which began its work in 1791. Schimmelmann was the joint owner of several plantations in the West Indies. At this time the number of slaves decreased on St. Croix, even though the slavers brought hundreds of slaves every year. The death-rate was high among the slaves and the birth-rate was low. The plantation owners feared a future with a shortage of slaves, not least if the transport of slaves from Africa was prohibited. They awaited the outcome of the Commission's work in suspense. It appeared in the form of a Royal Ordinance of 16 March 1792 which declared that the slave transports would cease on 31 December 1802. By stealing a march on England, Denmark-Norway was the first to pass such a resolution.

The Ordinance led to a considerable increase in the slave transport; it was a question of bringing as many slaves over as possible before the prohibition took effect. Now every nation was free to transport slaves to the Danish-Norwegian colonies in the West Indies, and they were also tempted by export bounties. In the hope that the islands would become self-sufficient with slaves, the tax was abolished for girls and females, but was doubled for males. In the period up to the time when the prohibition took effect, fully laden slave ships made trip after trip. Many sailed directly back to Africa to fetch a new cargo.

After the import of slaves came to an end, conditions for the slaves were slightly improved – it was important that their lifespan be increased! Peter Carl Frederik von Scholten was appointed acting Governor General in 1827. He initiated several measures which improved the situation of the free Negroes and also appointed several to public offices.

At the next crossroads, the British Parliament acted in advance of the Danes when they gave all the slaves in the British possessions their freedom in August 1833. The fact that great numbers of slaves in the West Indies were now free exerted considerable pressure on the Danish colonies. In 1847 – thirteen years after the English law – King Christian VIII also decided to abolish slavery. Children born of slaves were to be free at once, while the others were to receive their freedom 12 years later. Von Scholten was aware of the growing resistance to this, and barely a year after the ordinance had been proclaimed, a rebellion erupted on St. Croix that forced the Governor General to declare a general emancipation.

We are back on St. Croix and on our way along Centerline Road, the highway between Christiansted and Frederiksted. Tamarind trees and Royal Palms sporadically form beautiful allées, while from time to time a flamboyant, flaming-red tree brightens the landscape. In some of the fields sugar cane is growing, for which there is no longer any use. Now it grows wild on the old plantations, with their very special names. Here lie Aldershvile (Old Age Rest), "Work & Rest", "Fredensborg". Then we find "Upper Love" and "Lower Love", which is the nearest neighbour to "Jealousy" – naturally! "Jerusalem" and "Sion Farm" along with "Blessing" indicate a strong faith; others counted on luck and hope with "Wheel of Fortune" and "Good Hope". The most fitting name, from the standpoint of the wretched slaves, was undoubtedly the plantation "Hard Labour.

Among the ruins of the old plantations the sugar mills are the most visible in the landscape. The conical brickwork of the mills remains, while the top and the wings have rotted or been blown down by violent hurricanes. There are also many ruins of main buildings, cookhouses and slave huts. On the Bethlehem Plantation the slave houses are for sale, and on the William Estate many of the houses are still inhabited by blacks.

Frederiksted is a pleasant little town with well-regulated streets and charming houses in colonial style. Fort Frederiksværn is situated by Strandgaden with its many arcades. The Fort is duly identified by Frederik V's monogram and the year 1760 in black wrought iron against a dark red brick background. Now it is a museum. On a bus stop alongside the Fort I read: "Free the Black People from the

*The opening page of the "Resolution".*

*Governor General Peter von Scholten wrote this proclamation which was printed on St. Croix and St. Thomas.*

# Hans Kongelige Majestæts

til Danmark, de Venders og Gothers, Hertug til Slesvig, Holsteen, Stormarn, Ditmarsken

Lauenborg og Oldenborg

## Bestalter

Excellence, Generalmajor, Kammerherre, Storkors af Dannebroge og Dannebrogsmand, Storkors af Isabella den Catholskes Orden, Storofficeer af Æreslegionen, Commandeur af Guelphe Ordenen, Ridder af Ordenen du merite militaire, General Gouverneur over de danske vestindiske Öer,

J E G

# Peter Carl Frederik v. Scholten

| *Giör vitterligt :* | *Maketh known :* |
|---|---|
| 1. | 1. |
| Alle Ufrie paa de danske vestindiske Öer ere fra Dags Dato frigivne. | All Unfree in the danish westindia Islands are from to-day emancipated. |
| 2. | 2. |
| Negerne paa Plantagerne beholde i 3 Maaneder fra Dato Brugen af de Huse og Provisionsgrunde, hvoraf de nu ere i Besiddelse. | The Estate Negroes retain for three months from date the use of the houses and provisiongrounds, of which they have hitherto been possessed. |
| 3. | 3. |
| Arbeide betales for Fremtiden etter Overeenskomst, hvorimod Allowance ophörer. | Labour is in future to be paid for by agreement, but allowance is to cease. |
| 4. | 4. |
| Underholdningen af Gamle og Svage, som ere ude af Stand til at arbeide, afholdes indtil nærmere Bestemmelse af deres forrige Eiere. | The maintainance of old and infirm, who are not able to work, is until farther determination to be furnished by the late owners. |

Givet under General Gouvernementets Segl og min Haand, General Gouvernementet over de danske vestindiske Öer, St. Croix den 3die Juli 1848.

[L. S.] **P. v. Scholten.**

Chain". This is not a battle cry from the nineteenth century. It has been freshly painted! It appears as if the dissatisfaction among the black population on St. Croix is a never-ending problem.

It was here, in the square in front of the red walls of Fort Fredriksværn, that the above-mentioned revolt erupted in July 1848. Around 8,000 slaves gathered under the command of a slave who was called "General Buddho". The slaves were armed and the situation was critical. The town was occupied; they stormed the police headquarters and a trading house was looted. All the soldiers on St. Croix were placed on the alert, and everyone feared a terrible bloodbath. It was in this situation that Peter von Scholten intervened and headed for Frederiksted. As the Governor-General's coach rolled into the square in front of the fort, the slaves cried "Massa Peter!" and demanded their freedom immediately. He climbed out of his coach and raised his arms, and in the ensuing silence he shouted: "Now you are free! You are hereby emancipated!"

The emancipated slaves faced a difficult period and lived below the subsistence level for decades. On 1 October 1878 a rebellion broke out, also in Frederiksted, and many lives were lost in the struggles against the authorities. A military court sentenced twelve of the assumed leaders to death, and the execution was carried out immediately by firing squad. The authorities gained control of the situation, but there had been considerable destruction, and several plantations had been set on fire by the rebels, including Høgensborg, the plantation belonging to the Søbødker family.

A little to the west of Christiansted we find Friedensthal with its old church from 1755. Missionaries from the Herrnhuter or United Brethren's Negro mission preached the Gospel among the slaves. Many were converted and it was claimed that this subdued the urge to revolt. The Christian slaves were far more tractable and dutiful. The local pastor welcomes us warmly and takes us inside the church. He plays the old organ, which fills the church with its tinny notes. Yearning souls once sat here and sought comfort from the Holy Scriptures in order to keep up their courage.

The old mission station took care not only of the living but also of the dead. The pastor leads the way to the old churchyard which is surrounded by a wall.

*The Herrnhuter's mission station in Friedensthal on St. Croix in May 1768, about two months before the* Fredensborg *delivered its cargo of slaves. The church is to the left, the living quarters of the missionaries are in the background, while a "Negro hut" is to the right. The blacks in white in front of the church are waiting to be christened. The local church register may be an important source of information for many descendants of slaves who are searching for their African roots.*

*Friedensthal in St. Croix an einem Bettage, da die Taufflinge zur Taufe in die Kirche geführt worden 1768 zu Anfang May und zu Mittage, da die Sonne ub Scheitel stehet, aller Schatten senckrecht fällt; überhaupt wenig Schatten ist. Hinter dies Wohnhaus zur lincken die Neue Kirche zur rechten Negerhäuser.*

*The social conditions of the liberated slaves were poor, and most of them lived below the subsistence level. 1 October 1878, on the so-called "Contract Day", a rebellion broke out in Frederiksted. The authorities proceeded with the utmost severity and many of the rebels died in the battles. Twelve of the assumed leaders were executed by firing squad.*

Here lie the whites who could afford a brick vault and a tombstone. Can we find the grave belonging to the possible "TBM" from the signet in the wreck of the *Fredensborg*? The dead are lying in rows under their white monuments. On fallen stone slabs we read the usual condensed information about an entire life: name, title and dates of birth and death. On grave no. 31 I find "Gouverneur General" Thomas Bordeaux Malleville. But to my surprise he is also lying in grave no. 32! The inscriptions on the two graves are identical, but one stone is slightly larger than the other. No one there is able to provide a sensible explanation of Malleville's two graves, but I have found the one I was looking for – and then some.

The number of slaves on the three Danish-Norwegian islands reached its peak in 1802, as a result of the hectic import before the transport of slaves was prohibited. By then the number of slaves had reached of 35,235. On St. Croix alone there were 27,006! Gradually the problems became greater than the profits, and during the nineteenth century a sale of the islands was heatedly debated. In 1917 the three Danish colonial islands were sold to the United States for 25 million dollars. Thus Abraham Markoe's old plantation Spanish Town came under the Stars and Stripes to which he had contributed. Today the U.S. Virgin Islands are a popular tourist attraction with beautiful beaches and first-class hotels.

My journey to the West Indies had answered many questions. The traces of the colonial period and the slave trade were clear in many ways, with forts, plantations, slave villages and other buildings from the time of the *Fredensborg*. But the wake of the *Fredensborg* did not end there. In order to get to the bottom of the question, I had to continue to the Gold Coast in Africa.

# CHAPTER 11

# A Journey to the Gold Coast

THE TROPICAL NIGHT HAS SUNK over the African landscape as I arrive at the fabled Gold Coast in 1995. In my imagination – as I examined the ship's logs of Kiønig, Ferentz and Hoffmann – I had been here many times earlier, as a stowaway on board the *Fredensborg*. Day after day I was there, while the frigate lay at anchor outside of Fort Christiansborg. Based on reports written by merchants, ministers, officials and sailors during the years 1697–1814 as a source, my knowledge of Ghana is in truth somewhat out-of-date.

"Ghana" was originally the name of an ancient regime which bordered on the River Niger. The Ghana of today is in West Africa, on the Bay of Guinea, between the nations Togo and Côte d'Ivoire, a little north of the equator. This former British colony, which became an independent state in 1957, is a republic with a population that exceeds 17 million. The country has valuable natural resources and is one of the world's greatest producers of cocoa. Here we also find manganese, bauxite, rich diamond fields and – of course – gold.

The capital, Accra, is a bustling city of a million inhabitants, spread over a large area in the flat, coastal landscape. It is an exciting city with colourful markets, modern and ancient buildings, and thousands of aggressive street vendours. The most remarkable fact is that Accra, which lies on the coast, has only one small pier. The city runs out into sandy beaches, and the boats look very much as they did in the eighteenth century.

With my headquarters in a bungalow at the University of Ghana I am strategically located in a lovely area on Legon Hill, on the outskirts of Accra. Up on a hill there is still a short allée of tamarind trees. These, planted by the Danes, bordered a road leading from the fort all the way to the plantation Frederiksgave, which was established in 1832 at the foot of the Akwapim hills. To the south I can see down to the coast where Fort Christiansborg appears as a small white dot in the light morning mist.

It was at Christiansborg that most things happened then, and they still do. As the seat of government and office of the president, Christiansborg – now simply

"The Castle" – is still a busy place of work. For security reasons few are allowed to enter the well-guarded walls, but I have been granted permission.

Soon I am walking through the gates of "The Castle", passing well-armed guards. Great changes have occurred here since the *Fredensborg's* time. The flint-lock muskets of the guards have been replaced by machine guns, and a single ancient cannon stands in sharp contrast to the modern armoured tank. In the area where the Negeriet lay there are now parking lots and a lovely park. Asioke's hut is gone forever. Now I am standing in front of the old main entrance, which still boasts the monogram of Christian VII over the massive black doors.

I enter the old courtyard. The Danish-Norwegian fort has endured much since 1768, but in spite of earthquakes, additions and annexes, the courtyard itself has retained much of its original appearance. Directly in front of me is the stairway up to the old governor's residence where those prominent gentlemen once lived. Under the floor of the governor's residence were the vaults where the important goods were stored. When a ship arrived with its hold full of goods, including 30,000–40,000 *potter* of brandy "there was not enough room in the warehouses, so we had to store the casks full of brandy in the rooms of the employees; this resulted in extreme leakage, or rather, drinkage."

The old cistern with its characteristic form still stands in the same place in the fore court. Rømer, who has just been quoted above, and all the others had need of great

*Christiansborg is beautifully located on a cliff facing the ocean. Seen from the east we can still get a good impression of the old Danish-Norwegian headquarters. It was on this side of the fort that goods from the* Fredensborg *were brought ashore, and the cargo of slaves later taken out. The canoes under the palms reinforce the impression of life in the past on the Gold Coast, even though the roadstead is empty.*

*The main entrance to old Christiansborg is still decorated with Christian VII's monogram. As a four-year-old he lent his name to the slave ship* Cron Prindz Christian, *which was later rechristened the* Fredensborg.

*Governor Carl Engmann, who built this cistern with its baroque style in 1753, later became one of the directors of the Guinea Company which owned the* Fredensborg.

amounts of water in the tropical heat. The inscription on the cistern has been overpainted many times, but I can spell my way through what is still comprehensible: THIS WATER BANK WHOSE DEPTH IS 28 FEET AND LENGTH 28 FEET WHILE THE WIDTH IS 32 FEET. WAS BEGUN IN THE YEAR 1753 THE 25 MARCH AND COMPLETED ON THE 31 MAY ANNO 1753. CARL ENGMANN

When the building of the cistern was begun, the *Fredensborg,* or *Cron Prindz Christian,* as she was then called, had had water under her keel for 49 days! Carl Engmann was the Governor *pro tem* during the years 1752–1757. He survived his stay on the Gold Coast later to become one of the directors of the *Fredensborg's* Company.

Engmann's cistern was a good hatchery for malaria mosquitoes and certainly the reason that so many at the fort became infected. Not even on board the slave ships which lay anchored in the roadsteads were they safe. The mosquito larvae, which live in water, were brought out to the ships in the water barrels, and certainly many a bloodthirsty mosquito flew up out of the ration barrels on deck. There were surely carriers among the crew and the deck slaves and remidors, and that spread the diseases throughout the ship.

*The courtyard of Christiansborg contains much history. Here there was extensive trade in human beings. In spite of structural changes in the upper storeys, the courtyard itself has been changed very little since the Danish-Norwegian period. At the left we see the characteristic cistern. The slave dungeons are still on both sides of the stairway that led up to the governor's residence, while the warehouses were placed in the arched openings in front. The yellow-brown flagstones on both sides of the main walk are made of Accra sandstone.*

The whites managed badly on the Gold Coast, and the great majority of them died after a short time. Fort Chaplain H.C. Monrad had disturbing experiences at Christiansborg:

"During their stay in the country even the appearance of the Europeans bore witness to the fact that they would not grow old. I shall never forget my first impression at the sight of them. Through the courtyard of the fort, where the unexpected rattling of the chains of many slaves pained the eye, the ear, and heart, I proceeded into the government reception room where many Europeans were assembled. Yellow, emaciated, they appeared to me to be already prepared for death. Later I came to understand that they were sentenced to life, as it was lived there, and the climate-fever soon gave me a similar appearance as well." Medical Officer Paul Erdmann Isert, who lost his own life on the Coast, was of the opinion that Norwegians, of whom there were always several at the fort, were especially vulnerable: "They give the impression of freshwater fish having been placed in salt water." I am relieved to be well-protected by vaccinations and anti-malaria tablets.

Some of the flagstones in the fore court have the unmistakable yellow-brown colour that I recognize from the stone mortar that we found in the wreck. That type of stone is called Accra sandstone. Chaplain Monrad has a word to put in here:

"The sandstone is the most common sort there. It is very easy to quarry with iron rods, and with a hammer and a wide chisel one can form whatever shape one desires. Of that sort of stone, which is found extensively even at the shore, there are large quarries worked by slaves; and further up-country all the European forts and their buildings are built largely of this stone. When newly worked, sandstone has a greyish colour, but after it has been exposed to weather for a long time it becomes dark brown." I wander around a bit on my own and come to a stop at the left of the stairs leading to the governor's residence. Two openings in the white masonry wall are provided with heavy doors having frames and bars of thick iron. These are the infamous slave dungeons which were packed full of Africans, day after day, year after year. They are empty now, but still locked.

On 19 April 1768 it was very lively here in the courtyard of the fort. Early in the morning the cannons on board the Guinea Company's good ship *Fredensborg* had thundered, and loading had begun. The great main gate was closed and locked when forty full-grown male slaves were led out of the dungeons and bound with ropes. When everything was under complete control, the gate was opened and the slaves moved in a long row down to the fort's large canoe which was waiting on the beach. The smith went along in order to fasten them to the footshackles on board the *Fredensborg*. During the course of two days the slave dungeons were emptied of women and men, boys and girls, a total of 265 slaves.

How many times the slave dungeons here at Fort Christiansborg were filled and emptied is not known precisely. As the chief Danish fort from 1694 to 1850 it was here that there was the most activity. It is a strange feeling to stand in the fort's courtyard which holds so much history. The slave dungeons, the water cistern, the warehouses – all these were in use during the *Fredenborg*'s 205-day stay on the Coast.

Christiansborg, according to Rømer, was served by "30 Europeans and 300 Negroes". It was fortified by "forty-some iron cannons". He had great faith in its construction and effectiveness, and wrote optimistically that "the fort is invincible and impregnable against the entire might of Africa!" But this had not always been the case. In 1693 the Akwamus had taken control of the fort with a sly trick. *Danne-brog* was replaced by a "blue flag with a black Moor holding a hatchet in his hand". One year later the Danes regained Christiansborg upon payment of a suitable "tax" in the form of goods to a value of 3,000 rixdaler. However, the Akwamu retained the keys to the fort as a trophy.

Close cooperation with the Africans was the basis of all commerce in what was called the Gold Coast, the land between Cape Appolonia in the west and River Volta in the east. An inter-dependency developed, of which both partners took full advantage. Christiansborg and the other forts and trading stations were entirely dependent upon local labour and provisions in order to continue to function. From a purely commercial view the Africans of the coastal areas were the masters in a favourable position. They acted as middlemen between the interior and the Europeans. This widespread operation had an influence on economic, political, social and cultural relationships. By the time of the *Fredensborg* the European presence had become an important element in the

*Solid barred doors lead into the fort's slave dungeons which have vaulted ceilings. The slaves were kept behind these bars before being taken on board the* Fredensborg *in April 1768. Like the other European forts on the Gold Coast, Christiansborg was designed for trade in slaves, as well as in goods.*

local power structure of a well-developed trading area. This having been said, it was claimed that the power of the whites, in the final analysis, extended no further than their cannons could reach.

The gate of the fort's courtyard represents, in a way, a meeting between past and present. Everyone had to go through this gate, whether slave or free, black or white, living or dead. A proud Captain Ferentz strolled through here after his appointment, while Ship's Assistant Hoffmann hurried by with a tight grip on his important journal. Young Erich Ancker from Christiania, pale and emaciated after his bout with "climate fever", undoubtedly walked more slowly. Cargo after cargo of Europeans goods was carried in and exchanged for slaves, ivory and gold. In the wreck of the *Fredensborg* I myself have picked up ivory which passed through this gate on Monday 19 April 1768.

On that very day, exactly 228 years ago, I would have met the mates Messrs. Lundberg and Gad who had come out together with Aye in order to go aboard. Later that year it was a fever-ridden Captain Kiønig who stumbled in here to die. He was then carried out through the gate opening which was just wide enough for his coffin and its bearers to pass through, before turning to the left towards the fort's cemetery.

I now follow the same route, accompanied by a security guard. On a green plain west of the fort, two old brick walls meet to form a right angle. Set into the wall on the left are six gravestones dating from 1830 to 1845. These gravestones and the brick walls are all that remain of the old Danish-Norwegian cemetery. There are no longer any traces of the graves from the eighteenth century, but I know that I am close to the place where Captain Kiønig, Chief Officer Lundberg

*Fort Christiansborg has been rebuilt extensively since the Danish-Norwegian times, but inside the gate bearing Christian VII's monogram the old fort yard remains with its mementoes.*

and nine other members of the crew found their final resting place. Among them were Abraham Engmann and the Norwegian, Ole Nicolaysen, who had had their altercation at the beer barrel on deck.

From the eastern wall of the fort I take a last look at the fort's landing place. Under the palms there is a cluster of large canoes, and I see some fishermen mending their nets. Everything appears to be the same as before, but when I turn my gaze out to sea, the roadstead is empty. Only the sound of the breakers is the same, as they roll in toward land and break on the slaves' coast. The ancient black iron cannons, aimed toward the old anchoring place, are silent forever.

There is something enchanting about old Christiansborg which, with its favourable position and through changing times, has been the centre of events. After the Danes sold both their forts and trading rights to the British in 1850, Christiansborg was the headquarters of that colonial power for many years. Indeed, even in our time it is still a

centre of power; here, as in Denmark, the country's highest authorities have their seat in their Christiansborg Castle.

Mementoes from "the Danish period" in Accra comprise not only "The Castle" and the remainders of two allées of tamarind trees on the road to Akwapim. Several officials had private residences in the vicinity of Christiansborg. On Labadi Road I find the well-preserved portal of Richter's residence. Over the portal there is a coat of arms containing the initials 'HR&CR' and the date 1809.

Henrich Richter was born in 1785. His father was the Danish Governor Johan Emanuel Richter and his mother was African. After the death of his father in 1817, Henrich travelled to Copenhagen to claim his inheritance, and with this inheritance as initial capital he established an extensive trading business. With his private army of 115 men this industrious Mulatto merchant participated in the battle at Dodowa in 1826. As a reward for the victory against Asante he was appointed Chief Military Commissioner. In 1836 he was awarded the title "Knight of Dannebrog" after a military expedition against the Krobo people.

Within the courtyard, in a straight line from the entrance, we see a neat, white-washed stairway which once led up to the first storey of the residence. Now it ends in mid-air, making a strong contrast to the worn and rusty corrugated roof on the three sides around it. Inside the circular walls, which are quite intact, many families now have their homes. An old woman is sleeping on the ledge of a brick wall; a golden-brown chicken is tied to a stool. On the wall in the small bar on the inside of the portal there is a drawing showing the place as it once was, when there were "delightful times on the Coast". Henrich Richter was certainly far wealthier than today's inhabitants of what was once a complete, small fortress with bastions and

*On Labadi Road, in the section of the city called Christiansborg, is the entrance gate to Richter's residence. Most of the once so impressive private residence was destroyed in a powerful earthquake. The gate, the ring wall, parts of the lower storey and the impressive stairway, in typical Gold Coast style, are still preserved.*

*From the Danish settlement on Castle Drive, we see, from the left, Bannermann's house, then Wulff's house, "Frederichs Minde", Florence Lodge, and the Basel Mission's former house, with an arched façade.*

cannons. Just listen to what Wulff I. Wulff wrote in 1836: "Here lives a very rich man by the name of Richter, who evidently owns 8 to 10 barrels of gold. He has 400 slaves and carries on considerable trade. He is married to a princess from Asantee, which lies 100 miles in the interior. This man has performed many services for us. I have often been invited to his home, both for dinner and for an evening meal. He is the Chief Military Commissioner. I have never in my life seen so much gold and silver, as well as costly objects as I have seen in his home. The tables are set with silver service, and as his guest one enjoys all sorts of rare foods, which he orders from all the ends and corners of the earth."

Poor Wulff, who was an officer at Christiansborg, could by no means live up to the extravagance of his wealthy friend. However, he built a fine home for himself, which today comprises an important element of the old Danish settlement along Castle Drive.

*In the drawing room in Frederich's Minde on Castle Drive, hangs a painted portrait of Wulff I. Wulff.*

Some of the buildings are still inhabited by the coloured descendants of Danish officials. In "Frederichs Minde" I am politely received by Leslie Stanley Wulff-Cochrane. He invites me into Wulff's house, where a generous Mrs. Wulff-Cochrane welcomes me. Here, among other pictures, hangs a portrait of Wulff I. Wulff which was sent down from Denmark about one hundred years ago. The nameplate over the main door is still in place, bearing the inscription 'FREDERICHS MINDE 1840 W.I. WULFF'.

Wulff married the Mulatto woman Sara Malm and they had three children. He himself did not enjoy the house for long because he died as early as 1842. In his will Wulff wrote, "I request that the burial of my body take place in my own house, as long as there is nothing to hinder this." The grave is in a small room in the basement. A window provides light over Wulff's grave, which is marked by red floor tiles. His daughter, Wilhelmine, rests by his side, and her grave is marked by a smaller stone inserted there. She was married to Major Cochrane, thus the family name Wulff-Cochrane.

There is a special atmosphere in that little room on Castle Drive. How Wulff got the idea of burial in this manner shall remain unspoken, but it is not impossible that his wife had her say in this matter. It was the custom in the land to bury the dead in their own homes, which was also done in the case of Richter.

In old Ningo I see a boat sailing in towards the coast from the west. Can it be Mister Ferentz who is coming in the longboat with much-needed provisions for the fort, which stands so beautifully next to the lagoon? Here come the fine trade goods to speed up the slave trade, so the frigate *Fredensborg* can receive her cargo. The remidors who have boarded the longboat out in the roadstead now find the easiest entrance into the lagoon, where the water is deep enough for them to sail into calm waters. Then they lower the sails and paddle the rest of the way to the beach. Under supervision, the fort slaves carry the cases of muskets, the barrels of gunpowder, brandy and other goods into the magazines of the fort.

The image of my fantasy crumbles, and the most beautiful of all the Danish-Norwegian forts is again a ruin. I have finally come to Fort Fredensborg, which gave its name to the frigate that has meant so much to me. On a small rise in the terrain a masonry construction towers over the green vegetation. Two arched openings in the seven to eight metre long stone wall transform the entire structure into an attractive monument. A large block of masonry, originally part of the roof construction, has fallen down and is providing a foreground. The stairs leading through one of the

*Todays fishermen at Old Ningo reminds me of the remidors who boarded the* Fredensborg.

openings are still in good condition. It is clear that this must have been a room with a vaulted ceiling; could it have been a warehouse, or one of the fort's slave dungeons?

Close to the fort is the small village Old Ningo. Old Ningo's Nana, or chief, welcomes me. The elders, who have a position of authority in the African community, are also present, all wearing their beautiful "cloth", draped like a toga. They are extremely interested in the history of the slave ship which was named after the fort in the village, and I am soon a participant in a welcoming ceremony in the form of an offering. *Schnaps* is drunk from a coconut shell, and a suitable amount is poured on the ground as a libation to the ancestors. This was also done in the *Fredensborg's* time. It is therefore inevitable that I think back to the cargoes of brandy and the several casks whose contents were surely offered to the ancestors in this village!

I have been provided with three men familiar with the area who will show me the remainder of the fort and anything else that might be of interest. We pass a low building under the palm trees not far from the beach. It is one of the shrines of the village. In the masonry on each side of the door I see the figure of a winding snake. On the roof of the shrine there are two figures of hyenas facing each other. The hyena is Old Ningo's sacred animal. A newly-arrived night-guard at Fort Fredensborg found this out in the eighteenth century when he killed a hyena which was sneaking by. This led to a terrible commotion which cost the Company dearly. The hyena was buried in a roll of Danish cloth, while the people had to be treated generously with brandy. Both the night-guard and most of the fort are gone now, but the traditions live on.

*There is not much remaining of old Fort Fredensborg at Old Ningo. With its connection to the slave ship* Fredensborg *it is important to preserve the remains for future generations.*

Parallel to the beach there is a parapet with embrasures along the top. Tropical growths attempt to hide this as much as possible, but some of it is still visible. A few metres further in there is a cannon resting at a slant, on a rise along a masonry block. The elevation is hopeless, but a cannon ball would undoubtedly have fallen into the sea where the slave ships were anchored waiting for their spoils. It looks as if much of the rise in the terrain where we are standing is due to collapsed masonry. There has been mention of an underground tunnel through which the slaves were driven when they were to be loaded on board. When there were conflicts, the inhabitants of Old Ningo took refuge behind the walls of the fort.

Rømer, who was stationed at Fort Fredensborg, writes that there were only ten Europeans there, and in 1742 the Asante laid siege to the fort "with 20,000 men", resulting only in the capture during the night of some one hundred Africans. Remarkably, the fort successfully resisted the siege with its 20 cannons, of which some were only one and one-half pounders. We cannot dismiss the possibility that the entire exercise was a power demonstration on the part of the Asante. The motives for sparing the fort could have had both tactical and commercial aspects.

They hesitate when I ask if there were more cannons at the site. Then I am led further along a narrow path through brush in the direction of the lagoon. In an open area lies another shrine, and under a tree I see another of the cannons from old Fort Fredensborg. The cannon is lying flat on the ground and evidently is part of the shrine. The Europeans on the Gold Coast came into contact with traditional African religion from the very beginning. This was something that both Rømer and other slave traders had to take into consideration in their daily work. They used the term "fetish" as a somewhat condescending description of the Africans' religious practices.

*This cannon from Fort Fredensborg no longer presents a threat, either to the mighty or to the humble.*

Quietly I wander down the path towards the lagoon and pass the end of the parapet. It looks as if the entire Fort Fredensborg, built in 1736, rested on a sandy foundation. This may be the reason for its ruin, because by 1850 it was useless. At the old landing place there are many canoes of various sizes. All of them are hollowed out of large trunks of the wawa tree. That light-coloured, solid dense timber is easy to work out. First it is hollowed; then, after the hull is built up with planks, thwarts are set in; and finally a name is painted on along with colourful decorations. These long boats are extremely seaworthy and are still suitable to the local conditions in waters where such boats have been in operation for centuries.

As I am standing there admiring the decor and building techniques, a large canoe comes in from the sea with its course directly towards the beach and the breakers. Finally, I am actually going to see a landing as it was done when the *Fredensborg*'s cargo of goods was brought to land in precisely the same time of year in

*The lagoon is still there with its large canoes, but Fort Fredensborg and the houses in the background are gone forever.*

1767. Those on board the canoe scan the sea carefully for a suitable wave swell. Then they ride it to shore. One of the fishermen stands aft with a long steering oar. As soon as they reach the shallows, some of the men jump out into the foaming breakers. Now the boat is to be turned with its bow seaward before being hauled onto the beach, ready for its next launching. It looks almost as if time has stood still – except that now there is no one paddling as they come in from the sea. On

the starboard side, almost astern, hangs the explanation; a 40 horsepower Yamaha outboard motor. The motor is mounted on a small piece of wood nailed solidly to the hull. It is quickly unmounted and carried to a safe place, and then everything is as it was before. Accompanied by rhythmic song the boat is hauled up on the beach under the palms.

The location of Fort Fredensborg has been ideal in terms of both trade and a favourable landing place. For Johan Frantzen Ferentz the fort was to be his salvation. As captain of the slave ship *Christiansborg* in 1775 he had to struggle against 336 desperate slaves. Having seized control below deck, the slaves were willing to lose their lives – which indeed many of them did. Somehow the male slaves had managed to get loose and make their way through the wall dividing them from the female slaves. There they got hold of weapons and found their way through the hatches; "some had knives, some had various other things with which to attack us." In the fight that followed, Ferentz and his men struggled for their lives. The slaves found the guns and powder, then severed the tiller ropes. In that situation Ferentz had to mobilize all his experience as a sailor. He had to manoeuvre using the sails and set his course for land. When there was no more powder on deck the resourceful captain resorted to "boiling hot water, which was used by us in defence every time the slaves came storming in an attempt to come up through the hatches." In the roadstead off Fort Fredensborg Ferentz succeeded in setting out the sloop. He left the ship and soon was on his way back with several canoes manned by remidors and soldiers from the fort. Ferentz regained control on board, but the rebellion cost both rixdaler and lives. Approximately every fourth slave was lost on that ill-fated journey.

I look down at the large and small footprints in the moist sand. My thoughts go to the thousands of slaves who were driven on board the canoes like those in front

*Fort Fredensborg and the "Negeriet" were beautifully situated by the lagoon at Old Ningo. The site was rented from "Field Marshal" Orsu for 20 benda in gold.*

of me. It is almost unbelievable that this lovely place was the centre for trade in human beings on such a large scale. A letter written by fiscal Quist the same year that the *Fredensborg* arrived on the Gold Coast gives us a small glimpse into that trade:

"Noble and honourable Governor and Chief.

With reference to Mr. Governor's report of 14 February, concerning Merchant Kuhberg's purchase at Fredensborg of slaves that were sent up to the main fort: Of the eight male slaves, three have hernia and five have teeth missing and are of indifferent quality. Further, of the nine female slaves, four are only average, two are poor quality and three are old. In my opinion and according to my conscience the slaves are saleable for the following prices:

| | |
|---|---|
| *4 female slaves* | *88 rdl.* |
| *3 old slaves* | *56 rdl.* |
| *1 ditto* | *112 rdl.* |
| *3 ditto with hernia* | *80 rdl.* |
| *2 female slaves* | *64 rdl.* |
| *1 male slave* | *120 rdl.* |
| *2 ditto* | *104 rdl.* |

In setting the above prices I consider that the greatest moderation has been practiced…"

The conscience mentioned above hardly referred to humane conditions. The trade in human beings required special qualities, such as a good sense of business and sufficient callousness. Rømer was clearly in possession of these qualities, since he gained his most valuable experience in this trade here at Fort Fredensborg.

The fort's Chaplain Monrad passes judgement on Rømer and the other merchants on the Coast: "Truth forces me to admit that I have never known any sympathetic or tolerant slave trader. Indeed how could any noble individual take up this shameful and revolting occupation."

In addition to Christiansborg and Fredensborg the dual monarchy Denmark-Norway had other forts on the Coast: Augustaborg, Kongensten, and Prinsensten. In Teshie there are still some few remainders of Augustaborg. Kongensten in Ada – built in 1783 and located strategically at the mouth of the River Volta – disappeared several decades ago. But further east, 15 miles along the coast from Christiansborg, lies Fort Prinsensten on a spit outside of the great Keta lagoon.

It was a moving meeting with the old Danish-Norwegian fort, which was built in 1784 on the site of an old trading station. The well-known builder of forts Jens Adolph Kiøge was responsible for its construction, but forces of nature later brought about its destruction. In a violent storm in 1980 the waves were so powerful that the walls in the foremost part of the fort were undermined. This had fatal results. Parts of the fort, which was then being used as a prison, collapsed, and huge blocks of masonry remain lying on the beach. Fort Prinsensten is an attractive, but sad sight at sunset under a flaming red sky. A single cannon pointing southwest makes up the total armament, but the bastions toward the sea have been conquered for all time. I think about Boatswain Rosenborg who waded ashore on

*Fort Prinsensten is now a complete ruin. After a storm in 1980 waves washed away sections of the foundation; the bastions and walls collapsed. It would be a pity not to preserve what is left of the fort.*

this beach after a long journey along the coast in the longboat. Goods from the *Fredensborg* reached this place, goods that were traded for "60 good Crepe slaves or more."

The large, shallow lagoon behind the fort was a perfect hatchery for swarms of malaria mosquitoes. Rømer claims that, at worst, the local people had to bury themselves in the sand at night in order to be able to sleep. In all probability, it was here that the boatswain received the deadly injection that cost him his life later during the journey. Here sweated poor Lauritz Reimers, who was the vector until he fell out of favour and was sent home. Like the *Fredensborg* they both ended their days on the southern coast of Norway. Somewhere in the yellow sand Bernt Jensen Mørch lies buried, or does he? Perhaps the violent storm fetched the remains of

*Fort Prinsensten as it looked in 1847.*

the captain who took over the slave ship *Christiansborg* after Johan Frantzen Ferentz. It is said Captain Mørch died here of oyster poisoning.

After visiting Christiansborg, Fredensborg and Prinsensten and other sites, I have gained an overall view of the condition of the old Danish forts on the Gold Coast. Most of them have disappeared or are in ruins, apart from the historic sections of Christiansborg. In order to gain a complete picture of how these buildings were constructed and how they functioned I must travel further along the coast. Within the present boundaries of Ghana, along a stretch of some 500 kilometres, there once were more than 60 European forts and trading stations which carried on trade for gold, ivory and slaves. Most of them have disappeared, or are in ruins, but 14–15 miles along the coast west of Accra lie two of the best preserved – Elmina Castle and Cape Coast Castle.

Fort Elmina! It was there that it all started, before Columbus discovered America. The Portuguese, who built the fort, called it São Jorge da Mina, which became Mina de Ouro, or the Gold Mine. As mentioned before, gold was what it was all about, before the slave trade began in earnest. The fort, which later came to be called Elmina, is in the land of the Fante, a strong people whom even the powerful Asante dared not confront. The trade in slaves at Elmina was unstoppable, and many extensions have been added from the days of the first fort in 1482 up to today. On a rise a short distance from Elmina is the small redoubt St. Jago. It was this hill that the Dutch used when they seized Elmina from the Portuguese in 1637. After that the first massive trade in slaves began on the Coast.

Slowly I wander over the drawbridge. The courtyard is large, with buildings on all sides. An impressive stairway leads up to the governor's residence. At a short distance

*Fort Elmina is an attractive monument as it lies on a spit out toward the sea and the surf. In the middle of the white masonry wall there is a small opening where the slaves were driven out in order to be loaded on board the slave ships.*

226

from the fort chapel, near the main gate, there are two small rooms with doors of heavy wood. The heavy bars on the doors tell us that this was a dungeon. One of the two, the best ventilated one, is closest to the entrance of the fort and was used to punish the fort's employees. Above the door of the other cell there is a decoration of a skull and crossbones. This was the death cell for rebellious slaves who were too dangerous to handle; no one left this cell alive!

After having crossed the courtyard I turn to the left in a dark passage which leads to a small backyard. On three of the sides there are arched doorways which lead to the slave dungeons where the female slaves sat waiting for their fate. Through the small air vent in one of the short walls unhealthy fumes drift out of the powder chamber. In the corners there once stood

*In this courtyard were the dungeons for female slaves, provided with solid bars. From his airy residence the governor had a good overview and could choose as he wished among the women. When the slave ships were ready to take on cargo, women and children were led out first through the large arches, and further through the dark passages and taken on board.*

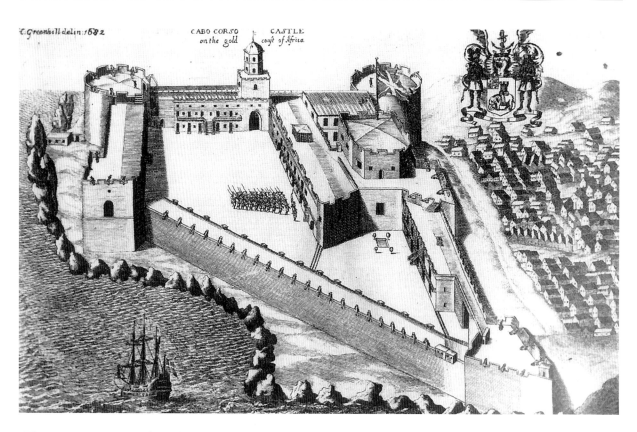

*C. Greenhill delin: 1682*   CABO CORSO CASTLE
on the gold coast of Africa

*The English head-
quarters, Cape Coast
Castle, as it appeared
in 1682.*

barrels stinking of excrement. Two cannon balls attached to leg irons, which were
once fastened to the legs of the slaves, are lying there as silent reminders in the slave
yard. On the last of the sides of this yard there is a solid door which leads to a stair-
case. This ends in an upper storey, and is provided with a secret trap door not far
from the governor's bedroom. It was here that trembling slave girls were brought up
to please the governors, and relieve their loneliness far from home…The luckiest
ones ended up with a house in town, as mothers of the children of the white men.

A dingy passageway in the back ends in a narrow opening in the wall of the fort.
This did not lead to freedom, but to the loading place for the transportation of the
slaves out to the slave ships. The internal stream of goods was well organized at
Elmina, with loading in on the one side and loading out on the other. I stare at the
narrow opening, where the bright daylight is streaming in. Every time a slave filled
the opening, it became dark in the passageway where the stone floor has been
worn smooth by thousands of bare feet.

Elmina is considered to be the oldest European building on the African continent south of the Sahara. There is now a strong movement underway to collect
means for a full restoration of both the fort and the buildings around it in the
town. It is a major project, not least to collect furnishings that are historically correct, because the interior of the fort has been completely stripped. But it is indeed
an important project. With its moat, its drawbridge and bastions holding old cannons, Elmina is a unique historical landmark.

Cape Coast Castle, some 12 km east of Elmina, was the headquarters for the
British engagement on the Gold Coast. The first fortified station on that site was
raised by the Swedes in 1649, and named Carolusborg. Thereafter, the Danes took

over and later the British. The fort was conquered by the Dutch and was in their hands for a short period. On a hill about one km northeast the Danes built their Fort Frederiksborg. After a few years, in order to pay off debts, the place was sold to the British who became the dominant power in the area, largely thanks to Cape Coast Castle. Like Elmina, this is an impressive structure. In front of the buildings, which form an L, there is an open, spacious courtyard which ends in a strong bastion. Rows of large cannons are aimed out to the sea, and piles of cannon balls lie there ready for use. The cast iron shows signs of the salty, hot air; corrosion is extensive and the balls no longer fit the barrels of the cannons.

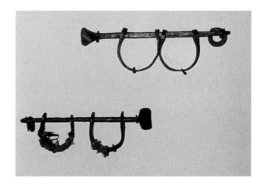

A dark passage snakes deep down under the fort. It ends in a large room with an arched ceiling where there was room for the male slaves. It is a gloomy "waiting room", naked cells where the slaves might have had to sit for weeks and months before being "processed" further.

Cape Coast Castle is an exciting structure, precisely as I had expected to find a typical tropical fort. In the fort's museum there is a fine and informative exhibit about the slave trade. Several West African states see great possibilities in tourism where the mementoes of the slave trade are expected to play an important rôle. The World Tourism Organization (WTO) and UNESCO are very much engaged in this work, and the two monumental buildings Elmina and Cape Coast Castle are on the World Heritage list of landmarks worthy of preservation.

*Cape Coast Castle, which is open to the public, offers both information on a film and a good museum with chief emphasis on the slave trade. Above are seen slave shackles of different sizes. The smallest ones are padded in order to prevent blisters.*

*The cannons at Cape Coast Castle point stubbornly out to sea where the Fredensborg passed 30 September 1767. Captain Kiønig ordered a nine-gun salute which was answered with only five, while Elmina had responded in full earlier in the day.*

After visiting the forts I have a greater insight into the activities of the Europeans on the Coast. I have seen how they built their forts and organized the slave trade. But where did the slaves come from? I shall try to follow the trail toward the north – after the Crepe and Akwamu slaves who found themselves on board the *Fredensborg*.

The flat coastal savannah changes to a more verdant landscape further inland east of the Akwapim hills. On the way I pass the famous Krobo Mountain, where, in earlier times, lone travellers were robbed and killed. I am in a state of suspense, wondering how the story of a slave ship from the eighteenth century will be received by the once so feared Akwamu. At the end of the seventeenth century and the beginning of the eighteenth century they dominated large sections of the coastal areas where the Denmark-Norway had its forts and trading stations. The Akwamu then controlled the important routes from the interior, a situation they exploited in such a manner that a number of other peoples grew weary of it, and rebelled. One of these peoples were the Akyem, who, together with allies, launched an attack. In a bloody war in 1730 their superior power was too great for the Akwamu.

The weakened Akwamu people were driven from their homes, and most of them settled somewhat further inland near the River Volta, where they again built up their strength. This was an advantage for the Danes in a battle later against the Asante in Dodowa, in 1826, where the Akwamu King Akotoh I made a successful ambush in the Akwapim hills. This contributed to a complete victory, and resulted in a treaty of friendship and oath of loyalty to King Frederik VI. In gratitude the Akwamu king was presented with a sword of honour for his contribution. With enemies in the vicinity it was inevitable that the Akwamu were constantly at war, which also happened while the *Fredensborg* was anchored at Christiansborg. Akwamu, having formed an alliance with Awuna, was then at war with its archenemy Akyem. There is reason to believe that some of the Akwamu were taken prisoner and thereby ended up as cargo on board. Captain Ferentz wrote a note that the king of Akwamu had a pawned slave on board, who was exchanged two days before departure.

Between the palms I catch sight of a large river. The River Volta! After having crossed the river I have finally arrived in Akwamuland. The landscape is extraordinarily beautiful; the river is bordered by fertile fields and the mountains are covered by green forest. A little way upriver, on the eastern bank, is the capital, Akwamufie. Further east I find the town of Adome and its chief, entitled Adomehene, or Nana. I am given a friendly reception at the Adome palace, which is a one-storey building, painted yellow, located a little way outside of the town. After we have exchanged greetings he invites me to take part in a welcoming ceremony similar to the one in Old Ningo. His traditional stool is decorated with the figure of an elephant, and his feet rest on an animal hide. Like his fellow Africans he is interested in the past, and he listens intently as I tell about the *Fredensborg*. Then he takes me to the old palace, originally built in 1733, only three years after the Akwamu came to this area. Around the large building, made of reddish brown dried clay, daily life goes on as usual. An older woman is busy preparing food over a newly-walled oven. It is quiet and peaceful here now, but in the courtyard in front of the old palace things happened in earlier times.

The existence of the Danish-Norwegian forts and trading stations on the coast was entirely dependent upon deliveries from the interior. From these areas there were well-used paths to the coast and the trading stations at Keta and Fort Fredensborg; others made use of the River Volta to travel down to Ada. The most important "goods" were slaves, which were acquired by various means. Most of them were prisoners of war; others were criminals who had been convicted; some were already slaves. Slavery was an aspect of the old social structure in Africa, and

*Between the palms I catch a glimpse of River Volta and the fertile landscape where the Akwamu live. On the other side of this fabled river are the towns of Akwamufie and Adome.*

in many cases slaves could own property and also advance in social status. A harsher existence awaited those who were sold to the Europeans. From the flat lands of the coast to the mighty forests and great savannahs in the north, there existed a conglomerate of large and small states. Wars were often waged, which affected the stream of slaves. Guns, bullets and powder were an important component of the payment for slaves, a fact which usually encouraged the desire for wars.

Elephant and hippopotamus tusks were another type of trade goods. The *Fredensborg*'s tusks cost the lives of roughly 35 elephants and 4 hippopotami. The hunt for these valuable tusks has resulted in the eradication of these animal species in large areas, but fortunately, both elephants and hippopotami are found in game reserves in Ghana.

It is Sunday, but not an ordinary Sunday in the realm of the Akwamu. First I am invited to participate in the celebration of *Akwasidae* at the home of the Adomehene, Apea Kwasi III. This is the traditional festival which is held nine times a year to honour the ancestors. Thereafter there is a festival in Akwamufie, and there I have been granted an audience with the king of Akwamu, the Paramount Chief of the Akwamu people.

*Akwasidae* is celebrated under the large, spreading tree in the courtyard behind

*The key ring from Christiansborg and the sword of honour, which was a gift from Frederik V, are costly mementoes for the Akwamu.*

*The reception by the paramount chief of the Akwamu was marked by dignity and formality. Here the Akwamuhene, Nana Otumfuo Ansah Sasraku VI, is seated, surrounded by his most influential men. The Akwamu nation includes thirty-five towns, large land areas and a population of about one million.*

the Adomehene's palace. There are eighteen of us altogether, members of the families, the elders, the linguist (interpreter) and, of course, the Adomehene himself. It is the linguist who leads the ceremonial rituals, which include prayers and offerings to the ancestors. After everyone has been given *schnapps* and poured a libation to the dead, a new ritual starts. This time it is yams that are offered, and I am given a mouthful, too. There is something beautiful about these rituals which are performed with elegance and dignity. This is an old culture with a meaningful content, which has its origin far back in time.

After the ceremonies I travel to Akwamufie with the Adomehene and his followers. It is he who has

arranged for the audience with his immediate superior, who is staying in a two-storey building. Both the palace and the other buildings in the vicinity are built of masonry. The town is in a flat stretch of country a little way from River Volta, where handsome canoes are moored at the riverside.

While I am waiting, I see a group of beautifully dressed women arriving at the festival grounds near the king's palace. I have not yet registered all the impressions before I am informed that the audience is to take place. It is an exciting moment when I am shown through the door into a literally royal reception. The entire room is covered in beautiful, traditional cloths, and in an armchair on a platform sits the Akwamuhene, Nana Otumfuo Ansah Sasraku. He is surrounded by his most important men and protected by watchful bodyguards with their upper torsos bare. On the floor in front of the king sits the executioner in his black cloth with his sword pointed to the ground, while the linguist – the king's spokesman – holds firmly to his staff decorated with a "wisdom knot" and two gilded figures at the top. Behind the stool where I was directed to sit are the Asafo corps, the warriors. While I shake hands with the king and his trusted men, I hear loud shouts. The corps of warriors responds with songs sung in four-part harmony, and someone plays on the "double bell". After the greeting ceremony and presentation is over, I am asked by the linguist to explain the purpose of my visit.

I tell them briefly about the *Fredensborg* and the discovery of objects in the wreck which have a connection to Ghana. Then I go into more detail about the enslaved Akwamu on board who had planned a revolt and takeover of the ship. According to the ship's log, it appears that the Akwamu were the only ones on board willing to fight for their freedom. I tell them that it was because of this that I wished to visit the place where some of the slaves came from, and greet the Akwamu of today.

*Like most Africans the Akwamu keep their culture alive. During the festivities in Akwamufie the elders and linguists have their own seats, and among them, one linguist holds the traditional linguist staff. It is beautifully made and the gilded figures and the wisdom knot represent important symbols.*

*A view of an idyllic African village overlooking the River Volta with the Adomehene, Apea Kwasi III, in front.*

My short speech is well-received. In the conversation which follows, it appears that the Akwamuhene is especially concerned about the Europeans' picture of Africa as a continent of misery, where hunger and catastrophe dominate the news reports. He emphasizes that this is highly incorrect, and he urges me to present Africa as it really is. Upon my question as to whether I can see the keys to Christiansborg and the sword of honour given to them as a gift from Frederik VI, he answers that, unfortunately, that is not possible on such short notice. These regalia represent some of the highlights of Akwamu history and their contact with the Danes, and they are kept well hidden from foreigners.

It has been a formal, but very pleasant meeting with the paramount chief of the Akwamu. They have preserved their old culture in a manner that could be a model for many, and which I experienced to the fullest as a guest at the festival.

I leave Akwamufie for this time. Near a small village on the River Volta I see a lone paddler in a neat canoe on his way towards the shore. The houses of dried clay with palm leaf roofing glide harmoniously into the landscape. Could this have been the home of some of the slaves on board the *Fredensborg*? Those who were seized and taken away lost almost everything: family, rituals, the earth of the ancestors. My thoughts range from this beautiful landscape to the poor slave houses I found on St. Croix, and the consequences of the slave trade stand out more clearly for me than ever before. I now understand the strength of the African culture and how parts of it could survive through all the brutality in the new continent and in more recent times. At the same time, I realize that I have come to the end of the road in my historical journey back into time. This is how far it was possible to follow the trail from the past after the *Fredensborg* and those who were on board.

I am back in Wulff's house on Castle Drive. As I stand in the small grave chamber there are strong forces on the move out of doors. Coming out into the backyard I see threatening dark blue clouds building up. Shall I actually be given a demonstration of a travat, the storm that caused so many problems for the *Fredensborg* and her crew? At a point closer to the beach I have a good view both out towards the roadstead and back towards Accra. It now builds up swiftly and dramatically. While powerful gusts tear at the palm trees, I realize that I am in the right place at the right time, here, close to Christiansborg! It begins to rain, and I experience a storm which is the worst I have ever known. Palm leaves whirl through the air, the woven baskets of sellers roll away, and visibility is reduced to near zero. The roads become rivers, lightning crackles and thunder rolls – Rømer was right, a cloudburst and thunderstorm in Europe cannot be compared to this frightening sight.

It was during just such a storm, almost precisely 228 years ago, that they had to secure the *Fredensborg* with an extra anchor when the travat hit. In the dark of the evening, with the ship rolling strongly and violent gusts of wind blowing, Chief Offiser Lundberg had little chance when he slid on the rain-wet deck and fell overboard. Nature's powerful demonstration gives me a clear picture of the strength of the travat and the problems it caused for the ships in the roadstead.

Evening approaches and the atmosphere becomes sombre. The contours of Christiansborg are wiped out by the storm and the dark of night, and soon it is all gone. Only an occasional flash of lightning illuminates the old trade fort in the Danish-Norwegian realm on the Gold Coast.

# Epilogue

THE *FREDENSBORG* SAILS ON! It turns out that the story of the Danish-Norwegian slave ship has attracted considerable attention when the dark history of the slave trade is to be told. A close collaboration with the Norwegian National Commission for UNESCO, as well as the author's membership in UNESCO's International Scientific Committee for the "Slave Route Project", has resulted in an internationalization of the Fredensborg Project.

Since the *Fredensborg* appears to be the best documented ship found as wreck of the transatlantic slave trade to be located so far, it has aroused considerable national and international interest. A working committee with interdisciplinary competence, consisting of Mari Hareide, Per Hernæs, Johan Kloster, Tove Storsveen, Leif Svalesen, George Tyson and Selena Winsnes, has supported the following and other projects:

A BOOK: *The Slave Ship Fredensborg and the Eighteenth Century Danish-Norwegian Slave Trade* by Leif Svalesen. In 1996 the book was published in Norway by J. W. Cappelen Forlag and in Denmark by Forlaget Hovedland.

A MONUMENT: On 1 December 1996 a stone monument with a plaque commemorating the slave ship *Fredensborg* was unveiled by representatives of Ghana on Tromøy near Arendal in Norway, at the site of the shipwreck.

A TRAVELLING EXHIBITION IN SCANDINAVIA: The Norwegian Maritime Museum has contributed a large travelling exhibition based on finds from the *Fredensborg*. The exhibition has been enthusiastically received in Norway, Denmark and Sweden. Permanent exhibitions have been mounted in the Aust-Agder County Museum in Arendal, and the Norwegian Maritime Museum in Oslo.

A CARTOON BOOK: *The Slaver Fredensborg, The Final Voyage 1767–68* by Kurt Aust, Leif Svalesen and Kin Wessel – a comic strip version for younger readers

with a factual section – was published in Norwegian and English by C. Huitfeldt Forlag and the Norwegian Maritime Museum in 1997.

AN EXHIBITION ON ST. CROIX. A compact, permanent *Fredensborg* exhibition has been mounted at the Fort Frederik Museum in Frederiksted on St. Croix, with assistance from the St. Croix Landmarks Society. This was Norway's gift to the 150th Anniversary Emancipation Celebration 3 July 1998.

AN EXHIBITION IN GHANA. A similar exhibition was presented as a gift from Norway to Ghana 16 February 1999. The exhibition is on permanent display at the National Museum in Accra.

Thus, exhibitions and other activities have been organized on the three continents that were affected by the final voyage of the *Fredensborg*.

As a result of the significance of the *Fredensborg* and the "Slave Route Project" in UNESCO's "Culture of Peace" program, NORAD, The Norwegian Agency for Development Cooperation, has made a large contribution. Among other things this has made possible the exhibitions on St. Croix and in Ghana as well as work with an international educational project about the slave trade for UNESCO's Associated Schools Project, ASP.

*After the opening of the exhibition in Ghana the Akwamu arranged a splendid and memorable durbar at the court in Akwamufie for the UNESCO-Fredensborg Team. In the middle of the picture we see the Paramount Chief, Nana Otumfuo Ansah Sasraku VI, with central representatives of the Akwamu people and other Ghanaians. Others are from Norway, St. Croix and France.*

# SOURCES

## *Quotations*

Owing to the verbosity and often complicated style of writing in the 18th century it has been necessary to shorten some of the quotations without affecting the meaning.

## *Bibliography*

Unpublished Sources

Nedenes Court Register no. 20, fol 1 B, National Archives in Kristiansand.

West Indian-Guinean Archives VA. XIV No. 475. Daily journal of New Construction No. 2: The Frigate Cron Prindz Christian. Pamphlet 1. Fol 71-178 March 1752-Feb. 1753. Danish National Archives, Copenhagen (RA).

West Indian-Guinean Archives. Account-book based on reports from the Company's repair site 1752-54 pp. 72-74 and 84-85. RA.

Rentekammeret V.G. Renteskriverkontor 1754-60. Correspondance register 1755–60 VA VII no. 2249.13.RA.

West Indian-Guinean Exchequer and General Customs House Records A no. 1650, 20 Aug. 1765 and A no. 1945. RA.

West Indian-Guinean Archives, 216. Ration and Scale of Victualling for the crew of the frigate Cron Prindz Christian 10/12 1753. RA.

West Indian-Guinean Archives, 216. Scale of Victualling for slaver Cron Prindz Christian's first voyage 31/8 1753.

Archives of the Guinea Company. VA XIV no. 52 fol. 24-36. Archive no. 53 pp. 1–39. Inventory, materials and commissions ledger for the Fredensborg, among others. RA.

Archives of the Guinea Company no 49. pp. 1-74. Daily journal for the the Fredensborg, among others. RA.

Archives of the Guinea Company no. 89. The Chief Officer's ship's journal for the Fredensborg 1767-68. RA.

Archives of the Guinean Company no. 109. Journal of the Ship's Assistant for the Fredensborg 1767-69. RA.

Archives of the Guinea Company no. 88. The Captain's journal for the Fredensborg 1767-69. RA.

Archives of the Guinea Company no. 7. Extra journal for incoming letters 1766-69, pp. 88-90 and 92. RA.

Archives of the Guinea Company no. 23. Agent Carl H. Thalbitzer's journal 1767–69, pp. 41-62. RA.

Archives of the Guinea Company no. 6. Instructions for the Captain. RA.

Archives of the Guinea Company no. 6. Instructions for the Ship's Assistant, RA.

Archives of the Guinea Company no. 12-21 1767-78. Coastal documents, letters to the Government 1767. RA.

Kay Larsen's archives, Danish National Library, Copenhagen.

Karsten Bundgaard. *Ludevig Ferdinand Rømer.* Unpublished manuscript 1976.

The author's own journals, diaries and notes 1973-1976.

## Published sources and literature

*Africa Pilot,* vol I, London 1967.

Anquandah, James. *Rediscovering Ghana's Past,* London 1982.

Bannermann-Richter, Gabriel. *The Practice of Witchcraft in Ghana,* Cal. USA 1982.

Bech, Niels. *Christiansborg i Ghana 1800-1850.* Article in Architectura, Yearbook of architectural history no. 11, Copenhagen 1989.

Berulfsen, Bjarne, Gundersen, Dag. *Fremmedordbok,* Oslo 1986.

Boaten, Nana Abayie Boaten I, *Notes on Akwasidae,* Research Review Supplement No. 6, 1993.

Bundgaard, Karsten. *To signeter fra slaveskipet Fredensborg.* Reports from the Norwegian Numismatics Association no. 3, Oslo 1980.

Børretzen, Børre A. *Den store boken om dykking,* Oslo 1986.

Clarkson, Thomas. *The History of the Abolition of the African Slave Trade,* London 1808.

Dannevig, Hartvig W. *Skipsforlis på Sørlandskysten,* Oslo 1969.

Dannevig, Hartwig W. *Slaveskipet Fredensborg,* Oslo 1978.

Eilstrup, Per and Boesgaard, Nils Erik. *Fjernt fra Denmark,* Copenhagen 1974.

Engeland, Sveinung. *Betal for slavehandelen,* A-magasinet, Oslo 08/1993.

Eriksen, Egon and Frantzen, Ole L. *Dansk artilleri i Napoleonstiden,* Museum of Arms and Uniforms Copenhagen 1989.

Fage, John D. *A History of West Africa,* Cambridge University Press, 1969.

Fisher, The Mel Fisher Maritime Heritage Society. *A Slave Ship Speaks. The Wreck of the Henrietta Marie,* USA 1995.

Green-Pedersen, Svend Erik. *Om forholdene på danske slaveskibe med særlig henblik på dødligheten 1777-1789.* Museum of Commerce and Shipping Yearbook, 1973.

Gøbel, Erik. *Sygdom og død under hundrede års kinafart.* Museum of Commerce and Shipping Yearbook, 1979.

Gøbel, Erik. *Dansk sejlads på Vestindien og Guinea 1671-1807.* Museum of Commerce and Shipping Yearbook, 1982.

Hair, Paul. *Barbot on Guinea. The Writings of Jean Barbot on West Africa. 1678–1712.* Vols. 1 and 2. Hakluyt Society, London 1992.

Hamran , Ruth. *Merdøgaard skjærgårdsmuseum.* Aust-Agder Museum, Arendal 1990.

Hansen, Torkild. *Slavenes kyst,* Denmark 1968.

Hansen, Torkild. *Slavenes skip,* Denmark 1968.

Hansen, Torkild. *Slavenes øer,* Denmark 1970.

Harboe, C.L.L. *Dansk Marine-ordbog, 1839,* reprinted Copenhagen 1979.

Henningsen, Henning. *Vagt til sjøss.* Museum of Commerce and Shipping Yearbook, 1967.

Henningsen, Henning. *Sømandens våde grav.* Museum of Commerce and Shipping Yearbook, 1987.

Henningsen, Henning. *Besøg på Guldkysten.* Museum of Commerce and Shipping Yearbook, 1970.

Hernæs, Per O. *The Danish Slave Trade from West Africa and Afro-Danish Relations on the 18th Century Gold Coast,* University of Trondheim 1992

*History of the First Troop Philadelphia City Cavalry. From its organization 1774 to its centennial anniversary,* USA 1874.

Hyland, Tony. *The Castles of Elmira,* Kumasi Ghana 1971.

Haagensen, Reimert. *Beskrivelse over Eilandet St. Croix, 1758.*

International Confederation of Free Trade Unions (ICFTU), ILO and FFI's campaign report, 1994.

Isert, Paul Erdmann. *Reise nach Guinea und den Karibäischen Inseln in Columbien,* Copenhagen 1788. Translated into English by Selina Axelrod Winsnes, Oxford University Press, 1992.

Bro-Jørgensen, J. O., Rasch, A. A. *Asiatiske, vestindiske og guineiske handelskompagnier.* Danish National Archives Copenhagen, 1969.

Klem, Knud. *Skibsbryggeriene i Danmark og Hertugdømmene i 1700-årene,* volumes I and II, Copenhagen, 1985, 1986.

Kondor, Daniel. *Ghanian Culture in Prespective,* Accra, Ghana, 1993.

Larsen, Kay. *Dansk Vestindien 1661-1917,* Copenhagen, 1928.

Larsen, Kay. *Krøniker fra Guinea,* Copenhagen, 1927.

Larsen, Hans. *Danmark og piratstatene.*

Lewisohn, Florence. *The Romantic History of St. Croix,* St. Croix, 1964.

Lewisohn, Florence. *Under Seven Flags,* Hollywood, Florida 1974.

Molaug, Svein. *Slaveskipet Fredensborg,* Norwegian Maritime Museum's Yearbook 1975.

Molden, Gunnar. *Arendal-Afrika-Narestø.* Aust-Agder-Arv, 1994.

Monrad, H. C. *Guinea-Kysten og dens Indbyggere,* Copenhagen, 1822.

Møen, Leiv I. *Tromøy kirke gjennom 800 år,* Tromøy Parochial Church Council, 1987.

Nilsen, Sigrid E. *Glemte Mestre. Kirkekunst og inventar i gamle Nedenes prosti,* Tvedestrand, 1992.

*Norsk historisk leksikon.* Edited by Rolf Fladby, Steinar Imsen, Harald Winge. J. W. Cappelens forlag, Oslo, 1981.

Norton, Graham. "Ghana's Crumbling Heritage," *History Today.* Oct. 95

Nørregaard, Georg. *Våre gamle tropekolonier,* volume 8, *Guldkysten,* Copenhagen, 1966.

Palmer, Colin. *The Cruelest Commerce,* National Geographic vol. 182, no. 3, Sept., 1992

Rask, Johannes. *En kort og sandferdig Rejse-Beskrivelse til og fra Guinea,* Trondheim 1754. Translated into New Norwegian, *Ferd til og fra Guinea 1708–13,* Oslo, 1969.

Remy, Mylene. *Ghana Today, 1993.*

Rømer, Ludevig Ferdinand. *Tilforladelig efterretning om Kysten Guinea.*Copenhagen, 1760.

Rønning, Bjørn R. *Myntene fra slaveskipet Fredensborg.* Report from Numismatic Association no. 3, Oslo, 1980.

*Salomonsens konversationsleksikon* II ed. vols. I-XXV, Copenhagen 1915.

Sarpong, Peter: *Ghana in Retrospect,* Ghana, 1974.

Stub, Karen Elisabeth. *Dansk slave i Marokko.* Siden Saxo no. 3, Damm 1994.

Svalesen, Leif. *Arendalsmann på slavetokt.* Aust-Agder-Arv, 1994.

Svalesen, Leif. *Kinakapteinene på Merdøgaard.* Aust-Agder-Arv, 1991.

Sætra, Gustav. *Adam - Herlofsons negerslave.* Aust-Agder-Arv. 1932.

Teisen, Michael. *NSM. Marinarkeologi. Kunnskapsbehov. Skips- og båtfunn som kultur-minner og kildemateriale.* FOK Oslo 1993.

Thestrup, Poul. *Pund og Alen.* Archives' Information Series, Danish National Archives, Copenhagen, 1991.

Thestrup, Poul. *Mark og skilling, kroner og øre.* Archives' Information Series Danish National Archives, Copenhagen, 1991.

Tillemann, Erick. *En liden enfoldig Beretning om det Landskab Guinea og dets Beskaf-fenhed langs ved Søkanten,* Copenhagen, 1697. Translated into English by Selena Axelrod Winsnes, University of Wisconsin- Madison, 1994.

Tønnesen, Kjeld. *Tollvesenets utvikling på Agderkysten,* Kristiansand, 1989.

The Unesco Courier, Paris, Oct. 1994.

Unesco nytt no. 4, Oslo, 1994.

Unesco nytt no. 2, Oslo, 1995.

Van Dantzig, Albert. *Forts and Castles of Ghana,* Accra, 1980.

Vibæk, Jens. *Våre gamle tropekolonier, vol. 2, Dansk Vestindien 1755– 1848,* Copen-hagen, 1966.

*Vore gamle tropekompanier, vols. I and II,* Copenhagen 1953.

West, Hans. *Bidrag til beskrivelse over St. Croix,* Copenhagen 1793.

Wikander, Johan A. *Gamle havner ved Grimstad.* Selskapet for Grimstad Bys Vel, 1985.

Winsnes, Selena Axelrod. Translated and edited, Paul Erdmann Isert, *Letters on West Africa and the Slave Trade,* Oxford University Press, 1992.

Winsnes, Selena Axelrod. Translated and edited, Erick Tilleman, *A Short and Sim-ple Account of the Country Guinea and its Nature.* University of Wisconsin-Madi-son, 1994.

The author would like to acknowledge with thanks the following individuals and institutions for their contributions to the work with the vessel *Fredensborg* and the book:

* Senior Conservator John K. Appiah-Baiden, Ghana Museums & Monuments Board. Accra.

* Historian, dir. George Tyson, St. Croix Landmark Society.

* Ghana Museums and Monuments Board.
* Professor Joe Nkrumah, Ghana Museums and Monuments Board.
* Dr. Akosua Perbi, Department of History, University of Ghana, Legon.
* Chairman Joseph K. Kwabbi, Akwamu Heritage Committee.
* Model-maker Teddy Andersen, Arendal.
* Aust-Agder Archives, Arendal.
* Aust-Agder Museum, Arendal.
* Architect Niels Bech, Denmark.
* Archivist Kjell J. Bråstad, National Archives Kristiansand.
* Section Leader Karsten Bundgaard, The Danish National Library, Copenhagen.
* George Busby, Accra.
* Dr. Isaac N. Debrah, Ghana Museums & Monuments Board, Accra.
* Professor Christopher DeCorse, Syracuse University, USA.
* Coastal Historian Hartvig W. Dannevig, Hisøy.
* The Danish National Library, Copenhagen.
* Dr. Felipe Fernández-Armesto, Oxford.
* Erik Falck-Therkelsen, England.
* Pilot Johan Frigstad, Arendal.
* Student of History Gariba Abdul-Korah, Ghana/Tromsø.
* Conservator Karl R. Gjertsen, Aust-Agder Museum, Arendal.
* Zoologist Dr. Chris Gordon, University of Ghana, Legon.
* Archivist Erik Gøbel, Danish National Archives, Copenhagen.
* Professor P.E.H. Hair, England.
* Curator Ruth Hamran, Aust-Agder Museum, Arendal.
* Director Ulf Hamran, Aust-Agder Museum, Arendal.
* Dr. Per O. Hernæs, University of Trondheim.
* Museum of Commerce and Shipping, Kronborg, Denmark.
* Secretary-General Mari Hareide, UNESCO, Oslo.
* Professor Svend Holsøe, USA.
* Architect Eirik Knudsen, Aust-Agder County Municipality.
* Photographer Tore Knudsen, Aust-Agder Archives, Arendal.
* Junior Executive Officer Rita Kvaal, Norwegian Maritime Museum, Oslo.
* Nana Otumfuo Ansah Sasraku VI, Akwamufie, Ghana.
* Museum Inspector Kaare Lauring, Museum of Commerce and Shipping, Helsingør.
* Captain and Marine Painter Ants Lepson, Arendal.
* Director Svein Molaug, Norwegian Maritime Museum, Oslo.
* Archivist Gunnar Molden, Aust-Agder Archives, Arendal.
* Photographer Arild Lange Nilsen, Arendal.
* Prof. Joe D.K. Nkrumah, Ghana Museums & Monuments Board.
* Norwegian Maritime Museum, Oslo.
* Nana Apea Kwasi III, Adome, Ghana.
* Adviser Dag Nævestad, Norwegian Maritime Museum, Oslo.
* Tina and Geir Ommundsen, Vegårshei.
* Diver Odd K. Osmundsen, Jonsvika.

* Nene Osroagbo-Djanmah II, Old Ningo, Ghana.
* Dir. Hans Pettersen. Langesund.
* Danish National Archives, Copenhagen.
* National Archives in Kristiansand.
* The Norwegian National Commission for UNESCO.
* Terje Svalesen, Tromøy.
* Diver Tore Svalesen, Tromøy.
* Conservator Michael Teisen, Norwegian Maritime Museum, Oslo.
* Editor Arve Torkelsen, Nesodden.
* UNESCO, Paris, Director Doudou Diène.
* Illustrator Ann-Carin Wessel, Horten.
* Diver Kenneth Ødegaard, Froland.
* Author Kurt Østergaard, Horten.
* The participants in the two marine archaeological excavations in 1975 and 1977, as well as everyone else who has contributed with assistance and information.

## Analyses, Preservation etc.

* Identification of the coins from the *Fredensborg:* Senior Curator Bjørn R. Rønning of the University Cabinet of Medals and Coins, Oslo.
* Analysis of the bones from the *Fredensborg:* Chief Curator Pirjo Lahtiperä of the Zoological Museum, University of Bergen.
* Analysis of "goose barnacles" and shells, Hans Brattstrøm, Dept. of Marine Biology, University of Bergen.
* Information about malaria mosquitoes, Professor Ole A. Sæther, Zoological Museum, University of Bergen.
* History of Narestø's Buildings, Architect Eirik Knudsen, Narestø.
* Alfred I. Thommesen, legends from Narestø.
* Conservation of finds from the *Fredensborg,* Engineer Ib. Kjølsen, Arendal; Chief Curator Trygve Skaug and Engineer Pål Thome, Norwegian Maritime Museum, Oslo.

## Transcriptions, Interpretations etc.

Kjell J. Bråstad, National Archives in Kristiansand; Gunnar Molden, Kjell Knudsen, Kjell-Olav Masdalen, Knut Skistad, Anne Tone Aanby, Aust-Agder Archives, Arendal; Erik Gøbel, Jørgen Nybo Rasmussen, Danish National Archives in Copenhagen; Kaare Lauring, Hanne Poulsen, Museum of Commerce and Shipping at Kronborg; Hartvig W. Dannevig, Gunnar Knudsen Asdal and Bergår Gundersen, all Arendal, and Historian George Tyson, St. Croix.

## Journeys to St. Croix and the Gold Coast

I would like to thank Architect William Chapman, Curator William F. Cissel, Historian Barbara Hagan-Smith and Historian Jeannie Pitts for assistance, historical guidance and local transportation during the trip to St. Croix. Credit must go to my brother Tore for valuable assistance and his enthusiasm as a travelling companion.

I would also like to thank Scancem International through President Tor Kjel-saas and Managing Director and Norwegian Consul-General Tor Nygård of Ghacem Ltd. who placed a car and driver at our disposal. This was of vital importance in order to carry out the planned program effectively.

I wish to thank Nana Professor Arhin Brempong and Director of Public Affairs Secretariat Valerie Sackey, The Castle, for their assistance in gaining admittance for me to Christiansborg Castle. And I would also like to thank Professor Albert van Dantzig of the University of Ghana and chauffeur Roland Nimako from Ghacem Ltd. who succeeded in locating the right places.

In conclusion I would like to thank Chief Curator Johan Kloster, Senior Editor Tove Storsveen and Author Selina Axelrod Winsnes. They made up the rest of the Fredensborg Team and were of invaluable assistance, both during the journey and in the work with this book.